A HISTORY OF
THE JESUITS

CHRISTOPHER HOLLIS

WEIDENFELD AND NICOLSON
5 WINSLEY STREET LONDON WI

ACKNOWLEDGEMENTS

We gratefully acknowledge permission to reproduce the following illustrations: 1, Leonard von Matt; 2, 6, 12, 19, 22, 23, from *The Power and Secret of the Jesuits*, by René Fülöp-Miller, by kind permission of Mrs Hedwig Fülöp-Miller; 3, 30, from Hubert Becher's *Die Jesuiten*, Kösel-Verlag, 1951; 4, 27, the Mary Evans Picture Library; 5, 13, 14, 17, 20, 21, 25, 26, 34, The Mansell Collection; 9, Mr Chen Chao-Ming; 10, Burns, Oates Ltd; 11, Vincent Cronin; 28, Gabinetto Fotografico Nazionale, Rome; 29, reproduced by gracious permission of Her Majesty the Queen; 31, photograph from Musei Communali, Rome; 32, photograph by the Rev. A. Powell; 33, the Vatican Museum; 35, 38, the Society of Jesus; 36, photograph by Yvonne Chevalier; 37, Geoffrey Chapman Ltd; 39, Felici.

SBN 297 76459 4

Printed by C. Tinling & Co. Ltd., Liverpool, London and Prescot

CONTENTS

ILLUSTRATIONS

MAPS

ONE

The coming of the Company

In the New Testament there is no invitation to Christ's disciples to look forward to a time when they would be the masters of a Christian society. On the contrary they are always spoken of as destined to be a small minority, misunderstood by the secular world around them, probably despised and persecuted, and bidden to be seriously alarmed if they should find that they are not despised. They are indeed to be the light shining in the darkness, but a light shining in a darkness that does not comprehend it. They are indeed to be the small leaven that may somehow hope to leaven the whole lump, but there is no suggestion that in doing so the leaven will itself become large, that they must ever expect to see a society in which Christians form a majority and occupy posts of political importance. Christ was no political rebel. Some rejected Him because He was not a political rebel, nor ready to strike a blow for the political deliverance of Israel. Others demanded His condemnation because He was a rebel – because He had proclaimed Himself a King. But that accusation, where it was sincerely made at all, was based on a misunderstanding. His kingdom was not of this world and His attitude to the principalities of this world was neither one of rebellion nor of enthusiastic loyalty. It was one of indifferent acceptance. The Christian should render to Caesar the things that are Caesar's because such worldly possessions as the shekel of the tribute were not important, nor was it important who claimed political dominion over Him. Such matters were not worth squabbling about. Let us pay our dues for the sake of peace.

This attitude of detachment was inherited by His first disciples. They were not concerned either with their own rights or with how the world was ordered. They were concerned only with spreading the Gospel of Christ. They quarrelled with official Judaism only

A*

when it opposed itself to Christian preaching. Those of them who were Jews accepted for themselves the obligation to keep the Jewish law. 'I wist not that it was the High Priest', was St Paul's reply when he was rebuked for having spoken to him with discourtesy. St Paul was willing enough to appeal to the Roman authorities and to take advantage of his Roman citizenship so long as he had hopes of support from the Romans for his activities. Later, when Rome had turned against and persecuted the Christians, the writer of the Apocalypse denounced its abominations. All other organizations were judged entirely by their attitude towards the Christian Church. They were neither good nor bad in themselves. The question whether their action made for the preservation or the disorganization of society was of little importance and of little meaning, since in their opinion the world was in any event destined to come to an end in a very few years.

So to the early Fathers of the Church such problems as whether a Christian might serve in the army were entirely personal ones. Was the Christian code such that he who served as a soldier committed a sin and would therefore be in danger at the Judgement? That was the only question that mattered. Such questions as whether, as the result of Christians refusing to serve, the frontiers would be insufficiently defended, the barbarians break in, the pattern of civilized life destroyed, many innocent lives lost, were never considered. It was God's business to preserve society if society was to be preserved. The world was probably coming to an end anyway, and in any event the number of Christians was so small that they could not make any notable difference to the strength of the army.

The first centuries passed by and the world did not end. The Roman Empire did not fall and the Christian Church made astonishing progress. The willingness of the Christians to suffer for their faith proved that they were at the least sincere in their belief in it. The empty secular world was hungry for a faith, and Christianity, based securely on its historical claims, was incomparably more capable of satisfying that hunger than were any of its mythological rivals. By the fourth century there was a new situation where Christians found themselves in positions of responsibility, where in their decisions they had to look not only to the satisfaction of their own personal consciences but to the general

effect on society. For them the question was no longer merely,
'Ought I to serve in the army and shed blood?' but, 'Ought I to
allow the barbarians to break in and to destroy society?' The
Emperor Constantine decided that there was no longer any
possibility either of ignoring or of suppressing the Christians. It
was better therefore, he thought, to form an alliance with them –
to declare the Empire Christian. *In hoc signo vinces.*

The Christians had of course to make certain concessions to, or
at least admit certain modifications of, their principles in return for
this privilege. No longer was a doctrine of total pacifism preached
from Christian pulpits. The Church of course – in theory at any
rate, whatever some Christians may have done in practice – by no
means surrendered to the other extreme of acclaiming all wars as
holy wars. But it accepted the principle that, though war was in
itself a great evil, yet there might be special circumstances where
to fight was the lesser evil. Under the guidance of St Augustine and
others it laid down the rigid conditions which must be satisfied
before a war could be called a just war. We need not enter here
into the details of these definitions. The point is that there came
into existence four hundred years after Christ something of which
Christ had never spoken – a Christian society, a society in which
Christians were in a position to make rules for a secular society,
rules supposedly to be made in accordance with Christian
principles. And this came about not by any person's choice, but
through the force of circumstance.

How far in practice over the next thousand years this mean that
secular society became Christianized and how far it meant that
Christianity became secularized we need not here inquire. It is only
necessary to make two points. First, this Christendom which now
came into existence was of course in no way a predominantly
European society. Christianity is clearly by no means an exclusively
European religion. The Incarnation did not take place in Europe.
In Christianity's early centuries its African and Asian provinces
were on the whole more vigorous than its European. The great
debates at which the creeds were fashioned took place in Asia.
The creeds themselves came out of Asia and Africa. There was
little European influence in their formation. The Empire by
Constantine's time was not a wholly European or Western Empire,
and by moving its capital from western Europe to his own city on

the Bosphorus Constantine moved its centre of gravity more firmly eastward. Secondly, while Constantine's ambition was perhaps to make the Empire Christian, it was by no means his purpose to make it papal. Later tradition might pretend to found the Pope's right to his temporal power on the supposed Donation of Constantine, but in fact Constantine in all his policies paid very little attention to the Pope and hardly ever mentioned him. Indeed the details of the Emperor's theological position were far from clear either to himself or to anybody else, nor was it at all certain whether the Christendom that he proposed to establish was to be Catholic or Arian.

Even without embarking on these controversies we can see by what accidents the wholly new and unforeseen notion of a Christian society emerged. In such a society, wherever orthodoxy might be it, was highly desirable for social and political rather than for strictly religious reasons that as many as possible and all those in positions of importance should be of the orthodox religion. Whatever the precise meaning of Pauline assertions that salvation could only be attained through faith in Jesus Christ, no one in apostolic times had believed that all those who did not explicitly profess the Christian faith would be condemned to everlasting fire. The doctrine of *extra ecclesiam nulla salus* acquired such a connotation only when Christendom had ceased to be a merely religious body but had also become a political unit. It was the political body which saw general orthodoxy as convenient.

Three hundred years after Constantine there arose in the Arabian desert the gigantic heresy of Mohammed. If we are tempted to say that the astonishing rise of Christianity in its early centuries is evidence of its divine origin, or perhaps that the almost equally astonishing rise and triumphs of the early Jesuits proves clearly that God was with them, we must face the fact that the rise and triumphs of Islam were every bit as sudden and as astonishing as were those of the Christian movements. Within a century the armies of Mohammed had spread over Asia and Africa and virtually destroyed those two great provinces of Christendom. They poured over the Straits of Gibraltar into Spain and made themselves masters of that country. They crossed the Pyrenees and advanced into the centre of France. It looked not impossible that all Europe might fall to them, as Asia and Africa had fallen, and

Christendom be utterly extinguished. Their attack was met and repulsed by Charles Martel at the Battle of Tours, but though the Muslims were driven back behind the Pyrenees, it was only after another seven hundred years, just before the death of Ignatius Loyola, the founder of the Society of Jesus, that they were finally expelled from Spain. Meanwhile, checked in the West, they had advanced in the East. After they had made themselves masters of all the territory which Asian Christendom had occupied, they had moved on into Europe, captured Constantinople, imposed their rule on the Balkan peninsula, and again by Ignatius' time it still appeared possible that they might make themselves the masters of Vienna and overrun Europe from the East as seven hundred years before they had threatened to overrun it from the West.

Thus Christendom was virtually confined within the boundaries of Europe. It was so confined not because there was anything in the nature of the Christian religion which made its message peculiarly suited to a European but simply because of the development of events. Christendom, which had become a society as the result of the action of Constantine and his successors, became as a result of the action of the Muslims a city under siege and, while it had been the intention of Constantine to establish his capital and the centre of civilization in the East and to relegate Rome to a secondary role, the unintended effect of the migration of secular government to Constantinople was to compel people in the West to look to the papacy for leadership even in secular affairs, as they probably would not have done had the Emperor remained in Rome. With the diminution of the power of the Eastern Emperors as the Muslims rose to threaten them, the importance of the Pope as Christendom's only secure master even of secular power inevitably increased.

The great need of medieval Europe was for peace. Europe cried out for peace not so much out of a belief in Christian doctrines of non-resistance as because of its need for unity in face of the Muslim menace. The peace that it imposed on itself was indeed a very brutal and by no means Christlike peace. As a besieged city, medieval Europe felt obliged to suppress vigorously the traitor within its gates. The Spanish Inquisition ruthlessly crushed Moors and Jews who were thought to have feigned their conversion and to be secretly working for Christendom's enemies.

As the story of almost every saint shows – and not least in a later day that of Ignatius – for all the intellectual vigour of the Middle Ages, every original speculator ran the risk that a heavy hand of suppression would fall upon him, and his acquittal depended more on chance and on the accident of having powerful friends than on any true orthodoxy. Even St Thomas Aquinas was at one time under suspicion. A terrible crusade – the Albigensian Crusade – was launched against the heretics of southern France, and they were suppressed in horror and massacre. A policy of repression was perhaps inevitable so long as the notion survived that it was desirable that there should be a uniform Christian society. Men do not of their nature think alike and any polity which seeks to make them do so is bound to be both oppressive and ineffective. So far was society at that time from being pacifist, as such early thinkers as St Clement of Alexandria or St Athanasius would have taken it for granted that any Christian society must be, that its system of organization – the feudal system – was a military one, and men took their titles – knights, lords, Emperors – from their military functions. Christians were not expected to be peace-loving. They were expected to be warlike and to keep peace only if there was a strong arbitrating authority which compelled them to do so. Society was hierarchical. Every man had a master to whom he could appeal for justice, and at the apex of the pyramid, in the high medieval theories of Hildebrand or Innocent III, stood the Pope, one of whose tasks was to arbitrate the disputes of princes.

Of course the theory was by no means consistently practised. The thirteenth century was not a period of untroubled peace, even between Christians. Still, at its peak the authority which Innocent III was able to exercise over the monarchs of Europe was remarkable and impressive, and the achievement of thirteenth-century Europe is certainly one of the highest to which the human race has attained. It has as good a claim as any to the title of the greatest of centuries. Yet, if so, the next two centuries were certainly centuries of decline. Scholastic philosophy, which in the hands of Scotus and St Thomas had been a great creative influence, in the hands of their decadent successors became little more than an exercise in word-chopping. The papal claims, which whether they were of divine origin or not had certainly at their height been one of the great cohesive forces of civilization, became instead a cause of weakness and division. The Pope could clearly only exercise his authority as the arbiter between princes if his own authority was unchallenged.

Innocent III's authority had been of that kind. Men might dispute who was king of this country or that. No one disputed who was Pope. He could claim to treat kings as his vassals because clearly he himself was vassal to no man. But when in the fourteenth century French kings set up the Popes as their vassals at Avignon, the situation was very different. This so-called Avignonese Captivity must in any event have had a damaging effect on papal prestige. It also happened to correspond with the Hundred Years' War between England and France. The Avignonese Popes, unable to pay their servants out of their own resources, paid them by appointing them to English benefices which they never in fact visited but whose revenues they demanded to have remitted to them in France. Naturally this seemed to Englishmen merely a device for robbing the English of their treasure in order to finance the enemy's war chest. It meant that long before Henry VIII's time English Catholicism was already anti-papal. In similar spirit, when the papacy returned to Rome Germans objected (again long before Luther) to being mulcted, by the 'sale' of indulgences, of money which was sent over the Alps to finance the rebuilding of Rome and the expenses of the Italian papacy. The papacy itself was in dispute between two claimants, and for a time between three. It was not surprising, indeed it was almost inevitable, that in such an atmosphere the claim could find support that a General Council was of greater authority than the Pope. Nationalism was growing. Papal prestige was falling. Long before the outbreak of the great Reformation there were signs that the unity of Catholic Christendom was breaking up. A man at the end of the fifteenth century might well have prophesied its imminent disruption.

It was into this fluctuating world that he who was afterwards to be known as Ignatius Loyola was born. His real name was not Ignatius but Inigo. The exact year of his birth is not quite certain but the most probable year was 1491. He was a Basque, born in his ancestral castle in the Pyrenees which lies between Azcoita and Azpeitia. This castle, which can still be seen, though it is now built over with great ecclesiastical buildings, is a very modest little affair hardly deserving of the title of castle. It is only fifty-six feet high and fifty-eight wide. The lower portion is of hewn stone, the upper of birch. Above the entrance is the family escutcheon of two wolves, rampant and lambent, having between them a cauldron suspended by a chain, crudely cut in stone.

The Loyolas were a very respectable but modest land-owning family, by no means grandees. Ignatius was the youngest of a family of thirteen. Of his early years we know little for certain. According to Maffei he was at one time at the court of King Ferdinand. By his own confession he was involved in youth in certain romantic affairs which it has been said went beyond the bounds of continence, and he left behind him a strange confession of a passing devotion to a lady who was, as he put it, no countess or duchess but of far higher station. Those who experience a dramatic conversion in later life sometimes like to exaggerate a little the sins and heedlessness of their youth. All that we can say about Ignatius is that he does not appear to have been remarkable in either direction: he was not in violent protest against religion, nor was he notable for any signs of sanctity or especial devotion. The career which he adopted was that of a soldier. The little Basque kingdom of Navarre straddled the Pyrenees and it was at issue whether the French or the Spaniards should obtain possession of it. The French were invading the country and Ignatius was one of the defenders of the fortress of Pampeluna against their attack. In what exact capacity he was serving – whether he was in command of the defence or a subordinate – is not clear. In any event he was wounded in the fighting, struck in the leg by a cannon-ball as he was rallying the defenders to repel the attack. The French treated him generously and took him to his home at Loyola.

The process of recovery was long and painful, and to pass the time he read all the scanty literature that was available in the ancestral home. Traditional works of romance like *Amadis de Gaul* were soon exhausted and he turned – at first for little more reason than that there was nothing else available – to works of piety, to Ludolph of Saxony's *Life of Christ* and to the *Flowers of the Saints*. These books aroused in him for the first time an ambition for sanctity. If God and Christianity were established truths, did it not follow as a necessity of logic that the only sensible life was one of devotion to religion? If Dominic and Francis had done such things as he found recorded of them, why should not he do likewise?

So, when he was recovered, he set off across the country down into Catalonia, to the famous monastery of Monserrat some miles up in the hills above Barcelona. There he gave his cavalier's uniform to a pilgrim, and clothed as a beggar made a night's Vigil of Arms before the ancient statue of Our Lady, dedicating his life to her. Then he went to the neighbouring little town of Manresa, in whose cave he composed his *Spiritual Exercises*.

As we have said, a variety of accidents over the centuries caused Christians to form themselves into a Christian society of which the New Testament gave no hint of a prevision. Ignatius of course entirely accepted the view of Christendom as a society and, not being a man of any deep historical learning or indeed at that stage of his life of any historical knowledge at all, he had probably never even thought that any other arrangement was possible. Christendom was to him an organized society under siege. It was the Christian's duty to help defend it. He was by training and instinct a soldier and therefore took it for granted that Christendom could best be defended by a military organization and, if necessary, by military means. Ignatius and the company which he formed proved themselves to be one of the great shaping forces of history. The most secular and unsympathetic of historians cannot fail to note their influence and it is right to discuss them as a great political force. Yet of course any historian would be greatly in error who wrote of them merely as a political force. Ignatius did think that the Church was a great social institution and that it must be efficiently organized to fulfil its social role, but such a work, though important, was only secondary. Man's prime business was not with this world at all, but with the establishment of a right relationship with God, and this world was in itself of no worth – a mere testing ground where man could fit himself for the final beatitude.

Therefore, as we read about the political and social achievements of Ignatius and his Company, it is only right to read that story aganst the background of the *Spiritual Exercises* – to remember that Ignatius had drawn these up long before he had ever decided what shape his activities in the world were to take, and that the *Spiritual Exercises* were left as a discipline to his disciples, upon whom was imposed the duty of daily meditation and an annual retreat, to remind them in the press of the world's business where the ultimate reality lay.

What then are the *Spiritual Exercises* and what is their importance? This is no place for a detailed description of the intricacies of the spiritual life. Such matters can only be described from within. But a description of their importance in the Jesuit scheme of things is called for, and also of the part that they have played in shaping the world's history. Ignatius was constantly revising his *Exercises* throughout his life and those which are used by the Jesuits of today are not the original composition of Manresa cave of 1522 but the final version of 1541. However, the changes are of secondary importance and it will be most convenient to consider the *Exercises* and their importance at this point – at the beginning of Ignatius' spiritual progress.

They have of course been criticized. Modern writers like William James have spoken of them as 'mysterious devices' and of those who have experienced them as 'emerging livid and haggard from the struggle'. It is difficult to draw any conclusion from such exaggerations except that James had never read the *Exercises* and never met a Jesuit. Those who have the advantage of him in this respect would find the epithets 'livid' and 'haggard' very surprising as descriptions of the Jesuits whom they happen to have met. Jesuits are common enough about the world. It is perhaps possible to like or to dislike them, individually or as a Society. Opinions may differ. But the part that they have played in the world has been such that no one can reasonably dismiss them as a society of idiots, or their method of training as a vulgar exercise in hocus-pocus. William James professed himself a pragmatist – a man who believed that the test of the truth of a system was whether or not it worked. A way of life or a system of training that has survived and exercised influence over many generations and in many parts of the globe, whose success has been so very much more than merely ephemeral and local, may not indeed embody the last work either of wisdom or of truth. But it has at least established its right to serious consideration. It must in some way have satisfied some enduring need of man. To dismiss it with gibes is merely vulgar and, of course, whatever else may be said of the *Spiritual Exercises*, to suggest that their devices are mysterious

– that they sought to capture their victim's allegiance by some species of pseudo-mysticism – is nonsense. They are a document of unimpassioned reasoning and sober psychological advice, to be considered and criticized. If it be true that some later Jesuits have been inclined to treat them as an almost inspired document in which the final answer to every spiritual problem is to be found, it is with no authority from Ignatius.

Other critics have complained that the exercises are not original – that they are deeply influenced by the *Ejercitatorio de la Vida Espiritual* of the monks of Monserrat – which Ignatius had been given by his Benedictine confessor at that monastery, or that they are based on Ludolph of Saxony's *Life of Christ* which he had read on his sick bed at Loyola. It is certainly true that some of the ideas for Ignatius' first week of meditation bear evidence of having been adopted from the Benedictine manual and some of those for the later weeks from Ludolph. What of it? Ignatius was making no claim to invent a new religion. There was no copyright in those days nor was he laying any claim to one. Man had been meditating on the Christian religion for fifteen hundred years and it would have been strange indeed had none of Ignatius' ideas been suggested to him by any previous writer. But the point of interest is not to what extent the *Exercises* are original but why they succeeded in making so enormous an impact upon the world – an impact which incidentally was not made by any of these other books to which Ignatius was indebted.

The pattern of the *Exercises* runs briefly as follows. The first week is dedicated to bringing home to the retreatant the supreme folly of mortal sin. The second and third weeks bid him, having conquered the negative problem of avoiding mortal sin, to seek out positively the particular task – the vocation – to which God calls him. The fourth week, with its hints of the higher mysticism, gives sure indication of the rewards that are likely to follow in the companionship of God from the acceptance of the vocation.

Ignatius tells him of the Two Standards – that of Christ and that of the world – and tells him that he must make a firm choice under which standard he enlists himself. What, it may be asked, is so very original in all this? It is of course true that it contains no teaching that has not been given many times before. Ignatius would have been the last to claim that it did. Its strength came from the logical coherence into which the teaching was all bound together, so that the final conclusions and premises of the fourth week followed inevitably from the assertions of the first. But apart from telling the retreatant what are the ends at which he ought to aim it gives him practical advice on how he is to achieve them. It commands a frequent Particular Examination of conscience. It enforces upon him the duties of obedience and humility. It analyses for him the nature of prayer, dividing it into its three natures.

The *Spiritual Exercises* is not a work of apologetics. It attempts no argument of conversion, no proof of the truth of the Christian faith. In it the truth of Christ is taken for granted. The *Exercises* are solely concerned with demonstrating, granted that the Christian religion is true, the logical consequences of its truth. That being so, they cannot of their nature be of great moment to one who denies the original premise of the Christian revelation. To one who fully accepts it, it might be argued, they should be largely unnecessary. But this second conclusion at any rate would be false. The world has never been divided into total believers and total disbelievers. There is a vast mass in between who are not prepared to deny that the Christian religion is in a certain sense true, that Christ was perhaps the Son of God. But, they ask, can we literally believe all the detailed threats and commands of orthodoxy? Can it really be true that he who breaks certain rules – some of them, he will say, of no overwhelming importance – and dies unshriven is in mortal sin and will go to hell? Such people believe after a fashion, but with reservations; as to the Judgement, they say, we cannot hope to understand what will happen but that it cannot be as crude as the official teaching. Somehow, they cannot but believe, things will sort themselves out all right –
      'Pish, he's a good fellow and 'twill all be well.'
To many there may perhaps be something a little stark in Ignatius' rigid condemnation of 'particular friendships' among his followers. Is it so grave a fault to prefer one friend to another and to show as much? Is it not likely that, if all preference is suppressed, then all too easily all affection will be suppressed? Did not Our Lord Himself have one especial 'beloved disciple'?

This is no place to argue what degree of truth those moderate believers may hold nor how far orthodox believers over the years may have damaged their own cause by describing it in too crude terms. But what is certain is that in the world of the sixteenth century, as perhaps in the world of today, the orthodox faith was slipping. The cause was not so much that a comparatively small number of enthusiasts, disedified by the practice of the religious, had seen fit violently to challenge religion's truth. It was much more that many who believed had during the years of their vigour kept their belief at the back of their minds, prepared perhaps to return to a full profession of it at the hour of their death but not believing that the hour was yet at hand. It was to such men – to those who had first welcomed the increase of freedom and then were beginning to feel their first fears of where it might lead – that Ignatius' appeal was especially potent. There are many such today – no opponents of reform, but at the same time a little anxious as to where the reforms will lead. As with all great books, the *Spiritual Exercises* owed its success to the coincidence of its own merits with the accident that it appeared at a time when there was a special demand for it.

The *homme moyen sensuel* is perhaps not so uncouth as brazenly to reject the large evidences of the Christian faith. He is willing to guard himself by obeying its absolute commandments – by attending Mass on Sunday, by refraining from a defiant commission of the flagrant sins – but he is not willing to order his whole life by obedience to religion. The saints alone are willing to do this. They are willing to break with all human relationships, utterly confident that the Christian promises are true and that they will really after death see again face to face those from whom they are divided. Who has ever dared to contemplate the awful sadness if that confidence should prove to be false and if it should be found that they have made their great sacrifices for no reward?

The Jesuits are perhaps thought of primarily as the men who checked and then turned back the attack of Protestantism. That was indeed their main achievement in the first half-century of their existence. But as with many other enterprises of history its architects achieved something quite different from what they had set out to do. It is true that Ignatius and Luther were virtually contemporaries. Luther was born in 1483, Ignatius, as we have said, probably in 1491. But Ignatius came from a territory where Lutheran doctrines had less currency than perhaps anywhere else in Europe. The financial grievances against the drain of German money to Italy was unimportant in the Basque country. He has left us no evidence that in those early years he had any curiosity about doings in lands that were distant from him. There is no reason to think that in those years when he was dedicating himself to God and laying the first foundations of his Society he had so much as heard of Luther or of Protestantism. On the contrary, to an enthusiastic Spanish Catholic the enemy of the faith was of course Islam. The last of the Moors had been expelled from Spain only with the conquest of Granada, coincident almost to the year with Ignatius' birth. Christendom, free at last in the West, was still gravely menaced in the East, and Ignatius' first idea was that it was towards the Muslims that his efforts must primarily be turned. Directly from Manresa he went to Palestine with the hope and intention of spending his life there in upholding the Christian cause against Islam. It was only on the direct command of the Franciscan authority in Jerusalem, who feared that his methods of proselytism would be more likely to endanger the Christians than to convert the Muslims, that he returned to Europe. He now saw that the great need of the Catholics, if the attacks on the faith were to be resisted, was better education, and that, if he was to teach or to organize the teaching of others, he must first of all be taught himself. He returned to school, and after that attended at the universities of Alcala and Salamanca. But he had at that time of course neither orders nor standing and Spain was a country in which all novelty was suspect. He soon found himself in the hands of the Inquisition, from which he escaped only with some difficulty. Authoritarian as he was, or at any rate thought himself, Ignatius was, though he did not fully know it himself, an innovator – a man who was going to teach the world how to revise its principles – and a spirit of innovation could not breathe in the Spanish atmosphere. Though in its origin the Society was so largely Spanish, and often in later years was to bear the tag of being a Spanish Society, it has never in fact been at ease in Spain as its chequered history there proves.

Ignatius left Spain and went to Paris, and it was there that he collected his first band of followers. On the memorable day of 15 August 1534, they gathered together in a little church on Montmartre. Faber, the only one among them who was a priest, said Mass and the rest communicated and took among themselves the vows of what was to become their new Society, though it had as yet no formal existence. A writer so little sympathetic as Balzac has written:

Who is there, that would not admire the extraordinary spectacle of this union of seven men animated by a noble purpose who turn towards heaven and under the roof of a chapel lay down their worldly wishes and hopes and consecrate themselves to the happiness of their fellow men? They offer themselves as a sacrifice to the work of charity that shall give them no property nor power nor pleasure; they renounce the present for the future, looking forward only to a hereafter in heaven, and content with no happiness on earth beyond what a pure conscience can bestow.

It was still Ignatius' hope and expectation that this new Company should work among the Muslims in the Holy Land. After their studies in Paris were finished in 1536 they agreed to disperse and make their ways by separate routes to Venice where they would foregather and whence they would sail to the East. Arrived at Venice, they were told first to go down to Rome and get the Pope's permission for their actions. The Pope blessed their enterprise. All those who were still laymen were ordained priests and they returned to Venice to wait for a boat to Palestine. But the time had not yet come when missionary enterprises into Muslim countries were possible. Indeed Christendom still stood on the defensive against the Turks and at Lepanto had to fight for its life. The battle was inevitable and Jesuits were to play their part in Pius v's Crusade in that campaign. Eight of them served as naval chaplains in the battle. In 1539 it became apparent that conditions were such that there was no chance of going to the Holy Land, and the Jesuits decided to return to Rome and put themselves entirely at the service of the Pope. Pope Paul III, the Farnese, gave his approval after some difficulty, and the Company of Jesus was finally constituted by the bull *Regimini Militantis Ecclesiae* of 27 September 1540. In the next years Ignatius drew up its Constitutions. The Company of Jesus – Ignatius never used the term Jesuit – in some ways resembled other religious Orders, though in others it differed markedly from them. The Jesuit, like the members of other Orders, takes the vows of poverty, chastity and obedience. But he does not, like the Benedictine, belong to a particular house. The term Company which Ignatius chose for his Society was a military term. It implied that the Jesuits were to be 'the light horse' of the Church – the special soldiers of the Pope, bound to him by a fourth vow of personal obedience which other religious do not take, ready to be sent at his command to any quarter of the globe. After the period of the schism and the General Councils, after the actions of some of the early Renaissance Popes, the prestige of the papacy did not stand high. Many even of those who thought themselves good Catholics paid scant obedience to papal commands and argued that General Councils were superior to Popes. Even St Thomas More, who was in the end to die for the papal claims, was inclined in his youth by his own confession to doubt whether the papal claims were of divine ordinance. It was Ignatius' typically military conclusion that a recovery of the body was not possible until there was first a recovery of the head, and that the first necessity was to put into the hands of the Pope a weapon which would enable him to carry through his policies of reform.

Unlike monks, the Jesuits do not say office in community. It is true that, as it developed, the Society for reasons of practical obedience divided itself up into territorial provinces, and the Jesuit, liable to be moved from house to house within his province, is not normally posted outside it. But he has no rights in this matter, and the Pope is free to send him wherever he wishes. Members of the Society are debarred from ecclesiastical honours. It is only under very special circumstances – usually in a missionary country where there is a shortage of priests – that a Jesuit is by command of the Pope made a bishop and, if raised to the episcopate, canon law releases him from his obligation of obedience to a superior. The Society of Jesus is an authoritarian Order. The Jesuit is under obedience. There is not – or at any rate was not until the recent constitutional reforms of 1966 – any taint of democracy in its constitution. The General is elected for life and resides at Rome so as to be in constant touch with the Pope, and he is supported by a body of Assistants appointed as representatives from each group of provinces. There is also an admonitor whose task it is to see to it that the General governs in obedience to the Constitutions. It is the General who appoints the Provincials of the various provinces and the Rectors of the various houses, and their appointments are for a term of years. No Jesuit can acquire any defined status. Thus one who has been a Provincial or a Rector has no emeritus rank. When his term of office is finished he must step down and accept the orders of his successor who can, if he wishes, pack him off to be a junior curate in the least distinguished of parishes. The Jesuit owes absolute obedience to his superior. He must obey him 'as if he were a stick in his hand', *'perinde ac cadaver'* – 'as if he were a dead body' – but only in so far as the command is not a sinful command, and the superior himself is of course under obligation to rule in accordance with the Constitution. The Jesuit Order is in this respect very different from a totalitarian tyranny, where the Führer can make up whatever morality he likes. The ultimate obligation of a Jesuit, as of every Christian, must be to his own conscience. 'Preserve always,' wrote Ignatius at the beginning of the *Spiritual Exercises*, 'your liberty of mind; see that you lose it not by anyone's authority nor by any event whatsoever.' He did not mean by these words to issue an invitation to irresponsible libertarianism. The will was in his view to a large extent the master of belief. A man could believe what he wished to believe and the Church asked of its subject not a wooden, unthinking, uncomplaining obedience. It asked him to 'think with the Church'.

In all Orders up to that time the novitiate lasted only one year. The Jesuit novitiate lasts two years. The training is given in a special house under a special officer, the Master of Novices. The most important part of it is the thirty days' *Spiritual Exercise*. After the novitiate comes a year or two of juniorate during which literary studies are followed, then three years of philosophy and a degree taken at a secular university. The scholastic, as the Jesuit who is not yet a priest is called, then usually teaches for a few years in a college. After that there are four years of theology, after the third of which he is ordained. His training is then rounded off by a year of the tertianship. At its completion the priest pronounces his final vows. Some take simple vows. Others – as it were the elite of the Society – take special vows and are 'professed'. It is they who elect the members of the General Congregation, who in their turn elect the General. He, as we have seen, is elected for life. The General Congregation has in theory the power to depose him but this power has never been exercised. The Society throughout the world is divided geographically into assistancies of several nations each. The assistancies are divided into provinces, one for each nation, or it may be, in such countries as the United States, France and Spain today, several provinces for a large nation. The Jesuit joins a particular province and, as I have said, as a general rule works within that province.

Eventually, after a hundred years of bitter fighting, the lines between Protestant and Catholic settled down virtually along the lines that divided the old Roman Empire from the barbarism beyond it, and such they have substantially remained from the Treaty of Westphalia in 1648 up till the present day. What was Roman has remained Catholic. What was outside the Empire has been lost to the Church. But in the first outbreak of Protestantism, while for nationalistic reasons the most vigorous protests against the Church's corrupt mishandling of finances came from the northern countries of Germany and England, theories of theological revolt were rife in all parts of Europe. Calvin was a Frenchman. Servetus whom he burnt was a Spaniard, and in Italy, while Protestantism was in the end to be wholly overcome, Protestant ideas in those early years were very much in the air. As has been said, there is no evidence that Ignatius was at all familiar with them. The first commission which the Pope gave the Company was to go to various cities in Italy where the new doctrines were showing signs of establishing themselves and to counter them. Brouet and Salmeron were sent to Siena, Faber and Laynez to Parma, Xavier and Bobadilla to the Campagna, Codure and Hoyes to Padua and Rodriguez and Le Jay to Ferrara. A Calvinist preacher, perhaps foreseeing the danger to his own doctrines if such a counter-attack should be fully launched, had been in Italy before the Jesuits, and had attempted to spread there tales accusing them of every manner of crime such as they have so frequently met from traducers.

On 5 April 1541, the Society held its first election of a General. As everybody expected the election went to Ignatius. He received every vote except his own. He demanded and was granted a second election, but it gave the same result. Ignatius was already fifty years old before he took up the main task of his life – an age at which, in those days, it was often considered that a man's active life was finished. The practical effect of his formal election was not

great, for Ignatius, remaining at Rome, had already been organiz-
ing the Society's growing activities throughout the world. From
Italy the Jesuits had already penetrated into Portugal, Spain,
France and Germany. In the same year, 1541, Salmeron and Brouet
made their way into Ireland where they hoped to organize resistance to Henry VIII's assertion of his own headship of the Church.
They went first to Scotland, then under the rule of James V, the
father of Mary Stuart, and thence crossed to Ireland, but arriving
there they found that their coming was already known to their
enemies and a price had been put on their heads. They were able
to stay only a month and could effect little.

On the continent of Europe at that time the probabilities were
indeed against a total apostasy of Spain and Italy from papal
obedience, grave as were the difficulties even in those countries.
But an observer might well have prophesied that the revolt against
Rome would by no means be confined to the northern countries
but might establish itself in the entire territories of France and
Germany, and many who were not deeply enamoured of Protestant
theology were most heartily sick of apparently interminable
religious wars and bloodshed. Many people were beginning to
deduce from the theologians' violent controversies that none of
these learned men knew as much as they pretended about the
ultimate truths; since we cannot be sure whether or not we have
the truth, such people argued, it would be more sensible to concentrate on the attainment of peace, which we can at least recognize
when we see it. The majority of the critics of the papacy did not at
that time think of themselves as persons who had left the Catholic
Church. They thought rather that the claims of the papacy were not
a necessary part of the Catholic faith and hoped to find some
compromising formula upon which all Christians could agree to
reunite. They did not think of Christians as sharply divided into
Protestants and Catholics. It is true that when it was decided to
summon a General Council at Trent, some hoped that there would
emerge from the Council clear Catholic definitions which all men
must accept or reject at the cost of exclusion from the Church;
however, others hoped that it would be possible to find compromises which both sides could accept, and which would make
possible a reunion of Christendom. The Jesuits of course belonged
to the first school. Ignatius had been invited by the Pope to be

present at it, but he preferred to remain in Rome. Laynez and
Salmeron went there as the Pope's special theologians. By the
Pope's command they were present at all the long-drawn-out
sessions of the Council which extended from 1545 to 1563, and
their hands were more powerful in shaping the decrees of the
Council than were those of any other man. No problems require
more careful judgement than decisions on what are essential
principles and what are secondary affairs on which, for the sake of
peace, it is desirable to compromise. Only a few years ago it was
taken for granted in Catholic circles that the Council of Trent by
its brave decisions had saved the integrity of the Catholic Church
and that those whom it excluded had been rightly and inevitably
excluded. The present ecumenical mood is more inclined to the
view that there were faults and virtues on both sides and that more
flexible policies should have been pursued. But neither rigidity
nor flexibility are in themselves absolute virtues. It is all a question
of timing. 'Ripeness is all.'

TWO

The early years in Europe

It may well be right today to approach the problems of the non-Catholic world in an ecumenical and understanding spirit, but concessions which can be made from an established position cannot be made by an army retreating in rout. If it be true that the present age calls for different policies from those of Trent, that does not in any way prove that the decisions of Trent were wrong. But of course, right or wrong, they were not decisions that could be taken without difficulty. Charles v, the Emperor, was a Catholic but by far the greater number of his German subjects were at that time hostile to the Church. It appeared to him, and it was not an unreasonable conclusion, that there was no alternative beyond civil war or a compromise. Even within the Jesuits' own ranks there was difference of opinion. To Laynez no concession should be made to heresy or rebellion and, although in itself no exact question of doctrine was involved by such a demand, he opposed any suggestion that the cup in Communion should be given to the laity. Peter Canisius, the young Jesuit of the rising generation who was destined to play a larger part than any other in the reconversion of Germany, took at first the opposite line and supported the concession and, doing so, earned for the time the goodwill of the Emperor. But for that very reason when later he changed his mind and sided with Laynez, the Emperor's hostility to him was all the more bitter.

Charles v's advocacy of compromise did not at that time seem unrealistic. It looked in these early years of the Reformation as if Catholicism had wholly lost the intellectual battle for Germany. Protestant doctrines seemed triumphant. A formal Catholic profession was found hardly anywhere save among some of the aristocratic Bishops and they made little pretence of sincerity and less at intellectual apologetics. To these new Jesuits who attempted to

bombard them with arguments they showed no favour. Who were
these young men who refused to be content with what was good
enough for their grandparents? In these early years of its history
the Society had not yet come to impose upon its members the
extended training which was later to become customary. As a
result the early Jesuits were much younger men than the Jesuits
in positions of authority at any later date. It is not impossible that
that is one of the reasons why they met with such spectacular
success. Old men do not naturally make good light horsemen.
Anyway at the time of the Council of Trent Canisius was only
twenty-six, Salmeron and Le Jay thirty-one, and Laynez thirty-
four.

Charles v's dilemma was that the only possible way, if there was
any way at all, in which he could resist or repel the Protestant
attack was by crude methods of violence – by defeating his
opponents in battle and by persecution – and, although in accordance with the spirit of the age he had no objection in principle to
violence or persecution, he was intelligent enough to see how
narrow were the limits of what it could achieve. One could, if one
had the guns, perhaps conquer a province. One could burn a
heresiarch, but, if the spirit of the people had wholly lost its
Catholic faith, one could not permanently hold them within
Catholic bounds by constraint. And the trouble with Germany, as
Charles saw it, was that the Catholic cause was wholly lost.
Catholicism's nominal leaders had no apostolic faith, no apologetic ambition. The people drifted between indifferentism and
Protestantism. The Emperor had no alternative but to compromise. If he did not, all that would happen would be that he
would go down to destruction along with the Pope.

All this reasoning was within its limits substantially plausible
and, had the German mind remained as Charles found it, there
would have been no alternative to a policy of surrender. It was the
greatness of Peter Canisius to see that the only solution was to
change the German mind, and the greatness of his achievement
that he succeeded in doing so. The field on which Catholicism
could substantially defeat Protestantism, if only it took the trouble,
was the field of debate. The battle must be won by education.
Ignatius advised Canisius that it was only necessary to execute a
few heretics and then heresy would collapse. Canisius, who knew

his Germany, knew better. Ignatius at the first foundation of the Society had had no thought of devoting his Fathers to the education of the laity. Canisius saw the necessity of undertaking such a task if anything was to be rescued. Faber, before Canisius, had already been engaged in apostolic work and had upheld the Catholic cause at the Diet of Ratisbon in 1541 when he confronted Bucer and Melanchthon. He had been succeeded by Le Jay and Bobadilla. Faber returned to Germany and disputed at Spires and Cologne. Le Jay was appointed a professor at Innsbruck and then at Augsburg persuaded the assembled bishops, with some difficulty, to refuse the discussion of differences of religion as a matter of open debate. Bobadilla was made Socius to the apostolic Nuncio at Nuremberg and afterwards attended and spoke at the Diet of Worms and subsequently in Vienna. But his impetuosity came near to undoing all the Jesuits' careful work. Three years after the Council of Trent had met, the Emperor Charles issued what he called an Interim forbidding anyone to change their religion until the Council had decided. Bobadilla, afire with apostolic zeal, denounced the Interim and as a result he, and through him the whole Society, earned the disfavour of the Emperor. Ignatius withdrew Bobadilla from Germany and posted him to Naples.

During all this time Canisius, then a very young man, had been labouring at Cologne to prevent the Archbishop, Herman von Wied, from openly apostatizing. When the Archbishop's defiance of orthodoxy had become too outrageous, Canisius hurried off to appeal against him to the Emperor and King Ferdinand, Charles' brother, the so-called King of the Romans. At Ferdinand's court he met Truchsess, the Cardinal of Augsburg, who was so impressed with his ability that he insisted on taking him with him as his personal theologian to Trent. When the Council was adjourned Canisius was sent first to Italy but then in 1550 was appointed Rector of the University of Ingolstadt It. was then that he started on his great work of educational foundation. He founded colleges at Vienna, Prague and Ingolstadt. He opened negotiations for the foundation of a college at Strasbourg. He took part in religious discussions at Worms and was sent by Pope Paul 1 to the imperial Diet of Pieterkov in Poland. In 1552 the Collegium Germanicum was established in Rome at his request. In 1559 Canisius was summoned to the Diet of Augsburg and remained based on that city until in 1562 he returned to the Council of Trent as papal theologian. His experience was that of practical German conditions; Laynez, who himself did not know a word of German, had the experience rather of the seminary class room. They differed, as has been said, over the question of the Communion cup for the laity. But in spite of his subsequent loss of favour with the Emperor when he changed his view in order to prevent dissension within the Society, Canisius was able to continue his work of educational foundation. In 1562 he opened the College of Innsbruck and became the spiritual director of Magdalena, Ferdinand's daughter. In 1564 he inaugurated the College of Dillingen. He was appointed secret papal Nuncio in Germany by Pius IV and, when Pius V succeeded to the throne, he wished to keep him in that post. But Canisius, who was sensitively aware of the great danger when a priest allows himself to become too intimately involved in politics, and particularly in the secret intrigues of politics, excused himself from the post.

Von Ranke has written:

At the beginning of 1551 the Jesuits had no fixed place in Germany – Le Jay was appointed Rector only in June of that year – but in 1566 they occupied Bavaria, Tyrol, Franconia, a great part of the Rhine Province and Austria and had penetrated into Hungary and Moravia. It was the first durable anti-Protestant check that Germany had received.*

In 1566 Canisius was theologian to the Legate at the Diet of Augsburg. The indifferentists wished for a declaration of religious peace between the denominations. Catholic intransigents denounced such a suggestion as a betrayal, but Canisius who had a political sense far more keen than most of his contemporaries saw clearly that, if peace was rejected, the inevitable result would be civil war and that even if the Catholics were to win that war the true Catholicism of their faith would inevitably be disastrously damaged by the fighting, and that a victory for Catholic arms over a population that had no Catholic spirit would be an empty and worthless victory. He saw on the other hand that owing to his educational foundations the Catholics were now at last beginning to win that intellectual debate which a few years before they were

* Quoted in J. Brodrick, *Peter Canisius*, London, 1935, p. 767.

so visibly losing and that his new colleges would almost certainly perish in the destruction of war. He persuaded the Legate not to denounce the peace and thus to plunge the country into war, and was thus able to continue his work of educational foundations. In 1567 he founded a college at Wurzburg. He evangelized Mayence and Spires and he established a college at Halle. In 1575 he was papal Legate at the Diet of Ratisbon. He introduced the Sodality of the Blessed Virgin at Innsbruck and finally at the Pope's command built a college at Freiburg where he remained for the rest of his life. Canisius saw the need for an organized literary defence of the Church, and cultivated the friendship of the great printers and publishers of the day such as Plantin, Cholm and Mayer. He brought out the first official reports of foreign missions, established a printing press at Freiburg, and was himself ceaselessly writing. He exposed the decrees of the Centuriators of Magdeburg who had falsified early Christian history in a pretended support of Lutheran doctrines, produced a full text of the works of St Cyril and St Leo, and drew up his famous Catechism which gave the answer to some two hundred and more doctrinal questions. He died at last on 21 November 1597.

The general effect of Canisius' work was immense. He turned the course of history. In each of the great colleges that he built there were up to a thousand students. He was the first Jesuit to enter Poland. By 1600 there were 466 Jesuits there. When he entered Germany in 1550 he entered with 2 Jesuits as his companions. When he left it over 30 years later there were 1,111 Jesuits at work in the country.* Macaulay has written in his critical but in some ways laudatory article on the History of the Popes:

While the Protestant Reformation proceeded rapidly at one extremity of Europe the Catholic revival went on as rapidly at the other. About half a century after the great separation there were throughout the north Protestant governments and Protestant nations. In the south were governments and nations actuated by the most intense zeal for the ancient Church. Between these two hostile regions lay, morally as well as geographically, a great debatable land. In France, Belgium, southern Germany, Hungary and Poland the contest was still undecided. The governments of those countries had not renounced their connection with Rome; but the Protestants were numerous, powerful, bold and active. In France they formed a commonwealth within the

* Ibid.

B*

realm, held fortresses, were able to bring great armies into the field and had treated with their sovereign on terms of equality. In Poland the king was still a Catholic, but the Protestants had the upper hand in the Diet, filled the chief offices in the administration and in the large towns took possession of the parish churches. 'It appeared', said the papal Nuncio, 'that in Poland Protestantism would completely supersede Catholicism.' In Bavaria the state of things was nearly the same. The Protestants had a majority in the Assembly of the States and demanded from the duke concessions in favour of their religion as the price of their subsidies. In Transylvania the House of Austria was unable to prevent the Diet from confiscating by one sweeping decree the estates of the Church. In Austria proper it was generally said that only one thirtieth part of the population could be counted on as good Catholics. In Belgium the adherents of the new opinions were reckoned by hundreds of thousands.

The history of the two succeeding generations is the history of the struggle between Protestantism possessed of the north of Europe and Catholicism possessed of the south for the doubtful territory which lay between. All the weapons of carnal and spiritual warfare were employed. Both sides may boast of great talents and of great virtues. Both have to blush for many follies and crimes. At first the chances seemed to be decidedly in favour of Protestantism; but the victory remained with the Church of Rome. On every point she was successful. If we overleap another half century we find her victorious and dominant in France, Belgium, Bavaria, Bohemia, Austria, Poland and Hungary. Nor has Protestantism in the course of two hundred years been able to reconquer any portion of what was then lost.

It is moreover not to be dissembled that this triumph of the papacy is to be chiefly attributed not to the force of arms but to a great reflux of public opinion. During the first half-century after the commencement of the Reformation the current of feeling in the countries on this side of the Alps and of the Pyrenees ran impetuously towards the new doctrines. Then the tide turned and rushed as fiercely in the opposite direction. Neither during the one period nor during the other did much depend upon the event of battles or sieges. The Protestant movement was hardly checked for an instant by the defeat at Muhlberg. The Catholic reaction went on at full speed in spite of the destruction of the Armada. It is difficult to say whether the violence of the first blow or of the recoil was the greater. Fifty years after the Lutheran separation Catholicism could scarcely maintain itself on the shores of the Mediterranean. A hundred years after the separation Protestantism could scarcely maintain itself on the shores of the Baltic. The history of the Order of Jesus, [Macaulay writes in explanation of this amazing reversal] is the history of the great Catholic reaction. The Order possessed itself once of all the strongholds which command the public mind, of the pulpit, of the press, of the confessional, of the academies. Wherever the Jesuit preached the church was too small for the audience. The name of Jesuit on a title-page secured the circulation of a book. It was in the ears of a Jesuit that the powerful, the noble, and the beautiful breathed the secret history of their lives. It was at the feet of the Jesuit that the youth of the higher and middle class were brought up from childhood to manhood, from the first rudiments to the courses of rhetoric and philosophy. Literature and science, lately associated with infidelity or with heresy, now became the allies of orthodoxy.*

It would be absurd to attribute this gigantic revolution in the German mind to one man alone, but most certainly Canisius was far more responsible for it than was any other single person. Its consequence was not of course to reconvert the whole of Germany to Catholicism, nor even indeed to save Germany from the terrible religious civil war of the next century. But it was to ensure that, when peace was to be made in the middle of the next century at Westphalia, it could be established on the formula that the religion of each principality should be the religion of its ruler: *Cuius regio eius religio*. This formula is often spoken of as an acceptance of defeat by the Catholic powers. So in a measure it was. To the high pretensions of such a Pope as Innocent III – indeed even as Pius v – the notion that the secular prince could be allowed to put his subjects out of the Catholic Church would have been intolerable. To them the rights of Catholicism were inherent and the only consequence of a ruler declaring himself Protestant should be that he should be excommunicated and deposed. Still, if the Catholic Church did not emerge from the German conflict with all its privileges, the formula of *cuius regio eius religio* preserved for it a great deal more than at one time looked probable. At least it meant that a Catholic prince could preserve Catholicism in his dominions. Before Canisius it looked only too likely that many Catholic princes would find themselves the rulers of obstinately Protestant subjects who might well demand privileges for their religion as the price of allowing their ruler to keep his throne.

In France the situation was somewhat different. The Protestants – the Huguenots – were of course prominent. But there was never

* Macaulay, Essay on von Ranke's *History of the Papacy*.

an imminent probability that they would make themselves total masters of the country. On the contrary, as Henry IV was later to show, it was convenient for anyone who wanted political power to declare himself a Catholic. But the consequence of Protestantism and religious conflict in France was not to persuade the majority to become Huguenot but to persuade a large number, particularly among the ruling classes, to become sceptical of the full claims of either religion. France was above all the country of the *politiques*, of those who thought ultimate truth unattainable and unknowable and that the most important service that a man could render to his people was peace. It was the country in which Montaigne was asking '*Que sais-je?*' and Descartes soon to answer '*Cogito, ergo sum*'. To such a spirit the aggressive counter-offensive of the Jesuits was not congenial. The Jesuits met with vigorous resistance from the Parlement and the University of Paris. Their friend was du Prat, Bishop of Clermont, but in Paris the Archbishop du Bellay was their opponent and they met with no good fortune. Spain was at that time at war with France and the Jesuits were suspect in France as being Spaniards. The university refused them affiliation on the ground that they were neither friars nor secular priests – men of no recognizable status. The Parlement refused them recognition. They had no funds. They were reduced for a time to the College of Clermont in Paris and the number of their pupils was reduced to four. In 1560 their friend, the Bishop of Clermont, died and left them a considerable legacy, but it was disallowed by the courts on the ground that they were not an authorized corporation.

Charles IX was on the throne and the reins of power were in the hands of his mother, Catherine de' Medici. She was essentially a *politique*, sceptical of the possibility of attaining truth and anxious only for peace. In defiance of the Pope's wishes she offered an amnesty to the Huguenots and in 1561 summoned a Colloquy at Poissy before which the rival religions were to state and, it was hoped, compose, their differences. The Pope sent Laynez, by then the Society's General, to state the uncompromising position. Laynez' argument was that it was beyond the competence of secular princes to settle where religious truth might lie. That was the business of the Pope alone. Laynez' intervention was a bold one. Catherine's delegate at the Council of Trent, Du Ferrier, had bluntly stated: 'As for Pius IV we withdraw from his rule; whatever decisions he may have made we reject, spit back at him and despise. We scorn and renounce him as Vicar of Christ, Head of the Church and Successor of Peter.'* There was a great possibility that, if crossed by the Pope and the Jesuits, Catherine would look across the sea to the example of Elizabeth and break the bonds with Rome altogether. The French Bishops had explicitly denied 'the Pope's plentitude of power to feed, rule and govern the universal Church'. On the other hand there were wheels within wheels, and the French Bishops, if reluctant to be recognized as wholly subject to the Pope, were equally reluctant to be wholly subject to the king. Nor had they for the most part any wish to be too closely associated with the unpopular Huguenots. They therefore were not willing to join in an attack on the Society, and in spite of the Archbishop of Paris' opposition, supported and carried a motion for the legalization of the Society. But one at any rate among the Jesuits, Edmond Auger, was not willing to compromise for popularity. A brilliant orator, he was unsparing in his denunciation of those with whom he disagreed and aroused both intense enthusiasm and intense hostility. At Valence, where the Bishop had just apostatized and the whole people had turned Huguenot, he denounced them with such vigour that they seized him and were proposing to burn him at the stake. But from the stake he delivered another sermon of such eloquence that a rival gang, moved to enthusiasm, boldly rescued him. At Lyons he denounced the League with such violence that his eloquence had the opposite effect. The populace which had begun by acclaiming him became hostile and threatened to throw him into the Rhone.

It is a general experience of mankind that revolutionary enthusiasm only lasts for a generation or so. In our own times for a period Communists were true apostles of their creed – truly anxious to overthrow all traditional society – and there was no wise policy but to oppose them without compromise. With a new generation a new type of Communist appeared which no longer had any strong purpose of revolution and Pope John XXIII and Pope Paul VI rightly judged that the time had come when it was wise to engage in dialogue with them, just as Pope Pius XI and Pope Pius XII were wise to refuse to engage in dialogue with their

* Martin, *Le Gallicanisme et la Réforme*, Strasburg, 1929, p. 28, note 4.

predecessors at the earlier date. So it was with the first French Revolutionary Jacobins anxious to overthrow all governments, and their petty bourgeois descendants of the Orleanist monarchy anxious only to cultivate their gardens, and so with the first wild Calvinist revolutionaries of three hundred years before demanding to overturn the world, and their descendants avid only to exploit it. The task of statesman, ecclesiastical or political, is to judge when the time has come when enthusiasm has abated and dialogue has become useful. Laynez was probably right in thinking that it had not yet come at the time of the Colloquy of Poissy.

When Aquaviva became General in 1580 he decided from the first that it was important that the Jesuits should not become involved in the internal politics of any country. He issued strict orders against any such activity and in obedience to them Auger desisted from his attacks on the League. However his abnegation did not protect the Society from the hostility of the Sorbonne and the Parlement. The centre of that storm was Maldonatus, a famous Spanish Jesuit, then lecturing at the University. Maldonatus, while expressing his own firm belief in the Immaculate Conception, opposed the custom of the university of requiring a declaration of such a belief as a condition of admission to it. Since the Immaculate Conception was not then an article of faith, the requirement of it as a condition was, argued Maldonatus, illegitimate. Oddly enough, ever since the Council of Basel in 1439 a dogmatic declaration on the Immaculate Conception had been demanded by the party which asserted the superiority of the General Council to the Pope. The Popes of that day opposed a definition as inopportune and it was natural enough that a Jesuit should support the Pope. Yet their hostility to the university brought down criticisms on their heads. Antoine Arnauld, the father of the two later Jansenist protagonists, pleaded against them as a lawyer in a property dispute concerned with the College of Clermont. He took the opportunity to denounce them as:

those trumpets of war, those torches of sedition, those roaring tempests that are perpetually disturbing the calm heaven of France. They are Spaniards, enemies of the state, the authors of all the excesses of the League, whose Bacchanalian and Catilinian orgies were held in the Jesuit college and church. The Society is the workshop of Satan and is filled with traitors and scoundrels, assassins of kings and public parricides. Who slew Henry III? The Jesuits.

The accusation was of course as absurd as it was irrelevant. It was the League, not the Jesuits, who had exulted over the assassination of Henry III and who had sworn that Henry IV should never be allowed to ascend the throne. It was the Jesuits, and Possevin in particular, who had urged the Pope to grant him absolution for his heresy. Nevertheless, when shortly afterwards Jean Chastel made an attack on Henry IV, the Parlement – again quite without basis – accused the Jesuits of connivance in the crime. One Father Gueret was racked. Another Father Guignard was hanged. In fact Henry IV was always the strong friend of the Society and invited them back to their College of Clermont.

In Spain and Italy the situation was different again. In Italy the city that threatened to follow the English example and establish a national Church independent of the Pope was Venice, which had a very long tradition of ecclesiastical independence. The Servite, Paul Sarpi, was the leader of the movement for secession. Henry IV intervened and was instrumental in preventing this, but the Venetians insisted as the condition of their remaining loyal to the Pope that the Jesuits should be excluded from their country. Aquaviva, not willing that the Jesuits should be a cause of embarrassment to the Church, insisted with the Pope that this condition be accepted.

Education in both Spain and Italy had been sadly neglected, and schools and colleges had to broaden their curricula if they were to keep pace with the new learning of the Renaissance. Numerous colleges were established in various places in Italy and the *Ratio Studiorum* on which Jesuit education was for so many years to be based was drawn up. In Spain Protestantism had little hold, and the Inquisition saw to it that there was little overt proclamation of heresy. But repression of course has only a limited effect. It can do no more than compel men to keep their doubts to themselves. He who can hold his tongue can hold anything and worldliness and cynicism were rife among the high ecclesiastics; Catholics, like other people, require the challenge of competition to make them live up to their standards. It is very often in countries whose population is nominally solid in its Catholicism that the Christian precepts are in reality least obeyed, and sixteenth-century Spain was no exception to this generalization. Nor was the disfavour with which, owing to his German quarrels, the Emperor Charles v now viewed the Society of advantage to it in Spain. But apart from the opposition of the worldly, the secular-minded and the cynical, the Society met in Spain the first of a peculiar class of enemies by whom its footsteps have been dogged throughout its life. Ignatius, at the Society's first foundation, prayed that it might 'never for long remain unharassed by the enmity of the world' and said that if ever there was a time when all the world spoke well of it that would certainly be a proof that it was not properly performing its task. His prayer has certainly been answered. Jesuits over the years have of course made their mistakes. They make no claim to perfection and the historian and critic is entitled to pass his verdict on this action and on that. But apart from reasoned criticism the Jesuits have throughout their history always had the capacity to arouse in some few people – sometimes Catholic, sometimes non-Catholic – hatred and denunciation of almost insane violence. Perhaps the Jesuits' way of talking of their fellow Jesuits as 'ours' and the rest of the world as 'externs', their habit at times of thinking of themselves almost as an ecclesia within an ecclesia, a foolish sense of loyalty which causes them to defend actions and sayings of colleagues which no one really believes them to approve in their hearts, have at times irritated and perhaps to some extent caused the reaction. But there can be no doubt that the reaction has been altogether more violent than the provocation warranted.

The first of these strange psychopaths appeared in these early years in Spain – a Dominican called Melchior Cano. The reason for his great hatred is impossible to understand. Controversies about grace were at that time still in the distant future. There was no general hostility between Dominicans and Jesuits. His own Dominican Provincial specifically repudiated him and forbade him to continue with his attacks, as did the Pope. They made him Bishop of the Canaries to get him out of the way but he resigned and returned to Spain to continue the hostilities. At his death he left a document in which he wrote, 'If the religious of the Society continue as they have begun there may come a time, which I hope God will avert, when the kings of Europe would wish to resist them but will be unable to do so.' This document naturally enough was much quoted two hundred years later when the European monarchs were asking for the destruction of the Society. But when we come to ask what was Cano's objection to the Society it does not seem easy to find anything except his opposition to their advocacy of more frequent Communions – a point on which even had he been right it is not easy to see why he should have become so inordinately heated.

In Portugal the troubles of the Jesuits in these early years came rather from their own follies than from the hostility and short-comings of others. The importance of Portugal at that time was of course that she was the great imperial power, and the Portuguese King John III asked for Jesuits to be sent to Portugal's territories overseas on missionary enterprises. This was exactly the sort of service for which in Ignatius' view the Society was most especially formed. The story of how those requests were met in the colonial fields will be told in the coming chapters. Our immediate concern is with the fortunes of the Jesuits who were left behind at base in Portugal to organize those activities. The Provincial there was Rodriguez, one of the original Jesuits. Rodriguez was for ever writing to Francis Xavier in the East saying how much he was longing to join him at the front. But in fact all the evidence was that he had taken a considerable liking to life in contact with a royal court.

The first task of a Provincial in Rodriguez' position was to make a wise choice of the Fathers whom he sent overseas to the missions. He did not prove himself adept at this and he sent out a number of Fathers who were not well suited to their tasks. Meanwhile he was introducing strange and morbid forms of discipline among the Jesuits under his command at home. Ignatius in the early days of his conversion had, like so many new enthusiasts, submitted himself to strange and violent forms of penitential discipline. His sturdy common sense soon taught him that such ascetic practices tended to be in reality forms of indulgence rather than of penitence and that, if practised at all, they should only be practised under the strict control of a spiritual director. Otherwise they might well do more harm than good, and the Jesuit way of life has always tended to be very suspicious of penitential extravagances. But Portugal at that time was rife with them and Rodriguez was indiscreetly willing to participate in them. Oblivious of the cardinal Jesuit rule of obedience, he encouraged his companions to carry indulgence in such practices far beyond any

B

bounds of which Ignatius would approve and it was, according to Brou's *Vie de St François Xavier*, common enough to see eight or ten thousand flagellants in the streets of Lisbon exercising themselves with a Jesuit to whip them on – a form of traffic-jam of a peculiar kind.

Ignatius recalled Rodriguez to Rome, but Rodriguez had been immensely popular both with the king, the people of Lisbon and the members of his own Society. Extravagance was in the air there at that time. The result of Rodriguez' recall was that a hundred and thirty-seven members of the Society in Portugal left or had to be dismissed. A special visitor had to be sent to the king to appease him and dissuade him from withdrawing his favour from the Society. It was well that the visitor succeeded, for a quarrel with the king of Portugal would have meant not only the destruction of the Society in Portugal, but, what was far more important, the destruction of its missionary enterprises.

THREE

The early Jesuits in Asia

With the discovery of the route round the Cape the Portuguese had been able to establish themselves as the world's leading colonizing power. Portuguese colonists had gone out to the East, but they had taken little of the spirit of their religion with them and John III's desire that missionaries should go out to the Portuguese colonies was not so much in the first instance to convert the natives as to make respectable and Christian the lives of the Portuguese settlers. It was of course Francis Xavier who was selected for this great task. He sailed from Lisbon as papal Nuncio and Portuguese ambassador to the Emperor of Ethiopia on 7 April 1541. Sailing down the west coast of Africa, rounding the Cape of Good Hope, he made first for Mozambique, and thence across the Indian Ocean to Goa. He remained five months at Goa, then sailed down the coast to Cochin and Cape Comorin and across to Ceylon: he visited the Pearl Fisheries and thence returned to Goa where he remained until the closing days of September 1545. He then sailed round the tip of India and across to Malacca in the Indonesian islands, turned north in the direction of China and Japan and sailed up as far as the Moluccan Islands which he reached in the middle of 1546. He remained there two years. Then he returned to Goa in 1548. He went back again to Malacca and thence sailed up to Japan which he reached on 15 August 1549, staying there till the end of November, when he returned to Goa, which he reached in 1551. On 17 April 1552 he set out again, intending to land in China, but he only got as far as the island of Sancian just thirty miles off the coast opposite China. He was never able to land on the mainland but died in Sancian on 2 December 1552. He was forty-six years old and it was eleven years and six months since he had sailed down the Tagus.

This record of travel under the conditions of that time is of

course astounding, and no one has ever challenged Xavier's title
to be the greatest Christian missionary since St Paul. Missionary
work of this kind and on such a scale was unknown before his day.
When he first arrived in Goa he found the condition of morals and
religion there appalling. The Christians made little pretence of
leading a Christian life. The major obstacle to all missionary success was indeed the unedifying example of the Catholics; for
example, the slave-owners flogged their slaves, counting the
number of strokes on their rosary beads. It is not to be expected
that those who go abroad to new countries will, unless they go for
a definitely missionary purpose, be edifying people. Barros, the
Treasurer of the Indies, gave as his opinion that 'the Moors and
Gentiles are outside the law of Jesus Christ. We Christians have no
duties towards them',* and his opinion seems to have been pretty
generally held by the Portuguese colonists of his day.

However, apart from the shortcomings of the Portuguese, conversion of the Indians was in Xavier's opinion almost impossible
because of the obstacles of the caste system and polygamy which
the convert would be required to abandon. In the first month of
his first visit to Goa Xavier was able to effect a considerable
improvement, though how much that improvement was likely to
survive his departure (and indeed how much it did) was clearly a
very open question. Nevertheless there were around the Indian
southern promontory at Cape Comorin among the inhabitants of
the Pearl Fisheries a population that had been baptized some years
before by visiting Franciscans and then abandoned. They were
despised and shunned by their neighbours first because they had
become Christians and secondly because in the Hindu hierarchy
they were of a very low caste. They lived a wholly degraded life.
Xavier lived with them for two years, baptized those of them who
had not been previously baptized and when he left sent them
missionaries to replace him so that they would never again be
abandoned. On his next journey he went first to Malacca – a
dangerous post, for the majority of the inhabitants were Muslims
whose toleration of his coming was uncertain. The Portuguese
Catholics who were there had been without priests for a long time
and their moral and religious practices had degenerated. Xavier
spent three days without food, ceaselessly hearing their confes-

* *Asia Portugueza,* Decade I, Book I, Chapter 1.

sions. He spent two years in the Moluccas, travelling up and down and establishing stations with the result that when du Beira was sent there ten years later he found forty-seven stations and three thousand Catholics.

Xavier then returned to Goa and found, as was almost inevitable, that things had not gone altogether smoothly in his absence. A certain Gomes had been made Rector of the college there and he, a man of volatile temperament, had succeeded in turning everything upside down and in quarrelling with his fellow-Jesuits. However, he was popular in the town and an eloquent preacher and to have removed him and sent him home would have aroused criticism. If Xavier was not willing to remain himself permanently in Goa, he could not afford to dismiss Gomes completely. He contented himself with restricting Gomes' authority to temporal matters and entrusting the spiritual authority of the community to another priest of the name of Cypriano.

For Xavier had reached the conclusion that there was no great work to be done in Goa. Christianity, he thought, could not hope to make great progress in the face of other established religions – of Muslims, or Jews, or Hindus. Its best hope lay among total pagans – among those who had never heard of the name of Christ and who had no perverted notion of Him because they had no notion of Him at all. He imagined that he would find such people in China and Japan and it was thither that he was now determined to go. On his way he passed Malacca, where he found that the missions that he had established were doing well. Thence in a miserable Chinese junk, with a few companions, of whom one was a Japanese convert called Xaca, he sailed for two months until he saw the mountains of Japan and on 15 August 1549 landed at Xaca's native city of Kagoshima. The legend that Xavier had some supernatural gift for tongues is quite untrue. He was always dependent on interpreters. He did indeed make it his first task to master the language as well as he could and, that done, drew up in collaboration with Xaca a Christian statement of faith. The Japanese authorities put no obstacle in his way and he and Xaca set out on a preaching mission. The Japanese boys, an ill-mannered lot, were the only inhabitants to show him hostility, pelting him with stones. Japanese religious life, which was Shinto, was under the control of religious leaders, called bonzes, who were men of little faith or respectability. The people at first looked on Xavier merely as another bonze, but, when they discovered that he at least had something different to say, the curiosity of some of them at any rate was aroused. But, whereas polygamy had been the obstacle in India, in Japan it was sodomy.

Rich men began to ask him to their houses. Xavier had up till now gone about in the rags of poverty, and on his voyage to India he had argued in response to a benefactor who had offered to provide him with a servant: 'It is credit and authority acquired by the means you suggest which have reduced the Church of God and her prelates to their present plight. The right way to acquire them is by washing one's own clothes and boiling one's own pot without being beholden to anybody.'* But now he came to the conclusion that this policy was a mistake and that he could only hope for a hearing if he dressed himself as a man of some influence.

It had always been the Jesuit belief that nations could best be converted through the conversion of their rulers. The Jesuit Suarez was amply to demonstrate, if demonstration was necessary, that this by no means meant that they thought that only the souls of the powerful were of value. It was simply a recognition of the fact that in the world as it was in the sixteenth century, whether in Europe or in Asia, it was not possible to carry out missionary work except with the goodwill of the secular authorities. There was obviously a danger in such policies – a danger that far from converting the poor the missionary would be perverted by the rich – and history has examples of men who could be suspected of such perversion. But Francis Xavier is obviously not among them.

It was for much the same reason that Xavier wished the Jesuits to display their scholarship. 'It was only because they believed we were scholars that they were disposed to listen to us on the subject of religion,' said Xavier.† The bonzes seem according to his account to have asked him some very reasonable questions. If the world contains both good and bad, they said, are there then two principles at work – a good and an evil principle? No, said Xavier, everything was made by the one good God. How then is there evil? they asked. Evil has come into the world, he said,

* 'Monumenta Xavierana', chapter II, pp. 836–7, in *Monumenta Historica Societatis Jesu* published by the Jesuits of Madrid, 1894.

† R. Rowbotham, *Missionary and Mandarin,* Berkeley, 1942, p. 213.

through man's evil. But why, they asked, did a good and omnipotent God make a man who was capable of evil? Why did He
not make a wholly good man? Besides there are many evils in the
world that are in no way the consequence of man's sin. Xavier
tells us that they raised these questions but that he answered them
satisfactorily. It would be interesting to know how, for they are
questions that have bothered man since the beginning of time and
to which no one has ever yet found a final answer.

At Yamaguchi a rich man gave Xavier a permanent home. He
remained there, preaching continually for some six months, and
made a number of converts. Then he went to the capital which was
then called Meaco, the present Kyoto, but made there little
impression.

At Meaco he received the news that things were not going well
at Goa and therefore, leaving two of his Jesuit companions, Torres
and Fernandes, behind in Japan, he returned to Goa. On his way
he passed Cape Comorin where he received the news that one of
his Jesuit priests, Criminali, whom he had left among the Pearl
Fishers, had been murdered – the first of the Jesuit martyrs. Reach-
ing Goa, he found that other missions that had been established
throughout the East were greatly flourishing; there was one, for
instance, at Ormuz off the coast of Arabia under the care of the
Belgian, Baertz. But at Goa the college over which Gomes had
been left to preside was in great disorder and Gomes had succeeded
in embroiling the Society with the Governor General. Xavier
therefore dismissed Gomes and recalled Baertz to make him Vice-
President in Gomes' place. Gomes resented his dismissal and
went home to appeal to Rome, but was drowned on the voyage.

As soon as Baertz was installed Xavier set out again – this time,
as he hoped, for China. Passing the Pearl Fisheries, he discovered
that the mission there was in great difficulty, but had no time to
do more than write back to Baertz, telling him of the situation
and bidding him find a remedy. Xavier's plan had been to sail to
China as the papal Nuncio to the Emperor of China in a large and
well-appointed vessel. Only by such an approach was there any
hope of being received by the Emperor. However the disreputable
Governor of Malacca who was deeply in debt seized Xavier's
vessel and its cargo and Xavier had to sail up the Chinese coast in
a much smaller, less well-appointed and less distinguished craft.

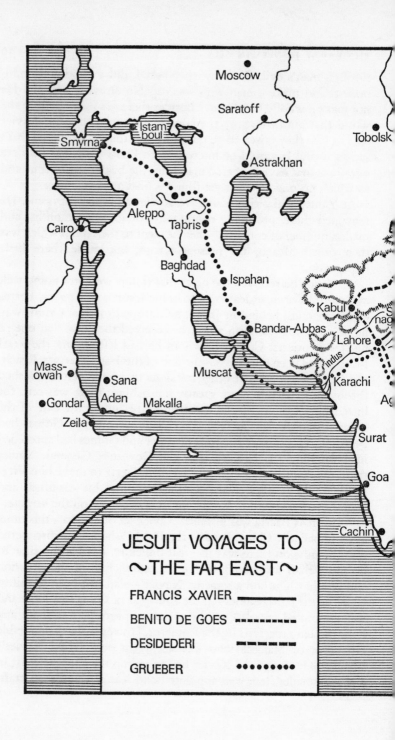

Moscow

Saratoff

Tobolsk

Istamboul

Smyrna

Astrakhan

Aleppo

Tabris

Cairo

Baghdad

Ispahan

Kabul

nag

Bandar-Abbas

Lahore

Indus

Mass-owah

Sana

Muscat

Karachi

Gondar

Aden

Makalla

Zeila

Ag

Surat

Goa

Cachin

JESUIT VOYAGES TO
~THE FAR EAST~

FRANCIS XAVIER ————

BENITO DE GOES - - - - - - - -

DESIDEDERI — — —

GRUEBER •••••••••

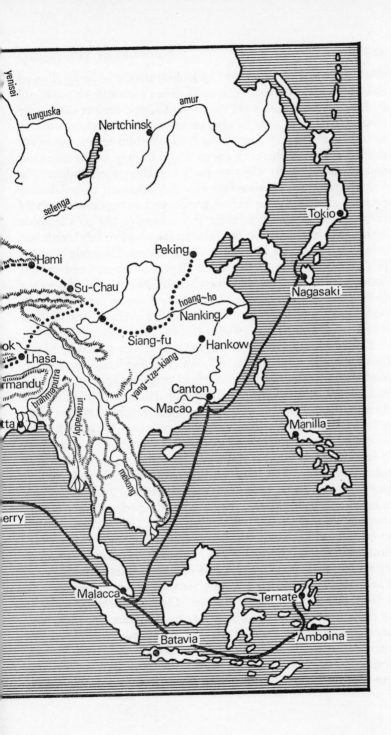

With an arrival of such a sort he had no chance of being allowed to land on the mainland. He landed, as has been said, on the island of Sancian, thirty miles off the coast. Chinese traders came over to the island from time to time and it was Xavier's hope that he would be able to get one of them to take him across. However death was the penalty both for an illegal landing on the mainland and for assisting to contrive such a landing for another. The Chinese traders were therefore naturally reluctant to collaborate even for money. Xavier waited, hoping that an opportunity would come, living in the meanwhile in a miserable hut on the shore which gave him no protection against the weather. His health was failing fast and on 2 December 1552, he died. His body was put in a pit of quicklime so that the flesh might be consumed and his bones buried. Two months later when the ship was about to return to Goa the grave was opened and to the onlookers' amazement the body was found quite uncorrupt. It was carried back to Goa where it remains in that state to this day.

This story of Xavier in death, as many stories of Xavier in life, illustrates one of the great difficulties of modern hagiography. Those who wrote the lives of saints in past ages were persons who had no doubt at all that God through His agents miraculously intervened in the affairs of this world. The modern age is in some ways more sceptical, if in others more credulous. We all of us now accept in general Hume's dictum, that, other things being equal, it is more probable that witnesses lie or are deceived than that miracles happen. The most credulous of us would today admit that for many events of the past that are claimed as miracles there is insufficient evidence that they happened – perhaps in some cases that later discoveries have shown that what was at the time thought to be miraculous was really susceptible of a natural explanation. Still, even though they may not happen as frequently as men of an earlier generation thought, it is obviously integral both to any Christian belief and to any unbiased approach to evidence to believe that they sometimes happen. The overwhelming majority of cures at Lourdes, for instance, are not miracles. But there have been a few miracles there. We do not expect miracles. We are not encouraged to expect them. But miracles do sometimes happen and unless one holds such a belief it is very difficult to see how one can read the New Testament with any appreciation at all. For the

New Testament was clearly written by men who believed, without any suspicion that they could be wrong, that miracles both could happen and had fairly frequently happened in their own experience. They may perhaps have been mistaken in this or that story but, if one takes the view that miracles are an impossibility and never happened, then the New Testament writers were so totally wrong on this gigantic point that there is no reason to think that they were right on anything else. There is no reason to accept them as serious historians at all.

Now, if God worked miracles two thousand years ago, is it common sense to imagine that He strangely ceased to perform them when the biblical period was finished? Therefore the general Christian view throughout the ages has been to imagine that miracles do happen from time to time, and when a great saint appears, to expect his sanctity to be signalized by God by some miracle. Credulous persons have doubtless often claimed as miracles events that were not miraculous or that never happened. But their errors do not invalidate the general reasoning. Now among those who are acclaimed as saints some have shown their sanctity by the achievement of some private, special, personal relationship with God. They have not greatly impinged on the secular world. A believer will find little difficulty in accepting that such persons were able to work miracles. The disbeliever will disbelieve as he chooses and give such psychological explanation of the illusion as he chooses, but he will not be greatly concerned because to him such a self-deceiving man or woman as the pretended saint will not be a person of great interest. But there is another sort of saint who forces himself on the historian's attention, whether the historian be Christian or sceptic, because he changed the face of history in a way that no historian can ignore. Joan of Arc was a saint of this sort, and so most notably were the early Jesuits – Ignatius himself, of course, and among his followers no one more so than Francis Xavier.

The secular historian cannot ignore Francis Xavier, though he may somewhat regret the stories of his miracles – think that all of them are untrue, as some of them most certainly are, think that he was a great man in spite of his miracles whereas his contemporaries thought that he was a great man because of his miracles. What are we to make of the story that when he had lost his crucifix overboard a crab retrieved it and brought it back to him? Did it happen at all? If it happened, was it a miracle or only a very strange coincidence? It does not greatly matter. Yet the stories are of sufficient interest to warn any inquirer against the vulgar notion that holiness and the company of the things that are unseen is in some way, as some think, an evidence of feebleness of mind and incompetence in the affairs of the world.

The world pays tribute to Francis Xavier's greatness and the most secular of historians is unstinted in admiration of the almost supernatural heroism which carried him through so many sufferings. Most justly so. Yet let us try and estimate and set out clearly what his achievement was. He did not succeed as he would have liked in winning the whole oriental world for Christ, or indeed even in laying the foundations for some such total conquest. Today there is a handful of Christians, some Goanese, some of other races, scattered through India. They are pitifully few. Christianity has made hardly any impact upon India. Such Christians as there are are scattered through the Indian peninsula and with very few exceptions are quite uninfluential. Bishop Mylne, Anglican Bishop of Bombay in the early years of this century, was a fervent admirer of Xavier, but records: 'Yet what is the result today? That the conversion of the country to Christianity is no nearer than it was when he left it, for anything that his followers have done; that they form but a Christian caste, unprogressive, incapable of evangelizing, observing distinctions of caste within the body of the Christian Church.'* He blames Xavier for travelling too widely, contrasting his wanderings with the missionary enterprises of such later Protestants as Schwartz and William Carey who found it profitable to confine their activities to a definite locality. Again there are Catholics of Portuguese or partly Portuguese blood in Malaysia and Indonesia. There are Catholics in Vietnam, but they do not derive from Xavier. In Japan and China they have never been in modern times, even when they have been permitted at all, more than a small fraction of the population, and suspect as unpatriotic.

It would, of course, be unfair to suggest that it was Xavier who was wholly, or perhaps even at all, to blame for these failures. In what proportion blame was to be divided between the short-

* Louis George Mylne, *Missions to Hindus*, London, Longmans, 1908, pp. 114–18.

comings of later Jesuits, the readiness of Dutch and English
Protestants to forswear their religion for commercial advantage,
the hostility of non-Jesuit Catholics from motives whether sincere
or jealous, will be discussed on a later page. Perhaps the task
was simply impossible of achievement. But we must face the two
criticisms that have been suggested against Xavier. The first is
this: Christianity, as we have said, was in its nature in no way a
special revelation to Europeans. Christendom was only forced
back into Europe by the course of history. When in the sixteenth
century for the first time for a thousand years Christendom had the
opportunity of making a large advance into continents outside
Europe, this was not a conquest of the other continents. It was the
expansion of the Catholic Church to reassume its true world-wide
Catholic nature, of which for a period it had been deprived. Yet
Xavier, willing to accept the Asian as a Catholic, was not willing
to grant to him at once the full privileges of Catholicism. He
would not have Indian priests. The caste system and polygamy, he
argued, made it extremely difficult for an Indian to become a
Catholic. This was clearly true, but was it not rather a reason for
taking special care in receiving Indians into the Church than for
refusing the priesthood to the exceptional Indian after he had been
admitted? He clearly thought the Japanese more ready for conversion than the Indians and allowed a number of Japanese
priests. Was it only because he knew them less well?

Yet it was suggested at the time that he would have been better
advised to stay in Goa and build a community there rather than
spread his apostolic butter so widely and so thinly. There were
those in Goa who complained that the misunderstandings between
the Jesuits and the civil authorities might have been avoided had
Xavier been there to attend to them, and when in the Pearl
Fisheries he gave baptism with little question to all who asked for
it, even Ignatius wrote to him that the instruction should precede
rather than follow baptism and that the well-being of the Church
was reckoned by quality rather than by quantity. It is necessary in
reply to understand Xavier's point of view. Later Jesuits, as we
shall see both in China and in India, were to see in the Confucianism and the Hinduism of their own day corruptions of
certain primal truths out of a development of which their devotees
could be led to Christ. Their critics were to complain of what they

stigmatized as excessive Jesuit laxity. Whatever the rights of that controversy, Xavier had no part in it. To him a Brahmin was an idolater, the Hindu religion abominable heathenry. Whether it was a corruption of truth or intrinsically false was a subtlety about which he neither knew or cared. *Extra ecclesiam nulla salus* was to him most directly and literally true and baptism was the necessary passport to salvation. Such beliefs, stark as we may think them, gave a terrible energy to his missionary work. Souls were to him desperately at stake, their fate dependent on the pace of the work. It is not possible for a man of another generation or another culture to judge such tactics. It is only valuable to record that such criticisms were made of Xavier's tactics at the time – even suggested by Ignatius himself. For canonization tends, understandably enough, to induce a suspension of judgement and we tend to think that a saint's every act was wise and thought to be so even at the time. Neither is necessarily so. Did Xavier despair of making Christians out of Indians too rapidly?

To form an opinion we must carry the story through to the succeeding years, to try and follow, to begin with, the ups and downs of fortune of the Jesuits in Japan in the years immediately after Xavier's death. The Jesuits in those years met with remarkable success and with most bitter opposition. By 1589 the number of Catholics in Japan had risen, it was said, to three hundred thousand, but in that year the Christian women refused to accept membership of the harem of the Shogun, Taicosama. He avenged himself by a campaign of persecution. All Jesuits were commanded to leave the country within twenty days. Every convert was bidden to abjure Christianity. Some did. Some refused. Two hundred and fifty churches were burnt. The Japanese religion, if such it can be called, was, and is, as has been said, Shintoist. It teaches no precise doctrines about the nature of God or the origin of the universe and imposes no precise code of morals. It inculcates ancestor-worship and teaches the transmigration of souls. The Christian Gospel had an intrinsic advantage when preached to the Japanese in that it offered at least an answer to these ultimate mysteries, by which it might be thought that every soul is perplexed. What proportion of those to whom the Jesuits preached were in fact concerned with such problems one cannot say. When primitive people are faced with the challenge of a religion different from that in which they have been brought up, they usually make their decision by observing which appears to be the stronger – which one it is which seems to bring them victory in war. Such considerations certainly played their part in helping the spread of Christianity in Japan. One of the Jesuits' converts, Sumitanda, a reigning prince, threw down a famous idol of the God of War before going into battle and, when he won the victory, it was of course only natural that the multitudes should join the Christian ranks. In general one might say that the two main reasons which induced converts to accept Christianity were that the Jesuits were manifestly men of a higher culture and of more ample scientific equipment than those to whom they preached and that they supplied a spiritual need of which the Japanese by their ancestral religion had been signally deprived.

The main obstacles to their success were the hostility of the bonzes, or native Shinto priests, who were naturally unwilling to see the people freed from superstitions which they were able so profitably to exploit, and the fear that the Jesuits were but the precursors of a European military conquest of Japan. Suarez in Europe might proclaim as a matter of theory that sovereignty was with the people. Vieira in Brazil might fearlessly fight the battle of the slaves against the oppression of the slave-holding landowners, but Ignatius was always careful to recognize reality and to work through such institutions as he found in existence. In the Europe of his day the common man had not as a rule education or opinions of his own. In order to convert a country it was necessary to convert the princes and the landowners. The rest would then follow. It was the same in Japan. When the Governor of Amaguchi was converted, more than three hundred of his vassals, even including two bonzes, almost automatically followed his example. The King Civandono who had been a friend of Xavier, although he did not himself become a Christian until later, supported the Jesuits even with arms. The king of Hirano became a Christian and hundreds of his subjects followed him.

The plausibility of the Japanese fear that the Jesuits would prove to be only the forerunners of military conquerors must be understood. As has been said, with the sixteenth century the European had for the first time advanced beyond the boundaries of his own continent. Everywhere else that he had advanced – in India or in America – he had advanced as a military, conquering power. The cross had indeed been taken to such countries and had played a very considerable part in mitigating the brutalities of military colonization. Still it had only gone there in the wake of the conqueror. The Japanese in their isolation were not very well acquainted with events in the world outside their islands, but they knew that the missionary enterprise without a military conquest which they were experiencing had happened nowhere else in the world and they feared – with good reason – that if the Jesuits should succeed in firmly establishing themselves in the country then, whether the Jesuits wished it or not, the soldiers would soon follow them and establish their military rule. They would have had reason enough to fear this in any event, but as it happened a number of particular incidents greatly sharpened their fears. In 1596 a Spanish captain whose ship had been wrecked on the Japanese coast most foolishly asserted that the Jesuits were only the forerunners of a gigantic Spanish and Portuguese invasion. What his motive was in this insane boast is not clear. Probably in simpleminded idiocy he thought that he would be more likely to be welltreated by the Japanese if they were convinced that his fellowcountrymen were not merely unarmed and innocent priests but fierce warriors who would wreak vengeance for any injuries that might be inflicted on him. If so, his calculation was singularly misplaced. What happened, as might have been expected, was a vigorous persecution of the Christians. Six Franciscans and three Jesuits were hanged on crosses in Nagasaki on 5 February 1597, and a general decree for the banishment of all Christian priests was issued.

When in 1605 the Shogun Diafusama heard that a Spanish fleet was sailing to the Philippines he suspected that its real purpose was the subjugation of Japan. The Dutch and English traders who wanted to get into the Japanese market gladly took advantage of the hostility to Christianity. They represented to the Japanese that the Jesuits were fanatical devotees of their religion, determined to turn upside down every tradition of Japanese life. The Dutch and English, they said, had no such ambition. If only they were allowed to trade they were quite willing to forswear their religion. In 1612 a Spanish ship from Mexico armed with instructions to explore the possibilities of trade put into port. On arriving there it took the usual soundings, a proceeding of which the Japanese knew nothing. The Shoguns had by that time seized real power from the Mikados. Diafusama, the regent or leading Shogun who had up till then been quite favourable to the Jesuits, asked what was the meaning of this operation and an English sea-captain explained to him: 'In Europe this is considered a hostile act. The captain is charting the harbour so as to allow a fleet to enter and invade Japan. The Jesuits are well known to be Spanish priests who have been hunted out of every nation in Europe as plotters and spies and the religion they teach is only a cloak to conceal their ulterior designs.'

On hearing this, Diafusama at once reversed his policy. The churches were all destroyed and the missionaries all ordered to leave the country. In 1616 Diafusama died and under his son a Dominican and a Franciscan took the risk of defying him by saying Mass in public, thinking that such an action would cause him to accept a *fait accompli* and reverse the order of prohibition. They were wrong. The Jesuits, who after the expulsion by Diafusama had slipped back into the country in disguise, had to take refuge in caves in the countryside from which they continued their instruction. A widespread and intense persecution of all Christians broke out but it was by no means wholly successful. It is certainly true that the Japanese, whether of the sixteenth century or of our day, seem to care much less about death and suffering than do other people. They are more ready than others both to inflict tortures and to endure them. Whether this is because they believe in the transmigration of souls, which means that there is no such thing as death in the sense in which we understand it, or whether some physical peculiarity has caused their metaphysical belief, who shall say? At any rate, the pious hope that the blood of the martyrs should be the seed of the Church was certainly realized in Japan. As a result of persecution at least as many people flocked into the Church as apostatized from it. Men and women queued up for the privilege of martyrdom. Those who went to the scaffold were accompanied there by cheering crowds, congratulating them and assuring them that they were ascending their scaffold to heaven. The Emperor in despair reduced the number of seven thousand who offered themselves for martyrdom and ordained that only

1700 should be executed. Kampfer, a Protestant historian, in his *History of Japan*,* has summed up the story:

The persecution was the worst in all history but did not produce the effect that the government expected. For, although according to the Jesuit accounts, 20,570 people suffered death for the Christian religion in 1590, yet in the following years, when all the churches were closed, there were 12,000 proselytes. Japanese writers do not deny that Hide-yori, Taicosama's son and intended successor, was suspected of being a Catholic and that the greater part of the court officials and officers of the army professed that religion. The joy that made the new converts suffer the most unimaginable tortures excited the public curiosity to such an extent that many wanted to know the religion that produced such happiness in the agonies of death; and when told about it, they also enthusiastically professed it.

In 1619 the Jesuits, Spinola and Fernandes, together with some Dominicans and Franciscans, were taken out of prison and put in a pen in the public street where there was no room to turn round and no protection from the elements. Spinola preached to the people from this pen and received converts. They took him out to be burnt, and when he was standing at the stake a little child whom he had baptized was put into his arms and perished with him. There was a kind of exultation in martyrdom among these Christians that is wonderful but at the same time almost horrible. In spite of the execution of so many of their comrades, in spite of the strict prohibition on their entry into the country, the Jesuits continued to smuggle themselves in, disguised sometimes as soldiers, sometimes as merchants. The English and the Dutch, who looked upon them as disturbers of commercial good relations, offered to search all incoming ships to see if there were any Jesuits aboard. Those who were captured suffered fates of unbelievable horror. Some had their feet cut off before they were burnt. Some were plunged naked into a freezing pool in mid-winter and left there to die of cold. The executioners were bidden to scourge them to the bone, to tear out their nails, to drive rods into their flesh, to throw them into pits filled with venomous snakes, to cut them up piece by piece, to roast them on gridirons, to hang them head downwards over a pit from which sulphurous fumes were emerg-

---

* Quoted by T. J. Campbell, *The Jesuits, 1534-1921*, London, Encyclopedia Press, 1921, vol. I, p. 189.

ing, to fill them with water and then to expel it by jumping on their stomachs. When even such methods did not suffice to prevent the Jesuits from smuggling themselves into the country, the Dutch and English merchants thought of and suggested to the Japanese a method by which the Jesuits would infallibly betray themselves. Let them at every port lay down a crucifix on the ground and demand of every immigrant that he trample upon it. The Dutch and the English were themselves ready to trample without scruple. The Jesuits of course would not be willing. One Mastrilli, a Neapolitan, decided boldly to put the matter to the challenge. He landed and before all spectators refused to trample on the crucifix. He was of course arrested, led through the streets of Nagasaki, hanged head downwards for sixty hours over the pit and then beheaded.

In general the Christian cause has not benefited as much as one might expect from the sufferings which Christians have been prepared to endure at the hands of persecutors on behalf of their cause, and the reason for this is obviously that critics have said: 'These men are doubtless brave and sincere but we cannot conclude that the Christians are therefore the unqualified foes of violence as they are required by their creed, for, were they in power, would they not employ violence against others as readily as others are employing it against them? They do not really believe that the ways of peace are superior to the ways of violence, whatever they may pretend.' And of course history has all too many examples of Christians who have not hesitated to use violence when they saw the chance of winning a short-term victory; and in so doing, they fatally handicapped Christianity's chance of winning an enduring victory. But in Japan, at any rate, the Christians suffered simply to do their duty as Christians by accepting suffering, and with no prospect of a day when they would have the opportunity to persecute and to inflict violence in their turn.

Among those who sat to watch the execution of Mastrilli was Father Ferrara, who had been Provincial of the Order in Japan. He, as far as records go, was the only Jesuit who apostatized under the threat of persecution. He was brought to Mastrilli's execution in 1637 and three years later was present at another execution of four more Jesuits. In 1643 he was even made to preside over the trial of five more. It was only nine years later when he was eighty

years old that Ferrara recanted his recantation, saying in his statement before his judges: 'I am one who has sinned against the King
of heaven and earth. I betrayed him out of fear of death. I am a
Christian and a Jesuit.' He was in his turn hung up over the pit
until his death.

It is estimated that two hundred thousand Christians were killed
in the Japanese persecutions. There is of course no way of verify-
ing the exact number. The effect was eventually to expel from
Japan all priests, Jesuits or other. In fact the Dutch and English
merchants by their tales of projected Spanish or Portuguese
invasions had overplayed their own hand and the Japanese, not
drawing much distinction between one European and another,
decided that all were dangerous and to be expelled from the
country. For two hundred years Japan was wholly closed to
Europeans.

It has been said that Catholicism might have survived in Japan
if only the Jesuits had ordained more Japanese priests. It is not
very easy to see how that accusation is justified. There were in
fact a large number of Japanese priests, and a considerable number
of the Jesuits who were martyred were Japanese. Xavier never
had the prejudice against the ordination of Japanese which he had,
rightly or wrongly, against the ordination of Indians. The
Japanese did not have the rigid caste system which in Xavier's
opinion made it impossible for an Indian to give the impartial
service to all souls which is required of a Catholic priest. The
reason why more Japanese were not ordained was purely practical.
There was no Bishop to ordain them. It was a series of accidents
rather than a decision of policy which was responsible for this defect.
Two Bishops who had been appointed died on the voyage out to
Japan. Two served there for a time and ordained priests but they,
too, soon died. A fifth who was sent to take their place again died
on the voyage out. Had there been a Bishop in Japan at the time
of the final persecution he would presumably have been killed and
what would have been the chances of preserving a secret native
hierarchy throughout the two long centuries of isolation from the
world? What happened at any rate was in some ways more extraordinary. Owing to the shortage of priests even at the time that
the missions were most flourishing, Japanese Catholicism was
always a somewhat unpriestly Catholicism. The missionary would

make his converts and baptize them, but he had then to go on his way. The convert only saw a priest at the rarest intervals and had to do the best that he could without the sacraments. There were, it need not be said, grave disadvantages in this but it also turned out that when the priests were finally expelled this lack of dependence on them had its advantages.

Of course many thousands dropped off who under happier circumstances doubtless would have preserved their religion. But when in 1859 Japanese ports were again opened to European commerce and the first missionaries were allowed in, it was found that a surprising number of Japanese had kept their religion, quite uncontaminated, it seems, by strange heresies, through these two hundred priestless years. Father Petitjean of the Foreign Missions has recorded how he was praying in 1865 in the little chapel which he had built in Nagasaki when he found three women kneeling by his side. 'Have you a Pope?' they asked him. 'Yes,' he answered. 'Do you pray to the Blessed Virgin?' 'Yes.' 'Are you married?' 'No.' 'Do you take the discipline?' 'Yes.' 'Then you are a Christian like ourselves.' These were, they thought, the marks of the Church. It is curious and perhaps a particularly Japanese choice, but at least Father Petitjean was able to discover that there were 2,500 Catholics in Nagasaki alone who had preserved their faith through these two hundred years, handing down their solitary sacrament of baptism from generation to generation.

The earlier record of the Jesuits in Japan was one to which no one has ever denied the title of unsullied heroism and sanctity. The story was not complicated there as it was in some other countries by disputes about secular loyalty or by disputes with other Catholics. Whether we look to the conflict with the Japanese persecutors or to the Dutch and English traders who abandoned their faith for commercial gain and trampled on the crucifix, the issue between the Jesuits and their opponents was as nearly an issue of a clear choice between good and evil as one could ever find. The common verdict is that, though the episode was heroic, it ended in total failure; however, as we can see, it was not quite total failure.

Xavier was doubtless right in thinking that polygamy and the caste system were enormous obstacles to any spread of Christianity in India. On the other hand the Hindu does not believe that God speaks exclusively through the Hindu revelation. He is more ready than many Christians would be to listen to teaching that comes from a source outside his own revelation, and therefore has no natural impulse to reject as folly or blasphemy all the teachings of Christ. God in the Hindu's view of His nature speaks in divers times and in sundry places. Also it is natural to the Hindu – more natural than it is to the European Christian – to respect poverty and asceticism.

Akbar, who ruled as Grand Mogul at the same time that Queen Elizabeth was Queen of England, was, as far as one can tie him to a creed, a sun worshipper, but his was a syncretistic sun worship. All religions were in his view aspects and emanations of his all embracing religion, and his curiosity was aroused about Christianity by the fact that one of the wives in his harem was a Christian. At his invitation the Jesuits came up from Goa to expound the Christian religion at his court. But it soon appeared that there was little prospect that curiosity would be carried so far as to induce Akbar to abandon his harem. The Jesuits left his court, seeing that there was no progress to be made, and went down instead to the Salsette peninsula where they were murdered. Akbar was horrified at the news, sent an embassy of condolence and begged the Jesuit superior to send him more missionaries. Jeronimo Xavier, Francis Xavier's nephew, was sent and won great favour with Akbar. Von Ranke records:

While the Jesuit was there the insurrections of the Mahommedans contributed to dispose the Emperor towards the Christians, for in the year 1599 Christmas was celebrated at Lahore with the utmost solemnity. The manger and the leading facts of the Nativity were represented for twenty days consecutively and numerous catechumens proceeded to the church with palms in their hands to receive baptism. The Emperor read with great pleasure a Life of Christ composed in Persian and a picture of the Virgin, copied from the *Madonna del Popolo* in Rome, was by his orders taken to the Palace that he might show it to the women of his household. *

Meanwhile down in the south of India one of the most remarkable of all the missionaries, the Italian, de Nobili, a nephew of Cardinal Bellarmine, was attacking the difficulty of caste with an

* *History of the Popes,* quoted by T. J. Campbell, *The Jesuits, 1534-1921,* London, Encyclopedia Press, 1921, vol. I, p. 229.

entirely new tactic. He discovered that his predecessor in that mission, Father Fernandes, had not made a single convert over fourteen years and de Nobili ascribed this largely to the fact that he was a Portuguese, or Prangui, as they were called, and was therefore in the Indian mind associated with the imperialistic system. De Nobili told the Indians that he himself was not a Portuguese and that, so as to make clear that he claimed no privilege, he would voluntarily submit himself to all the discipline of the Brahmins, abstain from wine and meat, live on rice, dress like a Brahmin and learn and study the languages of Telegu and Tamil and Sanskrit. He went to live in a hut, separated entirely from all Europeans, and soon showed himself better acquainted with the religious literature of the Brahmins than they were themselves. He soon started to receive converts and, like the Jesuits in China, he smoothed the path of entry for his converts by allowing them to continue to dress and behave in all external matters as Brahmins. The news aroused at first considerable alarm among his fellow Jesuits. Father Fernandes complained of him as a conniver in idolatry. Bellarmine and the General wrote to reprove him, but his explanations were accepted as satisfactory and he continued with his peculiar vocation for forty-two years, only desisting when he at last went blind. He then retired to Ceylon where he died in 1656.

De Nobili's tactics brought a steady stream of converts from all over southern India and there were many other Jesuits who followed his method, of whom the most famous was the martyr, de Britto. In 1700, a hundred years after de Nobili, there arrived in Madura Constant Breschi, who not only became a Brahmin but rose to the highest position of authority in Indian society. As long as he was at home he lived a life of the utmost asceticism. But when he went abroad he always travelled in a palanquin, seated upon tiger skins. A servant stood upon either side, fanning him with peacock feathers, while a third servant stood behind him holding over his head a silken parasol surmounted by a globe of gold. The Nabob of Trichinopoli made him his Prime Minister and thenceforth he never went abroad except accompanied by thirty horsemen, twelve banner bearers, a military band and followed by a train of camels. All whom he passed on the road, even including other Jesuits, had to prostrate themselves before him.

It is perhaps not altogether surprising that these extravagances should have been followed after Breschi's retirement by persecution. To follow the habits of the natives in all that was legitimate was sensible, and in their controversy about the Malabar rites the Jesuits were as certainly in the right as were the Jesuits who were involved in similar controversies in China. To ape native exaggerations was almost a mark of contempt for natives, indicating that he did not think them capable of anything better, and perhaps Breschi was deservedly punished.

In India, as in China, the Jesuit policy of treating oriental beliefs as imperfect hints of truth rather than as total errors, as the first missionaries had done, and their attempts to express their teaching as far as possible in the terminology to which their listeners were accustomed was meeting with increasingly vigorous criticism: in 1707 Bishop de Tournon was sent out from Rome to report on the whole situation. To the controversy in China we shall come in a few pages. The policy of adaptation met there with his vigorous condemnation. He condemned as vigorously the similar Jesuit enterprises in south India. There in the province of Malabar the Jesuits, de Nobili, de Britto, Breschi and others, had met with considerable success and, as we have seen, in order to attain it had not hesitated to adopt such native customs and forms of speech as seemed to them innocuous as they had done in China. They had established what was known as the Malabar rite. When the Jesuits became centres of strong controversy, their Indian policy came under attack along with other aspects of their policy. It was evident, alleged their critics, that the Jesuits were concerned only with the success of the Society by whatever means and were not really Christians. But in 1623 Gregory xv had ruled that their missionary methods were permissible and could be continued at any rate provisionally, and they therefore continued to employ them. Their policies extended to Pondicherry and the Carnatic, but in 1700 when Pondicherry, the French capital in India, was handed over entirely to the Jesuits, the whole matter was reopened. De Tournon, sent out on a general mission of investigation of their activities in the East, extended his investigation to southern India, and from Goa travelled across to Pondicherry. He was biased against the Jesuits there as elsewhere, and after a cursory inquiry he forbade the practice of the Malabar rite. The

1. The death mask of St Ignatius

2. St Ignatius at the age of thirty-three attends the school for boys in Barcelona (Ignatius is on the right)

3. St Peter Canisius

4. The first Jesuits take their vows at Montmartre

5. The Council of Trent

6. The Jesuit Father Martini, as a Chinese Mandarin, pays a visit to the Chinese Emperor

Pope supported de Tournon's decree subject only to the qualification 'in so far as the divine glory and salvation of souls would admit', and the matter was argued to and fro throughout two papacies until the final suppression of the rite by Benedict XIII in 1734.

The two sides to the important controversy were each clear, and the decision between them by no means easy. It is clear Christian teaching that Christ died for all men and that His command to us is that we despise riches. All Christians are, as Ignatius put it, obliged to 'spiritual poverty' – to the contempt of riches and to recognizing them as the root of all evil. But, though Jesuits and other religious are called to the actual renunciation of property, it has never been Christian teaching that all men are forbidden to own property. Even Ananias and Sapphira were told that they had every right to keep what was their own, had they wished; they sinned only in that they lied. If it be found convenient to order society in classes, the Church has never forbidden such a division.

Indeed it might be said that the medieval schoolmen went strangely far in feudal days by almost accepting class distinctions as if they were of divine ordinance. That being so, it was clearly but common sense that, when the Jesuits went to the Malabar coast, they should accept up to a point the social arrangements that they found in existence there. The Jesuit is under obligation to live in modest simplicity in his house. When he goes out into the world he should adopt the habits of those among whom he is called upon to work – dress decently, eat and drink with moderation what his host puts before him – being only careful in his self-examination that his own soul is not in any way corrupted by the vanities of the world. Thus, when Xavier found that he would not get a hearing in Japan if he went there dressed as a beggar but might be listened to if he dressed himself in style, he did not hesitate so to dress himself – and no sensible person could deny that he was right. Clearly, de Nobili and Breschi behaved sensibly in so far as they dressed and lived and accepted the diet of Brahmins because there was no chance that the Brahmins would listen to them if they lived as pariahs. The Christian religion was not of its essence an especially European religion and they did right to show the Indians that it could discard its European trappings.

C

Yet the question remained whether the caste system was merely an Indian version of the European class system. The most proud and class-conscious of Europeans did not pretend that God loved him more than He loved the peasant – that he would automatically be better treated than the peasant at the Last Judgement. The European class-system never pretended to be more than a system for this world. As symbol of their equality in the eyes of God, lord and serf knelt together at the altar. Could the same be said of the Indian caste system? The Brahmin was not willing to receive the sacraments side by side with the pariah. De Nobili was obliged to administer sacraments to the pariahs secretly. His Brahmin converts would not have tolerated it had they known. A number of the Jesuits joined the Padaram caste, which is alone allowed to have contact with persons of every caste, so that they might minister to both Brahmin and pariah.

In the same way when was a gesture towards an image a mere mark of social respect, and when did it become idolatry? There were, it is apparent enough, two sides to the question. Still it is hardly possible to doubt today that Rome's decision was wrong. On the pragmatic plane it was a disaster. It did not kill idolatry or the caste system in India. It merely killed Christianity, which perished in that part of India with the death of the Malabar rite. As for the idea that Christianity must not be corrupted, Christianity had gone so far in Europe in tolerating a reverence for wealth and habits of unbridled competition that are plainly in contradiction of the Gospel that it was hardly reasonable for it to take a rigid line against inequalities in India. The real truth was that Rome had come to look on the Church as a predominantly European institution and was not inclined to turn a tolerant eye on Christianity that was not dressed in European clothes: to this day it is paying a bitter price for its condemnation of the Jesuits. As for the accusation that the Jesuits were irresponsibly ecumenical and prepared to tolerate any evil which did not threaten their own power, we must remember that de Britto, one of the apostles of the Malabar rite, was beheaded for his condemnation of polygamy, which seems in itself sufficient evidence that they were prepared to draw the line somewhere.

There was hardly any corner of Asia to which in these extraordinary years Jesuit missionaries did not penetrate. At the same

time Jesuits were also going to Africa but there they met with
many martyrdoms and no success. Historically the most important
Jesuit in Africa in these early years was the Spaniard Pedro Paez.
Born in 1564, after ordination he went first to Goa and was ordered
to go thence to Abyssinia to convert the Empire of Prester John.
He started out disguised as an Armenian, was captured on his
way by an Arab slave-trader and had to spend seven years in the
galleys. Released at last, he returned to Goa and set out again for
Abyssinia. To equip himself he first entered a Monophysite
monastery there, and when he had learnt the language and
acquainted himself with the habits of the people, he began to
preach. He succeeded in the end in converting the Emperor and
travelled home down the Nile, whose sources are first recorded in
his book. But spiritually his success was short-lived. The Emperor
died. His successor rejected the Catholic faith and beheaded the
Jesuit missionaries whom Paez left behind. As Macaulay has recorded, 'they were catechizing and preaching in lands which no
white man had ever previously visited and in languages of which
no other white man understood a word.' Father Antonio de
Andrada and afterwards Brother Goes penetrated into Tibet over
the Himalayas. Father Johann Grueber entered it from the
Chinese side. They were found in every part of the Turkish Empire
– in Chaldaea reconciling the Nestorians to the Church, in Lebanon
disputing with the Maronites, in Persia, Constantinople, Ephesus,
Smyrna, Damascus, Thessaly, in India at Mylapore at the tomb of
St Thomas. The missionary activity of the Church outside Europe
before the sixteenth century had been nugatory. With that century,
and predominantly with the Jesuits, it burst out into every corner
of the world with this extraordinary exuberance. One of the most
remarkable of those missionaries, of whom all were remarkable,
was Alexandre de Rhodes, according to Fénelon the first inspirer
of the Missions Etrangères. His main work lay in what was then
called Cochin-China and Tonkin – what today we call Vietnam.
It is to him that the Catholics of Vietnam owe their religion.
Twenty-five years after his arrival there were no less than three
hundred thousand Catholics in the land. It was at any rate believed
that he was able, when conferring the sacrament of baptism, to
combine with it powers of thaumaturgy so that those who had
received baptism were able by the use of holy water to cure the

sick of their maladies. In what proportion faith-healing, exaggeration and genuine miracles were mixed to form those stories there is no way of knowing. They were certainly genuinely believed. When the time came for him to return to Rome, he decided to make the journey by land. He went first to Java where he was thrown in prison, but took advantage of the occasion to convert his godless gaolers. Condemned to solitary confinement, he gratefully seized the opportunity to make his retreat. He then walked alone, ignorant of the languages, through India and Turkey and eventually reached Rome to make his request to the General in 1648.

The first Catholic colonizing power in the East had been, as Xavier's career showed, Portugal, and the Portuguese had won from their priority some very extraordinary privileges. The Pope had agreed that no Bishop could take possession of his see throughout the whole Asian world without the agreement of the Portuguese government. Indeed no missionary could go out to the East without Portuguese consent. No papal bull could be issued without that consent. The missionaries received the support of the Portuguese in their labours but in return were required to support the Portuguese traders or Governors in any disputes into which they might fall with the native authorities. It was by no means always the case that the Portuguese were in the right in those disputes. The inevitable consequence was that the natives tended to think of the Christian religion as a peculiarly Portuguese religion to which other Europeans did not really belong and into which Asians were not really welcome. Alexandre de Rhodes, himself a Frenchman, thought it essential that this monopoly should be broken but naturally enough met with bitter hostility from the Portuguese when he attempted to fight the battle at Rome. After he had stated his case no Portuguese vessel was willing to take him back to the East, but, undaunted, he set out to make his return journey by foot and had got as far as Ispahan in Persia when he died in 1660 something over sixty years old. A French vicar apostolic of the name of Pallu was appointed for Cochin-China as a result of de Rhodes' representation, but again the Portuguese refused to give him transport and he never reached the country.

The most important and controversial of Jesuit missionary enterprises was in China. As has been said, it had been Xavier's clear ambition to go to China and he died in the island of Sancian off the Chinese coast without having ever reached the mainland. A Dominican, Gaspar de la Cruz, landed in the Chinese Empire four years after Xavier's death but was immediately expelled. The first Jesuit landing was in 1581. Thirty-six Jesuits had gathered on the Portuguese island of Macao off the mainland. Valignani, the Jesuit superior, decided that Chinese xenophobia and pride were such that there was no prospect that they would ever let Europeans into their country if they asked for entry merely as a favour to themselves. They would only be admitted if they could show that they were bringing the Chinese some benefit. He therefore took three of his young Jesuits, of whom the famous Matteo Ricci was one, and trained them to become the masters of every latest scientific discovery and device. Then, when the Governor and the Bishop of Macao were summoned to appear before the court of the Governor of Kwantung, these Jesuits were sent to represent them and took the occasion to astonish the Chinese by describing to them a wonderful clock which, if permitted, they would bring into China.

It may seem somewhat childish that it should have been necessary for the Jesuits to bribe their way into the country with petty toys. But of course in China they were faced with a problem different in kind from any which they had met in other missionary countries. Previously they had been face to face with people who were plainly their cultural inferiors: the Japanese Shoguns and kings were on the whole barbaric; the tribes around the Pearl Fisheries or in the Moluccas or Malacca were men without cultural pretensions; if Akbar the Grand Mogul could give himself the airs of a great monarch, he was in his own eyes an enlightened despot who was imposing culture on a barbaric people and he was grateful to other cultured people, like the Jesuits, who could help him do so. In China on the other hand the Jesuits found themselves face to face with people of a culture older than their own – with people who were convinced that theirs was a superior culture to that of the outer barbarians, among whom by their first instinct they were inclined to include the Jesuits. The Confucianism by which they regulated their lives was not indeed in reality a religion at all, but the Chinese did not think the worse of it for that. On the contrary they thought of religion as something which might be necessary for inferior barbarians but which cultured Chinese could do without. The teachings of the Christians seemed to them at first sight plain folly. A man might love his parents or his wife or his children, but love was of its nature a special relationship which could be offered only to a very few. To bid a man to love all mankind or to love his enemy was plain absurdity and such language could only be found on the lips of uncultured persons who were debasing language through an inability to use it properly. For a man to pretend to love someone called Jesus Christ, whom he had never seen and of whom he knew very little, above his ancestors, was both false and impious. To say that all men were equal and the soul of a man of the lower classes was of equal value in the sight of some putative God with that of a man of the upper class was equally absurd and, if taken seriously at all, could only result in the destruction of culture by dragging down the upper classes to the level of the lower, since it was manifestly impossible to raise the lower to the level of the upper. In Europe, as the Chinese understood, they might succeed in evading these patently ridiculous consequences of Christianity by paying lip-service to their creed while at the same time seeing to it that its teaching was not allowed to interfere with the serious arrangement of their lives, as Samuel Butler was later to imagine the inhabitants of Erewhon as doing. But there was no reason why the Chinese should allow themselves to be involved in these humiliating dilemmas when they were still happily able to avoid them.

Therefore the first task of the Jesuits was to persuade the Chinese that they, the Jesuits, whatever other Europeans might do, took their creed seriously. To this end they won their attention by showing that they were in some ways at any rate the superior of the Chinese in that there were certain inventions of which they were masters and of which the Chinese were ignorant:

A watch given at the right moment, a picture, a miniature, some little article in coral, enamel or crystal which in Europe is little more than a vain and useless ornament, presented in China to a governor or a Viceroy will serve as a support for our religion, will create protectors for us and will sometimes be the occasion of changing the situation in an entire province.*

They brought to the Chinese Western architecture and paintings in perspective.

* Bosmans, 'Ferdinand Verbiest', *Revue des Questions Scientifiques*, 1912, p. 232.

The Governor of Kwantung, tempted in the first instance by the clock, allowed the Jesuits to establish themselves in a converted temple at the island-town of Tschao-King. He soon fell from power and the Jesuits were at first compelled to return to Macao. However, shortly afterwards, in 1598, they were fetched back to Tschao-King, bringing with them maps and globes and astronomical instruments, on which Ricci took every opportunity to discourse to the Chinese mandarins. In 1595 Ricci had had the opportunity of being the first European to travel into the interior of China, but he had noticed the deep hostility of the people towards a foreigner and thought it wiser to return to Tschao-King and operate from there as a base. But after the end of a Chino-Japanese war which was then raging, xenophobia abated, and the people of Nankin, which Ricci had visited on his travels, insisted that he establish himself among them. Ricci had by then of course become very intimately acquainted with the habits and ways of thought of the Chinese and he saw, even more clearly than de Nobili had seen among the Brahmins, that there was no hope of making any impression on such men if one delivered no more than a direct frontal attack on all their customs. On the contrary, since the Christian revelation was for all men and since men were of an infinite variety, it was necessary to respect the customs of others wherever this was possible, and to interfere only where it was absolutely necessary. Many of the customs of European Christians were in reality more European than Christian and there was no reason why the non-European Christian should adopt them. Moreover, precisely because Confucianism was not a religion there was no need to interfere with its harmless, if meaningless, ritual of ancestor-worship. He thus had no scruples at all about allowing his converts to take part in the honours paid to Confucius.

In 1600 he moved from Nankin to Pekin, the capital, which was the scene of his greatest missionary triumphs. The greatest mandarin of the Emperor's court, Sin, became a Christian and a preacher of Christian doctrine. Converts from among the upper classes flocked in multitudes, their only apparent difficulty being in the requirement that they should believe that Christ had died not only for them but also for the lower classes. But, as was perhaps only to be expected here as elsewhere, success caused a reaction. Dark rumours began to be spread about that the Jesuits were planning to seize the Empire. Father Martinez in Canton was arrested and executed. But Ricci so long as he survived was able to ride the storm which did not finally break until after his death in 1610. Foreseeing the possibility of banishment one day, Ricci had been anxious to build up a native clergy and to obtain permission for the use of Chinese in the Mass, only specifying that the Chinese used be the language of scholars and not a patois.

The geographical labours performed in China by the Jesuits and other missionaries of the Roman Catholic faith will always command the gratitude and excite the wonders of all geographers. Portable chronometers and aneroid barometers, compasses and artificial horizons are, notwithstanding all possible care, frequently found to fail, yet one hundred and fifty years ago a few wandering European priests traversed the enormous state of China proper and laid down on their maps the positions of cities, the direction of rivers and the height of mountains with a correctness of detail and a general accuracy of outline that are absolutely marvellous. To this day all our maps are based on their observations.*

'Whatever is valuable in Chinese astronomical science,' Charles Gutzlaff† has recorded, 'has been borrowed from the treatises of Roman Catholic missionaries.'

The only weakness in Ricci's achievement was that it was so much a consequence of his own quite extraordinary personality. 'I leave you facing an open door,' he said to his companions on his death-bed. No sooner was he dead than the whole picture changed. In 1611 a general persecution broke out. The Jesuits by special imperial command were called out, publicly scourged and expelled to Macao. Their exclusion continued until 1620 when threats of a Tartar invasion compelled the Chinese to look to Portuguese assistance and caused them to summon back the Jesuits. Among this second band of Jesuits was Adam Schall, a mathematician as great as Ricci, who was employed by the Emperor to reform the Chinese calendar. He was accused by his critics of mixing astrology with astronomy, and to some extent he did so. It was an age in which the most pious of Catholics – and

---

* Thornton, *History of China,* Preface, p. 13, quoted by T. J. Campbell, *The Jesuits 1534-1921,* London, Encyclopedia Press, 1921, vol. I, p. 253.
† A modern Protestant missionary.

even sometimes Popes – had still a lurking belief in astrology. Such a man as the poet Dryden is a case in point.

Under this second invasion the missions prospered and the number of Catholics grew so large that the Jesuits were no longer able to serve them. The number of Catholics in China which, it has been estimated, was 13,000 in 1617, had grown to 150,000 in 1650 and 237,000 in 1664.* The quoted figures of conversions mean little as it was the habit of the Jesuits to baptize and count as converts all the abandoned babies whom they found and of whom the greater number died almost immediately.

The Jesuits called in other religious from the Philippines and it was with their arrival that the mission's real troubles began. Ricci, as has been said, made no scruple about Catholics joining in the ceremonies of Confucianism and the Jesuits had become so accustomed to such ceremonies that they no longer thought of them as in question. But to the new non-Jesuit priests the ceremonies were strange and, being regarded as a form of idolatry, shocking. They wrote back that the Jesuits indulged in idolatry and concealed from their converts the mysteries of the cross. In fact it was quite untrue to say that the Jesuits countenanced any Confucian superstition which they found existing. To the contrary the arguments of Ricci's most famous apologetic work, *The Teaching of the Lord in Heaven*, was that Confucians of his day, so far as they indulged in superstitions, did so because they had corrupted the original teaching of Confucius. Go back to the original teaching, he argued, and you will find that it leads much more logically to Christian conclusions than to the conclusions of its present followers.

Where the truth lay in these controversies only those very learned in early Chinese literature – of whom the present writer is most certainly not one – can have an opinion. When the first Japanese met the first missionaries with the question, 'If Christianity is true why was it not first revealed to the Chinese?' (since they thought of the Chinese as the final repositories of culture) the missionaries were happy to be able to point to the early Nestorian records to show that some of the earliest missionaries had made their first journeys to China. But the Nestorian records, it must be admitted, carried a warning as well as evidence. It is

---

* M. F. Harney, *The Jesuits in History*, Chicago, Loyola University Press, 1962, p. 230.

not easy to discover exactly what these early Nestorians came to believe but it is certain that they were taught by the Chinese as much as they taught to them and came to profess a very corrupted Christianity. It is true also that there were writers in Europe – Leibnitz, Voltaire and the Deists – who used the Jesuits' description of the Confucians to argue that Confucius without revelation could manage as well as Christians did with it; but the Jesuits could not be held responsible for the use which people made of their writings. Some of the more extravagant of the Jesuits indeed came to take up with the absurdity of the Noahcide theory, which taught that Japhet after the Flood went to China and taught the Chinese both the ancient law and the inevitable coming of the Messiah, and their extravagances indeed proved that there were dangers in giving a too indiscriminate welcome to all Chinese thought. The Jesuit habit of comparative apologetics originally came into being through an accident. No one was less sympathetic to suggestions that Christian hints were to be found in non-Christian teaching than Francis Xavier. He belonged to the old school of '*Chrétiens ont droit; paiens ont tort.*' Yet owing to the fact that his not very able Japanese convert told him through a mistranslation that the Japanese *Dainichi*, which means little more than 'the sum of things', signified God, as a Christian might use the word, he inaugurated a habit of this transference of language.

As for the controversy which grew up in China whether Shangti, the universal spirit, can properly be called God or whether he cannot be God since he is posterior to T'Ai Chi, the universal substance of things, the Jesuits on the whole had the better of the controversy. It was common Christian teaching that a belief in God in some sense was common to all mankind and that even polytheists always believed that there was a final God behind the gods. It would have been strange had the Chinese been alone an exception to this general rule and alone oblivious of conscience as the voice of God within them. The Emperor gave his solemn assurance that they held such beliefs and the Jesuits were surely wiser than their opponents in assuming that God spoke to all men, and in trying to understand and build on the language in which the Chinese described such beliefs rather than in denouncing them because their terminology was defective.

Yet whatever the rights or wrongs of the controversy it was

madness of the Christians to allow themselves to appear in bitter internecine quarrel before the Chinese. The Jesuits were not guiltless, but they were a great deal more sinned against than sinning. They were after all the men in position, carrying out a policy. Their opponents were people from outside coming in to spoil it. One can hardly dispute Jenkins' verdict.*

They had been founders and architects of the greatest missionary work which the world till then had seen. By the most consummate prudence and skilful diplomacy they had opened to the Western world an Empire which had hitherto been closed to every explorer. The method they had adopted had succeeded beyond their most sanguine expectations and now their life work was to be suddenly broken down and destroyed by Dominican and Franciscan rivals who were absolutely unable to estimate the plan upon which the building was laid out.

To estimate the relation of early Confucian to Christian thought there was required not only a deep knowledge of the Christian teaching but also a deep knowledge of Chinese teaching and life. The Jesuits could at least claim to have acquired such knowledge by many years of intimate experience. Rome sent out to judge them two bishops, de Tournon and Maigrot, who were not even acquainted with the characters of Chinese writing. 'One wonders,' said the Emperor K'Ang Hsi on reading the facile accusation which they levelled of Chinese atheism, 'how the ignorant and contemptible Europeans dare to speak of the Great Doctrine of the Chinese, these men who know nothing about either its rules or its practices and cannot perhaps even understand the characters in which they are written.' It is certain that the effect of the campaign against the Jesuits was to destroy utterly any prospect of successful Christian missionary activity in China or any chance of an abatement of the continuing stark antagonism between China and the rest of the world. Whether or not the Jesuits were right, there seems at least little question about it that their antagonists were wrong.

One of the new priests, speaking through an interpreter, told his congregation that Confucius and all his ancestors were in hell and that the Jesuits had taught them false doctrine. The result was, as was to be expected, persecution. The new priests were persecuted for having insulted, the Jesuits for having deceived. The

* J. E. Jenkins, *The Jesuits in China*, 1894, p. 101.

Emperor, it is true, remained faithful to Schall, made him a mandarin, and president of the board of mathematics of the Empire. He refused to become a Christian himself but appointed Schall as tutor to the young prince. It was not surprising perhaps that the appointment raised a great outcry among the enemies of Christianity. They said – and they could hardly be blamed for it – that under Schall's direction the young prince would certainly become a Christian and thus the whole Empire would be handed over to Christianity. There was an uprising and a persecution. All the missionaries were seized and put into prison, but one Navarrete, a Dominican, escaped and made his way to Europe where he began, in defiance of other members of his Order, to launch a vigorous attack on the Jesuits for their compromises with the Confucian rites. Schall, who was by then seventy-four years old, paralysed and dumb, was first arrested and then brought out of prison and put on trial for having perverted the young prince with Christian doctrine. It was his fate – a fate not altogether unusual for a Jesuit – that he should at the same time be charged in China for being too Christian and in Rome for being too un-Christian. He was condemned to be hacked to pieces, but before the sentence could be carried out a meteor appeared in the heavens and the imperial palace was burnt to ashes. The 'warning from heaven' was accepted by the Chinese and Schall's life was saved, but the divine intervention, if such it was, brought him little benefit, as he died naturally in the next year.

The leadership of the Jesuits in China passed from Schall to Verbiest. It was Verbiest's wish to carry further the task of accommodating Christianity as far as possible to Chinese tastes. He asked for permission to introduce a Chinese liturgy, but this was refused just as the Swedish liturgy had been refused a few years before. Shortly after his death in 1692 the Chinese Emperor K'Ang Hsi by a decree gave to the Christian religion the full toleration extended to Confucianism, Buddhism and Taoism. The troubles of the Jesuits after that were to be with their fellow-Christians much more than with the Chinese. The attacks on the Jesuit policy of Confucian accommodation at Rome were increasing and in 1707 de Tournon issued his order forbidding to Catholics the cult of ancestor-worship. The enterprise of the Jesuits thus ended in failure.

It is a story of immense importance, which is absurdly mis-

represented if it is depicted as a mere matter of introducing into
China some toys like performing clocks in order to attract the
attention of Chinese lovers of novelty. Any plan to dictate from
Rome the details of Catholic policy in China was in the conditions
of that time an absurdity. Men at Rome knew and could know
nothing of conditions in China. Communications were such that
policies of detailed administration were wholly impracticable.
Father Couplet, a Jesuit who after having spent many years in
China returned to Europe in these years, shattered in health, made
and published the careful calculation that out of six hundred who
had attempted to go out to China four hundred had died on the
voyage before they reached the country. If any success was to be
achieved, there was no alternative but to allow the men on the
spot who alone could know the conditions to take the decisions
for themselves.

It is the paradox of the Christian revelation that Our Lord was
a Jew and that His coming took place within the Jewish civilization. Yet He died for all men and left to His disciples the command
that they preach His Gospel to all nations. Pilate, little knowing
what he did, bore witness to the universal message when he wrote
up over the cross that Christ was the King of the Jews but wrote
it not only in Hebrew but also in Greek and Latin. One of the
first decisions which the disciples had to take was that their obligation was to preach the Gospel of Christ not only to the Jews but
also to the Gentiles. This meant in practice, in the conditions of
these early centuries, predominantly throughout the Roman world
and, on the intellectual plane, predominantly its restatement in
terms which made it intelligible and acceptable not only to Jews
but also to those of the Greek tradition, and of course the first
fifteen hundred years of Christian history were full of inquiry
about the relations between the Christian teaching and that of
Plato and Aristotle. The medieval scholastics, if anything, allowed
Aristotle to influence too greatly the shaping of their theories,
and it was common enough to explain that it was an error to think
that the Incarnation had taken place in a world that was utterly
unprepared for it; that on the contrary the Incarnation had been
delayed until it was in some vague shadowy way demanded; that
not only in Isaiah but also in Plato and Virgil there were to be
seen signs of a *praeparatio evangelica*.

Nevertheless, up till the sixteenth century no very serious attempt had been made to consider what can have been God's purposes in the great cultures that had grown up quite apart from the Mediterranean world. To some of these non-Europeans – to Red Indians, to Pearl Fishers on the Malabar Coast – it might perhaps not be ridiculous, even if it was a trifle arrogant, to explain that hitherto they had known nothing and that they now had everything to learn. It was absurd to use such language to such a man as Akbar, and had the claims of Christianity ever advanced to receiving serious attention at the court of the Great Mogul a more detailed attention would have been necessarily given to what a Christian could or could not believe and practise about Indian customs. As it was, the great challenge to the Christian missions came in China, the home of the most ancient of civilizations, as yet untouched by Christianity.

The tactics of the philistine anti-Jesuit who explained to the Chinese that both Confucius and all their ancestors were wholly without truth and certainly damned were obviously as childish as they were foolish. They betrayed not so much an insufficiency of technique as a radically inadequate understanding of the nature of Christian truth. God created all men – Confucius and all others – for a purpose. Somehow or other, little though they understood it, they must have been destined to play a part in preparing the way for the Christian Gospel. The notion of the Jesuits' enemies that God had created such pagans simply to be wrong and to be damned for ignorance of truths which they could not in the nature of things have known was obviously intolerable to any decent conception of Christian truth. How much that passes today for *aggiornamento* is really rather a return to ancient truths after the misapprehensions of the last few hundred years! The enunciation of the threats of an exclusive version of *extra ecclesiam nulla salus* did not frighten the Chinese into conversion but convinced them, in the circumstances quite rightly, that such a religion must be unworthy and imperfect. The Jesuit attempt to understand the Chinese beliefs, to see what hints and portions of Christian truth the Chinese had discovered for themselves, to encourage what was good, to tolerate what was harmless and only attack what was evil and false was clearly not only the prudent but also the Christian course. God had not spoken only through the prophets.

He had spoken at divers times and in sundry places. Hints of truth were to be found everywhere and so, just as, if it was to be accepted by the Greeks, the Christian truth had to be restated in the Greek language, so if it was to be accepted by the Chinese, it had to be restated in the Chinese language.

It is impossible to say whether or not, if the policies of Schall and Ricci had been allowed to continue, they would eventually have succeeded in Christianizing the Chinese at least to the extent that the Roman world was Christianized. Certainly at the time that the experiment was brought to an end an immense way still remained to be travelled. In China, unlike Japan, they had not as yet even begun to ordain Chinese priests. It is not to be imagined that any dramatic progress towards the conversion of China would have been possible until that defect had been remedied. But, if it is far from certain that the policies of Ricci and Schall would have been successful, it is entirely certain that the policies of their opponents were doomed from the first to failure. The disastrous results of it we can see today all around us. The missionaries were driven out of China. After a time the traders were able to force their way back into the country under the protection of the gun-boat. Europe was seen by the Chinese as a hostile, brutal, material-istic, barbarian civilization, to which the Chinese must yield, when he had to, but against which he would equip himself to strike back, industrially and perhaps even militarily, as soon as he was able. A world whose communications demand that it should be one world appears in our day to be irrevocably divided into two, and it has yet to be seen whether a consequence of this division will not be that each side destroys the other. Who knows but that the Jesuit missions, if they had not been interfered with, might have saved the world from this catastrophic schism?

The condemnation of the Jesuits' activity in China was more absurd than the Malabar condemnation, where there was at any rate a case for it in that the Indians practised idolatry and sup-ported a caste system that was in defiance of Christian teaching. But the Chinese had no beliefs about God. Their theology was simply a void waiting to be filled. Whatever exactly ancestor-worship meant – if on analysis it really meant anything more than a recom-mendation to people to preserve traditional customs – it clearly did not mean that they thought that their ancestors had created the

universe. In fact from India and China alike communications with
Rome were at the time so bad and information so scanty that it
was absurd that decisions on points of detail should be taken in
Rome, whether they were taken by the Holy See or by the General
of the Society. The controversy about ancestor-worship was
doubtless up to a point a sincere controversy, but it was exacer-
bated by national rivalries between the Jesuits, who were mainly
Spanish, and the Dominicans, who were mainly Portuguese.

The early Jesuits in America

As has been said, Christendom had been for a thousand years a city under siege, robbed of its Asian and African provinces, and in Europe defending itself against the Muslim attacks in the West and the East. In the Middle Ages there had of course been the sorties into Asia of the Crusades but they had been no more than sorties and had been in the end unsuccessful. The Jesuits came into existence at the beginning of a new era, the era of Europe's expansion. Ignatius' birth more or less corresponded with the discovery of America. The Portuguese traders were establishing themselves in Asia and Africa. Christendom, by accident almost exclusively European, was not so by nature. The Christian creed was of its nature a missionary creed; the Christian was under divine command to preach his Gospel to all nations. He could not be excused from fulfilling that task if its fulfilment was at all possible. It was only to be expected that such a man as Ignatius should accept the missionary opportunity as an obligation. As will be remembered, his first hope and expectation both for himself and for his Society had been to preach the Gospel in the Holy Land. The Spanish monarchy always took the view that American colonization and the exploitation of the natives was only justified if at the same time they gave the Indians their religion. Yet for the most part only crude and tough adventurers were willing to undertake such enterprises and, however edifying the instructions with which they might go armed to their adventures, there was no very easy way in which the distant government in Madrid or Lisbon could compel those orders to be obeyed. The only answer was to send out with them good and fearless priests, and in such straits it was natural to turn to the Jesuits.

The first enduring Jesuit enterprises in America were in the Portuguese colony of Brazil. A number of Portuguese nobles had

established settlements in what was to become that country. Some
French Calvinists had also established a settlement on the Rio de
Janeiro. It was therefore the policy of the Portuguese monarchy to
unite their settlement around the city of San Salvador. A force
was sent out under Thomas de Sousa and with it went six Jesuits of
whom the most important was Nobrega. They built the city of
São Paulo near to San Salvador and settled down to their apostolic
work. They found that they had plenty to do in instilling some
sort of decency and approximation to religion into the far from
edifying white settlers. They had also even more formidable
obstacles to surmount in Christianizing the native savages, who
were a race of cannibals. The whites had up till then been quite
indifferent to the natives' cannibalism, nor were Nobrega's
attempts at reformation universally successful. Often they only
tended to cause the natives to launch a general attack on all the
whites, confounding the more secular-minded lay settlers with the
Jesuits and thinking of all white men as busybodies anxious to
interfere with their ancestral habits. Fighting broke out. However
de Sousa, the Governor, was a humane and civilized man who took
seriously his duty to bring religion to the natives. Fighting was
sometimes inevitable but he avoided it wherever possible and
went out among the natives, accompanied by a priest carrying a
crucifix, and made peace with them wherever it was possible to do
so. The task was not easy, as the French Calvinists encouraged the
natives to attack the Portuguese. Indeed it began to look as if the
normal state of affairs was an unending war between the two
different groups of Europeans which would probably finish with
their destroying one another. Eventually Nobrega suggested that
he and his fellow-Jesuit Anchieta should go themselves to the
Indians and attempt to arrange a peace. 'Let me go,' said Nobrega,
'and see if I cannot arrange terms of peace with the enemy.' It was
a heroic offer as it was far from unlikely that the Indians would
merely put the Jesuit in the pot. However he was able to persuade
them to talk. They offered him terms which he was to take back to
de Sousa. Anchieta was left behind as a hostage. Again, only heroic
sanctity could have accepted such a role. But the Indians did
Anchieta no harm, and Nobrega was able to bring back terms of
peace. Both Nobrega and Anchieta lived on until the end of the
century and the missions flourished which they had thus heroically

founded. 'In the beginning of the seventeenth [century],' records von Ranke, 'we find the proud edifice of the Catholic Church completely reared in South America. There were five arch-bishoprics, twenty-seven bishoprics, four hundred monasteries and innumerable parish churches.'* It is true that not all of these ecclesiastics were Jesuits but it was the Jesuit who laid the founda-tions of Catholic life in Brazil.

What with the dangers of shipwreck and piracy on the voyage, the loneliness of exile, the perils of murder and sickness, only a very courageous man would make the journey from Europe to America in the sixteenth century. Those who made it were gener-ally either men who were compelled to flee their homeland, or who were driven by the lust for riches, or both. Naturally they were not for the most part deeply cultured men. The missionaries – Jesuit or other, but largely Jesuit – were the only people who made this journey for no personal gain. They were also very greatly the superiors in culture of those among whom they lived. Anchieta for instance – 'that great-hearted little hunchback of God', as Father Brodrick calls him† – living alone among the Indian savages, was a master of prose in Latin, Castilian and Portuguese, a qualified doctor, a considerable poet, an accomplished dramatist.

The crisis for the Jesuits in Mexico did not arise until some half-century later. Palafox, the then Archbishop of Mexico, was a man who according to his own account had lived a careless and worldly youth. In 1628 he experienced a 'conversion'. He entered the priesthood and his rise in the Church was rapid. Eleven years later in 1639 he was consecrated Bishop of Puebla in Mexico and went out there, armed with extraordinary powers of discipline over all civil officials. He had the right even to dismiss the Viceroy – a right which he almost immediately exercised. He quarrelled at once with the new Viceroy Salvatierra and for five years the country was in turmoil owing to the dispute between these two. Up till then however his relations with the Jesuits had been good and he even had a Jesuit confessor. But in 1641 he quarrelled with the Jesuits over the ownership of a farm near Vera Cruz. As a result of this controversy he ordered that no property should be

* Quoted by T. J. Campbell *The Jesuits, 1534–1921*, London, Encyclopedia Press, 1921, vol. I, p. 90.
† J. Brodrick, *Origin of the Jesuits*, London, Longmans, 1940, p. 225.

transferred to a religious Order unless the Order agreed to pay tithes to the Bishop, and he ordered all the Jesuits of Puebla to deliver up their faculties within twenty-four hours for inspection under pain of excommunication. When the Jesuits replied that they must refer the matter to their Provincial he excommunicated them. It was the custom in Spanish colonies to refer ecclesiastical quarrels to a commission of judges. The commission decided against Palafox. Palafox in full pontificals then drove to the cathedral and appealed for peace, but at the same time excommunicated all those who opposed him. When Salvatierra attempted to intervene Palafox simply disappeared and, according to a letter from him to Rome, lived for ten days in the forest without food or shelter and exposed to serpents and wild beasts. Then, returning to Puebla, he repudiated all that had been done in his absence, repeated his excommunication of the Jesuits, insisted that they appear in penitential garb and proclaimed that to listen to a sermon by a Jesuit or to go to confession to one was itself a matter for confession. He also wrote to Rome a letter of violent calumny against the Jesuits, accusing them of taking possession of vast estates and silver mines. Palafox was by then clearly mad. He was recalled to Spain by Philip iv and a commission at Rome decided that the Jesuits had been nowhere at fault except in neglecting at once to provide the Bishop with the evidence for their faculties. Nevertheless Palafox's letters, though evidently worthless as evidence, and indeed as to one of them not even certain in its authenticity, were kept to play an important part in the campaign against the Jesuits a hundred years later.

However, for the moment the Jesuits were victorious and still firmly established in the country. In the early years of the seventeenth century the colourful Irish Father Michael Wadding, born in Waterford, arrived in the country and pushed up into the northern territory where he established the first missions and converted the Basiruas tribe. The greatest adventures of the second half of the century were the expeditions up into Lower California, a country so little known and explored that it was generally thought to be an island. The three great names associated with that mission were Kino, Salvatierra and Ugarte. Kino was probably an Italian who spelt his name with a K rather than a Ch to make sure that people did not mistake him for a Chinaman. He arrived in Mexico in 1681, and in 1683 with a few companions sailed up into Lower California and established himself at La Paz in that peninsula. However, this settlement failed and he spent the rest of his life among the Indians of the neighbouring mainland of Sonora, to whom he taught the principles of horsemanship. In 1694 Kino, having then discovered that Lower California was a peninsula and not an island, set out towards it. On the way there he discovered the famous Casa Grande on the Gila River, said to have been a home established by Montezuma's ancestors on their way south to Mexico, and he said Mass in its ruins. Three leagues from it he found the basin of a reservoir large enough to furnish water for a great city. But this was the country of the most blood-thirsty of all American Indian tribes, the Apaches, and the result of Kino's advance was a war in which many of the mission stations were attacked and troops had to be brought into action to repel the attacks. When peace was restored Kino made in 1698 and 1700 two further attempts to penetrate to the mouth of the Colorado River and thence to enter Lower California by land, but though he got within sight of the peninsula he was never himself able to reach it.

Meanwhile his fellow-Jesuit Salvatierra had crossed the Gulf by sea and established many mission stations in the southern part of the peninsula. Salvatierra was assisted by Ugarte and eventually when Salvatierra returned to Mexico Ugarte became superior. The Spanish Jesuits were never in any way supported by the Spanish government and were entirely dependent on the private charity of what was known as the Pious Fund. Salvatierra died in 1717 but Ugarte lived on until 1729, and both the exploration and the first settlement of Lower California owe more to him and his fellow-Jesuits than to any other men. Bancroft, who was no especial friend of the Jesuits or of Catholicism, wrote* of their work in Mexico:

Without discussing the merits of the charges preferred against them, it must be confessed that the service of God in their churches was reverent and dignified. They spread education among all classes, their libraries were open to all and they incessantly taught the natives religion in its true spirit, as well as the mode of earning an honest living. Among

* Hubert Howe Bancroft, *Native Races of the Pacific States of North America,* New York, London, 1875-6, vol. XI, p. 436.

the most notable in the support of this last assertion were those of Nayarit, Sonora, Chihuahua and Lower California, where their efforts in the conversion of the natives were marked by perseverance and disinterestedness, united with love for humanity and prayer. Had the Jesuits been left alone it is doubtful whether the Spanish-American province would have revolted so soon, for they were devoted servants of the crown and had great influence with all classes – too great to suit royalty but such as might after all have saved royalty in these parts.*

Mexico was of course to Spaniards the half-way house to the Philippines, and there also in these years the Jesuits established themselves.

The task of the Jesuits in America was very different from that in Asia. In Asia they found themselves in thickly populated countries, possessed of their own sophisticated and ancient cultures, in which for climatic reasons Europeans were not likely to establish themselves in large numbers or as permanent citizens. Their task was to persuade the Asians that it was in the logic of their own beliefs to accept Christianity. The American continents were entirely inhabited by native Indians. There was no climatic reason why the European who went there as a colonist should not bring up his family and stay there permanently. The countries were obviously destined to become white-inhabited countries. In so far as the blood was mixed, the mixture was more likely to be that of imported blacks than of Red Indians. The Indians had no sophisticated culture which could be used as a starting-point on the road to Christianity. If they were to be taught the Christian religion they must be taught it from the beginning. The main obstacle to conversion was not any intellectual unwillingness of the Indians to accept Christianity but the patent and appalling contrast between the conduct of the nominally Christian colonists and any Christian code of conduct. The contrast was such that it was difficult to persuade the Indians that the Christians seriously believed their own religion. To the colonist the Indian existed only to be exploited and enslaved. The question was whether in face of the white man's onslaught the Indian would survive at all. The task of the missionary in such a society was to fight the battle of the Indian, to protect him so far as he was able against gross cruelty and oppression. Performing that task, he was inevitably

* Hubert Howe Bancroft, *op. cit.*, vol. II, p. 436.

in bitter conflict with the white colonists whose only interest in the native was to exploit him. This same pattern was repeated in country after country in America.

In 1567 Philip II asked for Jesuits to evangelize Peru. The request was granted. The Jesuits went there, established schools, preached, heard confessions, visited hospitals and prisons. After some years they were persuaded at the insistence of the Viceroy and somewhat against their better judgement to take on parishes also. The greatest Jesuit figure in Peruvian history in those years was Father Luis de Valdivia. Father de Valdivia vigorously championed the cause of the Indian slaves against the white exploiters. As usual the royal government at Madrid was theoretically benevolent but at the same time a little at its wits' end how to show its benevolence. Father de Valdivia returned to Madrid to lay before King Philip III the appalling conditions of his American colonies. Philip was much moved, and made him royal visitor and administrator of Chile. Arriving there at the height of a period of Indian rebellion, he at once gave ten thousand Indian slaves their freedom and persuaded the rebel chief U Tablame and sixty of his caciques to lay down their arms on 8 December 1612. Naturally enough de Valdivia met with hostility from the slave-owning colonists, but he succeeded in establishing four central Indian missions. He opened a mission to tame the wild Araucanian savages who had up till then resisted all attempts to convert them. The task was not easy and three of the Jesuits were murdered. The colonists argued that these murders exposed the folly of de Valdivia's hope of converting the Araucanians and advocated a war of extermination as the only realistic policy. De Valdivia refused and in the end persuaded not only the Araucanians but also the even wilder Guagas to lay down their arms and to accept baptism.

As we all know today, the problem of the proper relationship between persons of widely different races is one of the most difficult of all problems for a Christian. The brotherhood of man and the equality of all men in the sight of God are obviously the most fundamental of Christian beliefs and, where it is possible, it is clearly best to ignore racial difficulties – to bid men to live together in amity and forget their differences. But, though an integrated society must necessarily be the ideal to which a Christian must look, it is not necessarily at all times a wise policy immediately to mix the races indiscriminately. If there is in fact, whether or not there ought to be, bitter hostility between races, if the one is patently the superior of the other, it may be wise for the moment to keep them apart. So it was the Jesuit belief that in South America the white colonists were so deeply corrupted by power and avarice that there was no chance, if the races were mixed, that the Indians would receive decent treatment at their hands, while it was certain that the colonists would by the exercise of irresponsible power be yet more deeply corrupted. So the Jesuits collected what Indians they could and established them in what were known as the Reductions in Paraguay – communities into which no white man other than a missionary or a government official was allowed to enter and in which no white trader was allowed to establish his business. Eleven such Reductions were established in what is today Paraguay and some in the present Brazilian province of Parana. The Jesuits of course understood that these Reductions must be made self-supporting and to that end the Indians must be taught all the necessary trades. They taught them how to become carpenters, joiners, painters, sculptors, masons, tanners, and masters of every other variety of trade. They became cultivators of the soil. They became herdsmen and some of the Reductions had as many as thirty thousand sheep or a hundred thousand head of cattle. They built good roads to connect one Reduction with another. Equipped by the royal government, they created an army to defend themselves and drove off incursions both from the Portuguese in Brazil and from vagabond marauders. Philip v declared in a decree that he had no more loyal subjects than the Indians of Paraguay and the Bishop of Buenos Aires wrote that he did not believe that a venial sin was ever committed in any of the Reductions. By the end of the seventeenth century some one hundred thousand Indians were living in them. The imagination of many writers has been captured by this romantic story of a polity based on what Montesquieu, no special friend of Jesuits, described as the principle of *'ce sentiment exquis pour ce qu'ils appellent honneur.'* Perhaps the most attractive and lively account is that of Cunningham Grahame, no Catholic himself, in his *Vanished Arcadia.**

* New York, 1941.

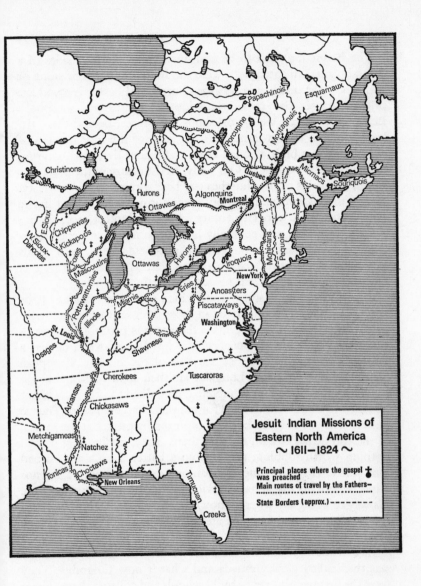

Jesuit Indian Missions of Eastern North America
~ 1611-1824 ~

Principal places where the gospel ☩
was preached
Main routes of travel by the Fathers—·········

State Borders (approx.) --------

Christinons

Hurons

Algonquins

Quebec
Montreal

Porcupine

Papachinois

Esquamaux

Montagnais

Micmacs

Souriquois

E.Sioux
W.Sioux
Dahcotas

Chippewas
Kickapoos
Foxes
Mascoutins
Pottawattomies

Ottawas

Ottawas

Hurons

Iroquois

Mohicans

Pequois

New York

Eries

Anoasters

Piscataways

Washington

Miamis

Illinos

St. Louis

Osages

Shawnese

Cherokees

Tuscaroras

Arkansas

Chickasaws

Metchigameas

Natchez

Tonicas

Choctaws

New Orleans

Timucuan

Creeks

The Reduction used to be laid out around the four sides of a
central plaza. On three sides were the Indians' houses of stone or
adobe. On the north side was the church, and beside it stood the
priest's house, the cemetery, widows' houses and hospitals.
Behind the church were workshops and stores, behind them the
houses of the Indian farmhands. At each of the four corners of
the plaza was a high wooden cross and before the street entering
from the south a statue of Our Lady. In the centre of the plaza was
a well. The ruins of the churches still bear witness to their majesty.
Music, processions and mystery plays formed a large part in the
village life. There were elementary schools and sometimes printing
presses. The land was generally held in common and trade confined to the exchange of the Indians' products against such goods
as they could not produce for themselves. The ideal was that as
far as possible they should be self-supporting.

A very remarkable story – one which gives a good idea of the
sort of life that the Jesuits lived in those days – is that of the Irish-
man Father Filds. Father Filds – the name is probably a corruption, it is not quite certain of what – left Ireland when he was a
young man and studied at various places on the European
continent – Paris, Douai, Louvain. He then went to Rome to do
his Jesuit novitiate. That completed, he walked to Lisbon, whence
he sailed to Brazil and worked for ten years in the mission. Thence
he was sent to Paraguay but was captured by pirates at the mouth
of the Rio de la Plata on the way there. They, finding that he had
nothing worth robbing, put him on a battered hulk and turned
him adrift. He and some companions drifted ashore at Buenos
Aires, where his missionary services were of use. He finally made
his way to Paraguay where, known to all as Father Tom, he spent
the last forty years of his life and died on 8 May 1624, at the age
of seventy-eight.

As early as 1598 there were other Jesuits further north in what
was then called New Granada and what is now Colombia. They
were the first people ever to build schools and colleges there. There
also they set up Reductions for the Indians, but unfortunately their
relations with the ecclesiastical authorities were not as happy as
further south. The white colonists disliked them for the usual
reason that the Jesuits stood between them and the exploitation of
the Indians. The colonists in Bogota were able to persuade the

Bishop that the Jesuit Reductions were a money-making affair and he suppressed them.

Nobody could make such an accusation against Peter Claver. Peter Claver gave himself especially to the ministry of the African slaves who, having been kidnapped in their own country, were transferred and discharged at Cartagena. A less attractive assignation, humanly speaking, it would be hard to imagine. These brutalized, diseased, half-starved Negroes arrived at Cartagena in their thousands. As soon as a vessel put into port, Claver made his way down to the harbour, armed with food, clothing and medicines which he had begged from citizens of the town. When they were sick – as they so frequently were – he would carry them on his back to the hospital where he would nurse them, baptize them and, as very frequently proved necessary, bury them. When any of them showed any signs of recovery he brought music to play to them and, since they were hardly of sufficient education to follow the story of the Gospel from a merely verbal exposition, he would hand round among them pictures of Christian stories to illustrate his message. He himself led a life of almost extravagant asceticism.

The Caribbean islands were of course not in the hands of the Spaniards but divided between the French and the English. The French islands were inhabited by French settlers and Negro and Indian slaves. All were nominally Catholic, but the first missionaries who went to those islands, the Dominicans, in fact kept entirely to the company of the French colonists and never learnt the native languages. The first Jesuits to go to Martinique were two priests and a lay brother who arrived there in 1638. Two of them were promptly murdered by the savages but more Jesuits followed them and by the middle of the century the Jesuits were firmly established in the French islands. In the English islands the story was different and more complicated. Naturally enough the English government of that day – and the Cromwellian government in particular – had no mind to tolerate Jesuit or other Catholic missionaries in their possessions. On the other hand a considerable proportion of the population was Catholic – or at any rate would-be Catholic – as West Indian islands were at that time used by the English governments as a transportation home for convicts, and Cromwell sent to St Kitts and Montserrat in particular a considerable number of Irish Catholics whom he had evicted from their homes after his campaign in Ireland. Some Irish transportees had already gone to the islands during the reigns of the first two Stuarts, but the numbers were greatly increased in Cromwellian times when in 1653 the London Council gave 'licence to Sir John Clotworthy to transport to America five hundred natural Irishmen'. Shortly after, Richard Netherway of Bristol received permission to transport 'one hundred Irish tories' that is to say, supporters of King Charles 1. When Jamaica was captured by the English from the Spaniards in 1655 one thousand Irish boys and one thousand Irish girls were sent there. A Jesuit who figures in the records under a variety of names, doubtless because he had to appear under a number of disguises, but who is most generally called Father Bathe, visited Montserrat disguised as a rubber merchant. He spread the word among the Irish that he was really a priest and they flocked out into the forests where he was able to say Mass for them until one day some Caribs discovered and murdered a number of them. Father Bathe went to St Kitts, where again he said Mass in secret but again was discovered. A hundred and twenty-five of his congregation were abandoned on the deserted Crab Island without food or water. A passing ship was able to rescue a few of them but most were left behind and were never heard of again. Later in Charles 11's time a Catholic of the name of Stapleton was made Governor of Montserrat and he saw to it that the Catholics were properly served.

From Martinique the French Jesuits went in the middle of the nineteenth century to Guiana but they had hardly established themselves there when the territory was conquered by the Dutch and all Catholic organizations were suppressed. However, when the British captured a portion of the land, the Jesuit Father Grillet received more humane treatment in the English colony from the English Governor, Lord Willoughby, and was eventually also able to establish quite a flourishing station at Cayenne in French Guiana, where the Jesuits remained in some strength right up to the expulsion of the Society from French territory in the time of Choiseul.

In North America the Jesuits were of course not allowed in these years to establish themselves in the British colonies. In Canada the majority of the inhabitants were still Indian and, as in

Spanish America, the main task of the Jesuits was that of protecting the Indians against the exploitation of the white man. The first Jesuits arrived in Arcadia in 1613 and in Quebec in 1625. The only Jesuit in those years who penetrated beyond the boundaries of Quebec was Brebeuf, who established himself to the north of what is today Toronto and made himself apostle to the populous Huron tribe. Brebeuf, accompanied by Chaumonot, pushed on to Lake Erie. Jogues and Raymbault went to Lake Superior and started on the work of converting the Objibways. It was the handicap of the Jesuits alike in North and South America that, while they were unpopular with the white man because they fought against white exploitation of the Indian, they were also very often suspect to the Indians who had a reasonable distrust of the white man and equally reasonably did not at first acquaintance understand that the Jesuits were of a different kind from other white men. On 3 August 1642, Father Jogues was passing near Three Rivers on his way from Quebec with supplies for the starving missionaries who had been left on Lake Superior. He and his companion Goupil were captured by the Iroquois who murdered Goupil but kept Jogues with them in captivity for thirteen months, torturing and mutilating him. He eventually escaped and got to New York whence he returned to France. He came back twice more to Canada and on his second return in 1646 was captured with his companion Lalande by Mohawks at Lake George. He and Lalande were murdered on the ground that they were Manitoos, bringers of bad luck. The Mohawks contented themselves with torturing the two other Jesuits of the company. The Iroquois were the great enemies of the Hurons and in 1649 they attacked and utterly destroyed them. Attacking the Hurons, they of course incidentally attacked their Jesuit chaplains. Three, Daniel, Garnier and Chabanel, were killed immediately. The two superiors, Brebeuf and Lalemant, were tied to stakes and burnt to death, the Iroquois during the course of the roasting cutting slices off their flesh, pouring scalding water on their heads in mockery of baptism, cutting the sign of the cross on their flesh, placing live coals in their eyes and the like. When they were dead, their hearts were cut out and eaten. Yet five years later the Jesuits were back again among the Iroquois. Father Le Moyne, to whom there is today a statue in the city of Syracuse, established a chain of missions through their country and many of the Iroquois were converted. The missions were eventually destroyed by a combination of English hostility and the ill will of French Governors in Quebec. Neither government had any great interest in seeing missions prosper too vigorously.

There were other missions in other parts of North America, all of them producing martyrs. There were missions among the Algonquins to the north of the St Lawrence and among the Ottawas to the west of Montreal. Father Menard, a very old man, penetrated as far as what is now Wisconsin, where he perished. Marquette and Juliet travelled down the Mississippi to the Arkansas and for the first time established with certainty that the Mississippi River flowed into the Gulf of Mexico.

The story of the Jesuits in America in this first period of the Society from 1610 to 1791 is recorded in the seventy-three volumes of the fascinating *Jesuit Relations*.* They are the reports of Fathers concerning their missionary journeys among the Indians in these early years. The English edition records in its preface:

Many of the *Relations* were written in Indian camps amid a chaos of distractions. Insects innumerable tormented the journalists; they were immersed in scenes of squalor and degradation, overcome by fatigue and lack of proper sustenance, often suffering from wounds and disease, maltreated in a hundred ways by hosts who at times might more properly be called jailers; and not seldom had savage superstition risen to such heights that to be seen making a memorandum was certain to arouse the ferocious enmity of the band. It is not surprising that the composition of these journals is sometimes crude; the wonder is that they could be written at all. From these writings we gain a vivid picture of life in the primaeval forests. Not only do these devoted missionaries – never in any field has been witnessed greater personal heroism than theirs – live and breathe before us in these *Relations* but we have in them our first competent account of the Red Indian when relatively uncontaminated by contact with Europeans. Few periods of history are so well illuminated as the French regime in North America. This we owe in a large measure to the existence of the *Jesuit Relations*.

The only English American colonies where the Jesuits had an opportunity of establishing themselves were Maryland and Pennsylvania. When the Catholic Calvert, brother of Lord Balti-

* Reuben Gold Thwaites (ed.), *The Jesuit Relations and Allied Documents,* Cleveland, 1896–1901 (73 vols.).

more, established the colony of Maryland in which it was proposed that Catholics and people of all other religions should enjoy total freedom, he brought with him two Jesuits, White and Altham. But the experiment was not successful. The neighbouring colony of Virginia was bitterly anti-Catholic and in 1644 and again in 1650 the Virginians invaded Maryland, seized it, repealed the laws of religious toleration and expelled the Jesuits. The record of toleration in Quaker-founded Pennsylvania was far superior to that of any of the other colonies.

FIVE

The first conflicts

Ignatius, with all the prestige of a founder and with his extraordinary strength of personality, was able to impose upon his Society a discipline that was quite unchallenged. Of all strong personal rulers everyone asks if a successor will be able to obtain for himself the same degree of authority, and it was so with the Jesuits. Ignatius died in 1556, so little expecting death that he did not ask for extreme unction on his death-bed. The election of a successor was hindered because there was at that time a quarrel between the Pope and Philip II – 'the heretic Philip', as the Pope called him in a phrase that is surprising to English ears – and Philip made trouble about allowing the Spanish Jesuits to come to Rome for the election. But in the end Laynez was elected on 2 July 1558.

Laynez had some difficulty with the Pope, Paul IV, who insisted on the Fathers saying their office in choir like other Orders – an insistence which was waived by Paul's successor, Pius IV. He also had trouble in Spain, Italy, and France (over the Colloquy of Poissy in particular). Laynez had his difficulties in preventing cranks from bringing the Society into discredit – for instance Father Manuel Goes in Genoa, who taught that it was a mortal sin to shave. There were at the same time two martyrdoms in India but these were not by themselves sufficient to still all criticism. The forceful personality of Ignatius removed, criticism was beginning to grow about the prominence of what seemed to some an upstart Society.

Laynez died in 1565 and the third General was the remarkable Francis Borgia, who had been Governor of Catalonia and one of the leading grandees of Spain. When he became a Jesuit, Ignatius had always given him a special position different from that of his fellow-Jesuits. He belonged to no province but was at the special

MATTHEVS RICCIVS MACERATENSIS, QVI PRIMVS E SOCIETAE
.SV EVANGELIVM IN SINAS INVEXIT OBIIT ANNO SALVTIS
1610 ÆTATIS. 60.

7. Father Matteo Ricci. This portrait is in the Jesuit residence of the Gesù,
Rome

8. Father Adam Schall, from Kiercher's *China . . . Illustrata*

9. Brother Castiglione, in half-European, half-Chinese costume. A self-portrait

10. St Peter Claver

11. Father Robert
de Nobili, wearing
sannyāsī dress. By
Baltazar da Costa

12. Fathers Brebeuf and Lallemant, tortured by Canadian Indians

13. The tomb of St. Francis Xavier in Goa

command of the General, as Ignatius' Commissary General. A man of great holiness and apostolic zeal, he was by no means without his faults and was strongly opposed by Father Araoz, the Jesuits' Spanish Provincial and Ignatius' nephew, and Father Nadal, the Commissary General of Spain. Borgia bitterly resented it if anyone questioned his orders. As if still possessed of unlimited personal wealth, he founded twenty new Jesuit houses in Spain but made no proper arrangements to see that these houses were supplied with either money or staff. He also attempted to impose upon members of the Society extravagant mortifications which were wholly contrary to the spirit of Ignatius. It was perhaps surprising that he should have been elected General on Laynez' death and indeed it is hardly likely that he would have been so elected had it not been for his family name, but it was an age where a great name still carried enormous importance.

When Borgia died in 1572 many thought that the election would go to Polanco who had been Ignatius' secretary. But Polanco's election would have meant that the first four Generals had all been Spaniards, and Polanco, like Laynez, was a Jew. The Pope of the time, Gregory XIII, saw the danger in the Society appearing, as it might thus so easily have appeared, a Society of Spanish priests, and procured the election of the Belgian Mercurian who ruled up till his death in 1580. Mercurian's reign was troubled by a curious and unpleasant controversy in the Society's affairs in Spain. There were plenty of abuses in other religious Orders in that country at that time and Ormaneto, the papal legate, suggested to Philip II that Melendez, the Jesuit Provincial, should be employed as a spy to report on what was going on in these other Orders. Melendez objected and appealed to Mercurian; in his turn Mercurian appealed to the Pope Gregory XIII who rescinded Ormaneto's order. But meanwhile Melendez had felt himself under obedience to obey and, doing so, had naturally raised against himself a storm of protest, which compelled him to leave the country.

Mercurian died in 1580 and Aquaviva, a member of a noble Italian family, was elected to succeed him in 1581. It was under his generalship that the Society had to meet a most serious attack from within which threatened for a time entirely to disrupt it. It is always the danger of a rigidly authoritarian organization that the prize of the key positions is so great that from time to time intense

D

competition is inevitable. Aquaviva thought that the time had
come to define the Society's scheme of policy on a number of
points. After fifteen years of examination there appeared the *Ratio
Studiorum* which laid down the whole scheme of Jesuit education
from theology down to the grammar of the lowest classes. Under
his inspiration there was also produced the *Directorium*, or guide
to the *Spiritual Exercises*. To a large extent the *Ratio* merely gave
statutory form to the classical cursus which the Renaissance had
made the usual curriculum of schools. Its original feature was the
strict division of Jesuits on the staff of a school into those who
taught and those – the Prefects – who were responsible for discipline and activities outside the class-room. In very recent years
the wisdom of that separation has come to be doubted and it has
today been generally modified, but it remained unchallenged in
Jesuit schools until a very few years ago.

Yet it was in fighting the Society's internal battles that
Aquaviva's energies were most fully engaged. The Society, as has
been said, was of its nature a universal Catholic Society, a society,
to quote Paul III's words, for the regiment of the fighting Church –
regimini militantis ecclesiae. But one of the most dangerous and most
persistent of all the temptations of the Church has been a false
notion of nationalism: no one can deny the Church's theoretical
universality or that Christ died for all men, yet just as with
exaggerated nationalism outside the Church, whereby for example
the German nation under Hitler claimed that it was a superior
nation, so the 'nationalist' within the Church is tempted to claim
that his is the only truly Catholic nation, and that others have but
half a faith and are little more than second-class Catholics. In the
sixteenth century the Europeans in general were, and perhaps to
some extent still are, guilty of this fault towards the non-European
world. 'The Faith is Europe and Europe is the Faith', wrote
Hilaire Belloc in the early years of this century, and there is no
Catholic nation that has not at one time made this arrogant claim
for itself. Certainly in the sixteenth century the Spaniards tended
to boast that their nation alone had not been infected by the
poison of Protestantism and that the Spaniards were the only true
Catholics.

The Jesuit Society was of course founded for the service of the
whole world but it had been founded by a Spaniard. Under its

first three Generals it was under Spanish direction, as was entirely reasonable. But the Spanish Jesuits bitterly resented it when with unconcealed papal encouragement a Belgian and not a Spaniard was elected as the fourth General, and they were bitterly disappointed when on Mercurian's death the generalship instead of reverting to Spanish hands went to an Italian. There was even a certain danger that the Society would establish itself as a family possession. It was Father Araoz, Ignatius' nephew, who put himself at the head of the Spanish opposition to Aquaviva. Araoz sought to introduce a limited constitution into the Society. He claimed that Generals should not be elected for life, that Provincials and Rectors should be voted for like Abbots in Benedictine monasteries, that there should be a General Chapter in Spain for the regulation of Spanish affairs and that above all there should be no communication of any sort between Spanish and non-Spanish Jesuits. Some of the Spanish Jesuits a little enjoyed haunting court circles and high society and resented it when Aquaviva called their attention to the dangers of such company and to the rules which bade them be very cautious of indulging in it. Araoz' argument was that all non-Spaniards were so infected with heresy that it was a danger to any Spaniard to be contaminated with them. A more direct defiance of the whole purpose of Ignatius, with his conception of the Jesuit as a man to be sent out to preach the Gospel of Christ in any quarter of the world, it would be hard to imagine.

The king, Philip II, whose Catholicism was not of the kind that liked to take orders from Rome or from any place outside Spain, was on Araoz' side. The most energetic propagandist of these views was a certain Jewish Jesuit, Father Dionisio Vasquez. Vasquez' complaints were frankly nationalist. It was, he argued, intolerable that Spaniards should be governed from Rome, since Rome was manifestly ignorant of Spaniards, and yet more intolerable that money should be drained out of Spain to satisfy Roman demands. Other countries were full of pestilential heretics with whom Spaniards should have nothing to do. So long as Spaniards were kept in Spain all danger of their falling into heresy could be satisfactorily avoided by the rigours of the Inquisition.

A certain Enrique Enriquez, one of the Jesuit dissidents, did indeed invoke the Inquisition – a Dominican body – and get four of the Fathers put into its prisons and others expelled from Valladolid and Castile and the Inquisition called for copies of the Bulls of the Society and its *Ratio Studiorum*. It also forbade thirty Jesuits who had been ordered on a mission to Transylvania from leaving Spain for fear that their faith would be contaminated by contact with heretics. The Pope Sixtus V took sides against the dissidents and the Inquisition and compelled it to release its prisoners and restore its seized documents. The dissidents replied by getting King Philip to demand a full investigation into all the affairs of the Society.

Naturally enough the vow to the Pope which all Jesuits are compelled to take caused Sixtus to take a special interest in the Society and therefore to be concerned at what appeared to be evidence that, far from the monolithic body of disciplined obedience which it had seemed to be under Ignatius, the Society was hopelessly divided by faction. He ordered an inquiry by the Roman Inquisition, which could be free of the special influences of Spain and at the same time independent. The Inquisition in its turn remitted the matter to four theologians. The general gist of their report was favourable to the Society. The suggestion that Provincials and Rectors should be elected was very firmly rejected. 'I don't want Chapters in the Society,' said the Pope. 'You would have one in every city and every family.' He warned the Jesuits about becoming heavily involved in secular politics but that was a warning that Aquaviva had already given them. The only positive order to the Jesuits that came out of the inquiry was that they change their name, which was thought to give offence, and this the Jesuits would have had to accept had not Sixtus died before his order was able to come into force. The dissidents demanded of the new Pope, Clement VIII, that he appoint a Commissary General for Spain and at King Philip's instance Loyasa, the tutor of Philip's heir, was appointed, but to the dissidents' dismay Loyasa reported entirely in favour of Aquaviva and against any constitutional devolution. 'One Pope is enough to govern the Church,' he said, 'and one General ought to be enough for the Society.' The dissidents then approached the Pope and persuaded him to call for a General Congregation, which duly met in November 1593. The result of the Congregation was a total vindication of Aquaviva, the exposure of the charges against him and the routing of his critics. The Congregation denounced the dissidents as:

false sons, disturbers of the common peace and revolutionists whose punishment had been asked for by many Provinces. The Congregation therefore, while grievously bewailing the loss of its spiritual sons, was nevertheless compelled in the interest of domestic union, religious obedience and the perpetuation of the Society to employ a severe remedy in the premises. Those suspected of being parties to such machinations shall make a solemn oath to support the Constitution as approved by the Popes and to do nothing against it. If they refuse to take the oath, or, having taken it, fail to keep it, they are to be expelled even if old and professed.

Yet the Congregation had one unfortunate consequence. Among the early Jesuits, convert Jews had been very prominent. As I have mentioned, Laynez, the second General, was a Jew, as was Polanco, Ignatius' secretary; so was Toletus, and also Acosta. But it so happened that a large proportion of those who had intrigued against Aquaviva with Vasquez at their head, were, or were thought to be, of Jewish origin and under the influence of this prejudice the Congregation passed a rule that men of Jewish origin were not be admitted to the Society – a prohibition that was main-tained until our own times. It had of course the unfortunate con-sequence of earning for the Society a reputation for anti-Semitism. It was a reputation that was by no means deserved in the Society's early days. Ignatius was no anti-Semite. He regarded Jewish blood as a privilege rather than a disgrace and Sacchini, the Jesuit historian of Aquaviva's time, was well in the Ignatian tradition when he recorded Laynez' Jewish blood. But Ignatius' broad-mindedness had by no means survived into the next generation of Jesuits. Spanish Jesuits who were not themselves Jews could not leave the matter alone. They thought to solve the problem of Laynez' origin by blunt denial of the facts.

For instance the province of Toledo sent to Father Vitelleschi, the General, the following protest:

The province of Toledo, united in a Congregation, unanimously petitions our Reverend Father General to see to it that what is written in the second volume of the History of the Society about the ancestry of Father James Laynez is deleted. We beg for the removal of so great a slur on the memory of so great a Father. Let there be no mention of it whatever in the second edition and in this first we ask that Father General would immediately cause the page containing this foul blot which damages the whole Society to be cut out and replaced by another asserting the purity and nobility of the Father's lineage. We give a few of the many reasons which may induce his Paternity to grant the petition. First, what the History discloses about the birth of this great man is false, as witnesses of the utmost probity who have investigated the matter testify. Secondly, even if true, it would serve no useful purpose but cause the greatest harm and be downright sinful to brand a General of the Society and one of its founders with that infamy.

Sacchini replied by quoting Laynez' own admission, but what is extraordinary and deplorable is not of course whether Laynez was a Jew but that the priests should have thought it 'an infamy' that he should have been so.

At the same time Aquaviva was under attack from some of his Italian colleagues who thought that the Fathers should practise more mortification and prayer than had been their custom. This was again of course in direct contrast with the Ignatian precept. As I have already mentioned, Ignatius in the days before he formed the Society had indulged in extreme asceticism but had reached the conclusion that the particular work of the Society was in the world, and to perform that work moderation in such practices was necessary. He discouraged extreme mortification and did not wish the Fathers, like monks, to say their office in common. Aquaviva was successful in winning his battle for the preservation of the Ignatian tradition.

In 1614 there appeared in Cracow the *Monita Secreta Societatis Jesu* – a document which purported to lay down the secret instructions given to all Jesuits to teach them how to acquire for themselves power over princes and legacies from rich widows. It was an absurd and palpable forgery, somewhat of the same kind as the Protocols of the Elders of Zion, and has been universally recognized as such even by scholars most critical of the Society. Its author was probably a disgruntled ex-Jesuit called Zahorowski.

While the Jesuits were thus divided among themselves they were attacked from the outside for their doctrine of grace. That attack came mainly from the Dominicans. The difficulty of reconciling a belief in God's omnipotence with a belief in man's free will is obvious enough and has perplexed mankind since the beginning of time. Perhaps there is at the last no more to be said about it than Johnson's judgement that 'all argument is against free will and all experience is for it', but, if so, it only solves a difficulty by plunging us into a further difficulty, for it seems to assert the insufficiency of reason. In any event the Jesuits maintained what they called the *Scientia Media* and asserted that man had a real freedom to choose whether or not he would cooperate with grace. The Dominicans asserted that such a doctrine was Pelagian. They asserted that man had no such freedom and his actions depended entirely on whether God chose to offer him grace or not and this, said the Jesuits, was Calvinism. The battle raged furiously between Molina on the Jesuit side and Ibaneza, a professor at the University of Salamanca, for the Dominicans. Pope Clement, seeing that there was no hope of an issue, imposed silence on both sides. In 1611 a decree was issued by the Inquisition forbidding anyone of either school from writing any treatise on grace, and this continued in force for the greater part of the seventeenth century. In the context of the sixteenth century, and since the Jesuits were the triumphant leaders of a very unexpected counter-attack in what was a primarily intellectual battle, it is hardly surprising that the Jesuits should have been the target of a large volume of pamphlet attacks both from Protestants and from Catholics who did not approve of their doings. The success of Canisius in Germany aroused a special fury. Nor indeed is it surprising, if we consider the literary habits of the time, that these attacks should often have been of a gross scurrility. But what is perhaps a little surprising is that so few of them should even have tried to deal with any serious issue. The great majority were mere catalogues of absurdity. Thus the first attack was the diatribe of Morlin which appeared in 1568. It accused the Jesuits in their schools of having intercourse with the devil:

God's Gospel was powerless before those creatures of the devil whom hell had vomited forth to poison the whole German Empire. They not only deal in witchcraft themselves but teach it to others and impart to their pupils the methods of getting rid of their foes by poisons, incantations and the like. . . . Those who send their boys to be educated by them are throwing their offspring into the jaws of wolves; or like the Hebrews of old immolating them to Moloch.*

* Janssen, *History of the German People*, English translation by Christie, 16 vols., London 1896–1910, vol. VIII, p. 339.

In 1575 Roding, a professor of the University of Heidelberg, wrote of them:

They are wild beasts who ought to be chased out of our cities. Though outwardly modest, simple, mortified and urbane, they are in reality furies and atheists – far worse indeed than atheists. The children confided to them are constrained to join with their swinish instructors in grunting at the Divine Majesty. They are not only poisoners but conspirators and assassins. Their purpose is to slay all those who have accepted the Confession of Augsburg. They have been seen in processions of armed men, disguised as courtiers, dressed in silks with gold chains around their necks, going from one end of Germany to the other. They caused the St Bartholomew massacre; they killed King Sebastian; in Peru they plunged red hot irons into the bodies of the Indians to make them reveal where they hid their treasures. In thirty years the Popes killed 900,000 people, the Jesuits two million; the cellars of all the colleges in Germany are packed with soldiers; and Canisius married an abbess.*

The *Historia Jesuitici Ordinis*, was published in 1593 and its authorship ascribed to an ex-novice, Elias Hasenmuller, in spite of the fact that Hasenmuller had been by that date six years dead. It asserted that 'the Jesuits were professional assassins, wild boars, robbers, traitors, snakes, vipers, etc. In their private lives they were lecherous goats, filthy pigs'. Bellarmine, asserted another such work, was 'an Epicurean of the worst type, who had already killed 1,642 victims, 562 of whom were married women. He used magic and poison and pitched the corpses into the Tiber. He died the death of the damned and his ghost was seen in the air in broad daylight flying away on a winged horse'. Pasquier in France, the Jesuits' great Jansenist enemy, was so ignorant that he thought that Pius IV, the Jesuits' great enemy, was a Jesuit. The Gunpowder Plot in the reign of James I produced a volume of literature in England at the head of which stood James' own *Conjuratio Sulphurae Quibus Ea Rationibus Et Authoribus Coeperit, Maturavit, Apparuit; Una Cum Reorum Examine*.

All this literature was so absurd that even if it attracted some attention at an excited moment one could hardly have expected that it would have had any very enduring effect. Nor indeed would it have had on its own merits, even though the Jesuits did not greatly

* Ibid.

help their own case when some of them, like Father Garasse, who replied to Pasquier, answered with almost as great ribaldry as that with which he had been attacked. But it was the misfortune of the Jesuits that at this time when some of the greatest minds of the time were engaged in their service, one of the most penetrating minds of all time should have turned itself to the attack on them. It is not because of his attack on the Jesuits that Pascal is today remembered as perhaps one of the greatest intellects of all time. His criticism of the Jesuits was beyond question his least considerable work. He was not adequately briefed and he used for his work other trivial pamphlets, little understanding how worthless they were. Nor was it the prime purpose of the *Lettres Provinciales* to attack the Jesuits. His concern was rather to defend his allies, the Jansenists, against the accusation of casuistry, and his method of defence was to show that casuistry was inescapable – had been employed by theologians of every school – and, as a proof of his thesis, he professed to give some examples of how it had been employed by the Jesuits. But, as Hilaire Belloc showed in an admirably exact analysis in the *Irish Quarterly Studies* of September 1920, of the eighteen *Lettres Provinciales* only those from five to ten are concerned with the Jesuits at all. There are in them eighty-nine alleged examples of Jesuit condonation of lax morality, and even in these the Jesuits are in no way advocating lax morality. It is a question not of what line of conduct they are advocating as desirable, but – a very different matter – what conduct is so plainly wrong that even where there are extenuating circumstances it must nevertheless be condemned as a mortal sin. When the accusations have been winnowed out, it comes to it that there were perhaps seven decisions which Jesuit casuists had given over the ages, of which the most important were that there might be extreme circumstances when duelling was permissible or where homicide was legitimate, which were open to challenge. The list is not very formidable and the Jesuits could legitimately answer that if their critics were honestly anxious to discover not what the Jesuits would pardon but what they advocated they should in fairness have gone to listen to the very strict and high-minded sermons of Bourdaloue, 'king of preachers and preacher of kings', who spoke for three decades from the pulpit of Notre Dame and won a reputation unparalleled both as orator and as spiritual father,

D*

rather than to the polemics of Pascal. Yet Pascal's name has remained justly as one of the glories of mankind and, though he wrote on this point not so much to condemn the Jesuits as to show that the Jansenists were not alone in employing casuistry, the effect of the *Lettres Provinciales* in forming opinion against the Jesuits was enormous.

The prejudice of the secular world against Jesuit casuistry, the belief that Jesuits teach that the end justifies the means and that they are very wicked to do so, is based on confusion. To the modern secular man the belief that there is such a thing as mortal sin, that there is any act so wicked that a man can go to hell for it, is too horrible to be acceptable. The Jesuits of course, like other Catholics, believed that mortal sin was possible. But, unable to say that it was impossible that any man should go to hell, they yet fully felt the horror of the doctrine. They rebuked those who spoke lightly of it as if it were a casual matter; and were unwilling to say that a penitent should be barred from the sacraments if there was any loophole of doubt about the wrongness of his action. It was a doctrine of mercy – or at least an expression of the unwillingness of a confessor to take it on himself to speak in the name of God when there was any possible doubt about God's verdict. It was the general teaching of the time that on a matter of morals, if the teaching of the Church was not certain, then a man was entitled to follow any opinion that had a sufficient weight of theological opinion behind it to give it probability. In the seventeenth century a Spanish Jesuit, Father Gonzalez, opposed to Probabilism the theory of 'Probabiliorism' and asserted that a man was only free to follow an opinion which had the greater weight of teaching to support it; but in the eighteenth century Alfonso Liguori, who in his youth had held to the more rigid opinion, confessed that he had seen so much suffering as the result of the insistence upon it that he adopted, and by his learning finally established, the theory of Probabilism which is now almost universally held.

The greatest Jesuit name of these years was that of Bellarmine. Bellarmine was born at Monte Pulciano in 1542 and began his theological studies at Padua in 1567. In his *De Controversiis* he championed what came to be accepted as the Catholic position of the time against the wholly Erastian theories of sovereignty of the English and the Venetians. The traditional medieval pretension of

Innocent III had of course claimed for the Pope a right to arbitrate between Christian princes. Bellarmine did not claim for the Pope a direct right to rule in the country of a Christian prince, but, since all authority derives from God, it followed, he argued, that any Christian prince forfeits his right to authority if he rules in defiance of the will of God – if his government is totally opposed to the rights of the Church – and, since the Pope is the Vicar of Christ, it naturally follows that it falls to the Pope to pronounce when a prince's rule is in total opposition to the will of God. Popes have of their nature the right to depose apostate princes, to relieve their subjects from any obligation of obedience to such princes, to call on their subjects to remove them from their thrones. Though there was no justification for accusing Bellarmine of advocating the lawfulness of the assassination of a defiant monarch whose authority had been declared forfeit, there could be no doubt that Mariana, the Spanish Jesuit, in his *De Rege et Regis Institutione*, published in 1599 when Elizabeth was still on the English throne, did argue that such action was permissible under the most extreme circumstances. It was of course pragmatically most unfortunate that he should have published such a book and Aquaviva condemned it, but, granted that he was to speak on such a topic at all, it is not so easy to fault the logic of his argument. One might of course argue that a Christian duty is one of absolute non-resistance – that the Christian should never take life even in self-defence and under whatever provocation. But neither the Jesuits nor the general body of Christian opinion has ever taken that view. And, if there are extreme circumstances where rebellion and killing are allowable, it is not easy to say that there are never circumstances in which assassination is allowable. Of course the assassination of the ordinary run-of-the-mill politician is not allowable because even if it be true that he is an evil man, there is no guarantee that his killing will change the policy. It is more likely that a worse tyrant will be substituted for the assassinated tyrant and the tyranny increased. But in the rare cases where a policy depends entirely on the life of one person the decision is not so easy. If it was legitimate to depose a Renaissance monarch, how could he be deposed except by killing him? He could not be voted out of office. There was no chance of persuading him to resign. Modern eyes find it indeed hard to see Elizabeth's rule as so plainly worse than that of all her rivals as to justify such means, but was there not good reason to think that the conspirators who tried to murder Hitler in 1944 might, had they succeeded, have brought the war to an end and saved countless lives? Can we with any confidence say that their attempt was certainly immoral?

It was of course on such principles as those of Bellarmine that Pius v sought to act against Elizabeth and that Bellarmine subsequently came into conflict with James i. Few would today, one fancies, deny that in asserting that sovereignty was legitimate only if it has some moral basis, Bellarmine was on considerably stronger ground than James in his championship of a divine and absolute right of kings, for which there was no title deed of evidence to be produced at all. The absolute right of the king might be self-evident to James i. It was less evident to the subjects of James' son. Yet Bellarmine himself on this point spoke the language of another age and by his writings did grave damage to both the Catholic and the Jesuit cause. When Innocent iii claimed arbitral rights for the papacy, he claimed those rights over a Europe in which the Catholic faith was universally accepted. It was not unreasonable that, when the Reformation revolts broke out, the Protestants should appear at first in Catholic eyes not merely as religious rebels but also as the enemies of all established order, men preaching a gospel that must inevitably perish and which the general good required to be suppressed as quickly as possible. Any new idea that makes seriously revolutionary claims has necessarily to run this gauntlet on its first appearance – first to prove that it is an enduring force, not merely an eccentricity destined to be preached today and forgotten tomorrow. But by Bellarmine's time it was evident that the new religion was not to be thus easily dismissed and suppressed. Perhaps it was by then evident that it was not going to conquer Italy, and Bellarmine was an Italian. It was his error to judge the situation in other countries by the situation in Italy. In fact, whether for better or for worse, the failure of the Church to keep any sort of peace or seriously to uphold any sort of moral order in international affairs in the years of the disputed papacy had created a situation where many men looked to the prince rather than to the Pope as the guarantor of order. It was reasonable for a Catholic – and especially reasonable for a Jesuit – to work for a day when the moral prestige of the papacy would be restored and when men would once more look to the Pope as the moral leader of Europe. It was idle for Bellarmine to pretend that that was the situation in his own day and to talk as if the Pope of his day had in fact a deposing power over princes. The only effect of a Pope attempting to claim such powers was, as English experience was to prove, to put Catholics into an impossible position – some of them reluctant to support foreign arms against their country and prepared to disobey the Pope rather than do so, others bearing such arms and earning for themselves and their religion a reputation for a lack of patriotism – and in the end the monarch was still on the throne and the Catholics were proscribed, persecuted and diminished.

The Church was in those years always engaged upon two battles. It had at the same time to fight against its declared public enemies and against the enemy within who was anxious to twist Catholic teaching in such a way as to cause it to deny the freedom of the will. The second battle was in many ways the more important of the two and Bellarmine was more happily engaged in it. Calvinists outside the Church and Jansenists within it were united in asserting that if God is omnipotent then men acted as they acted – well or ill – in accordance with whether God at His arbitrary choice saw fit to give them grace or to withhold it from them. The bare logical strength of the argument, the difficulty of seeing how man's free will can coexist with God's omnipotence, is clear enough, but the Christian tradition has always maintained that, difficult as it may be to explain, strong as are the conditioning forces of causation, nevertheless there is and must be some reality in the obstinate belief of man that he has some freedom. The Jesuits on this point fought for the Christian tradition. Baius, the theological Dean of Louvain, launched the first attacks on freedom. Bellarmine answered him and then, when he returned to the attack in 1579 Toletus, another member of the important band of Jews who played so large a part in the early years of Jesuit history – 'incontestably the most learned man living today', as Gregory XIII said – took up the task of reply.

Contemporary with these two was Suarez, who also crossed swords with James I. His argument was both more important and more cogent than that of Bellarmine. For Suarez, in order to answer James' assertion of the divine right of kings, was not content merely to invoke the Pope as the interpreter of the moral law – an invocation that would clearly be of little value to anyone who did not accept the Catholic position. He raised in his *Origin of Power* the fundamental question of sovereignty and asserted that the king, far from deriving his authority direct from God, possessed it only in so far as his rule was based upon general consent. It was, it is true, in accordance with the divine plan that there should be authority but the legitimacy of any particular claim to exercise sovereignty depended on the people's consent. Sovereignty was in the people. Where else could it be? Governments only survive so long as they have public consent to support them. What test is there but the test of fact?

The importance of this bold answer is clear. How large a part it has played in all subsequent political thinking from American independence, from Rousseau and the French Revolution up to the movements of self-determination of modern times! What was not quite clear is how far it helped or was indeed intended to help the Jesuit or the Catholic cause of his day. The Second Vatican Council might proclaim in unambiguous terms the rights of religious liberty, whatever a man's religious faith, and repudiate any suggestion that the Catholic Church should look for support or exclusive recognition to the state. But three hundred and fifty years were to elapse between Suarez and the Vatican Council. And, if it was in Suarez' day by no means certain that public opinion in England supported the claims of King James 1, it was by far less certain that it supported any claims of a Catholic restoration. Where did right lie when the people were against the Church?

To those names it would be possible to add others as distinguished or almost as distinguished – Lessius, Maldonatus, Lugo, Valencia, Petavius and others. Side by side with great scholars and philosophers the Society was also producing at this time men who were playing an extraordinary and colourful part in the diplomatic life of the time. Perhaps it would have been better had they been a little less colourful and more retiring. Later Jesuit superiors were to learn from experience and to be more careful how far they allowed their Fathers to involve themselves in such adventures. Yet we cannot tell the story of these years without adverting to the extraordinary lives of Warsewicz, Nikolai, Possevin and Vieira. Father Warsewicz was sent to Sweden not as a representative of the Pope but as the Polish ambassador – in order to persuade King John to become a Catholic. King John promised to do so provided that the cup was given to the laity, and a married clergy and a vernacular liturgy were permitted. These demands were not acceptable at Rome and indeed it is very doubtful whether even had a bargain been made with the king, that bargain would have been accepted by the Swedish people. After Warsewicz Father Nikolai was sent to continue negotiations. He confessed himself a priest but concealed the fact that he was a Jesuit. After him in 1577 came Father Possevin who arrived not as a priest but as the special envoy of the widow of Maximilian, the Holy Roman Emperor. He brought two other Jesuits with him. As a result of Possevin's persuasion the king was received into the Church but insisted that his reception be kept secret. He also asked that Possevin return to Rome and win for the Swedish people the three concessions that he had asked. Rome again refused the conditions, but Possevin on his return to Sweden no longer made any pretence that he was not a Jesuit. The Bishops and members of the royal family were up in arms at the king's conversion and in fear that he would lose his throne he reverted to Protestantism. Possevin also attempted to arrange peace between the Poles and the Russians who were fighting one another over Lithuania, and worked to persuade the Pope to absolve Henry IV of France.

Vieira was born in Lisbon in 1608 but was taken out to Brazil when still a child. In 1640 Portugal revolted from Spain, by whom it had been governed for sixty years. After a period of civil war, in which the Jesuits had been strictly enjoined to preserve neutrality but in which some of them had indiscreetly involved themselves on the nationalist side, John of Braganza was declared king of Portugal. Vieira, by then a leading Jesuit in Brazil, was summoned back to Lisbon to be made a court preacher and tutor to the infant Don Pedro. But he soon showed himself a man of practical competence of a sort uncommon at the poorly equipped Portuguese court, and was appointed a member of the royal council. He became virtually Prime Minister and reorganized the whole military and fiscal condition of the country. He represented the country abroad in embassies at Paris, the Hague, London and Rome. He also incidentally considerably restricted the powers of the Inquisition. Yet he was not a man avid of secular honours. He had only become involved in such affairs by accident and in spite of himself, and was always anxious to escape from courts to get back to Brazil and his missions. In 1652 he obtained leave to do so, but though free from personal ambition, he felt it a duty to use his name and prestige to fight the battle against injustice. The Brazilian landowners of Portuguese blood kept their Indians and Negroes under a rule of slavery. Vieira bluntly denounced them and was soon back in Lisbon to plead his cause against them. His influence at the court was such that that he had no difficulty in getting a verdict there. But, as always in the affairs of colonial South America, it was one thing to wring humane edicts out of the government of Madrid or Lisbon, and quite another, with the Atlantic between them and quite insufficient police forces, to find any way of getting the colonial landowners to obey such edicts.

Returning to Brazil, Vieira fought a not very successful battle for six years against colonial oppressors, travelling, catechizing, preaching incessantly. Then at last the landowners rose against him, took him prisoner and shipped him out of the country. He was sent to Lisbon. The former King John was dead and had been succeeded by Alfonso. The Inquisition had regained its power and its officers bore no goodwill towards Vieira because of his attacks on them. He no longer had the protection which he had enjoyed in the last reign. Church and state combined to refuse to receive him in Portugal and he had to go to Rome. There he made the acquaintance of Queen Christina of Sweden. After John III, with whom Possevin had negotiated, Gustavus Adolphus had succeeded to the Swedish throne. He of course had been a Protestant and had indeed been the great Protestant champion of the Thirty Years' War, but had been succeeded by his daughter Christina who from the first had been strangely attracted to the Catholic religion. The Portuguese ambassador in Stockholm, Pereira, brought with him as his confessor the Jesuit Macedo. Macedo like Possevin, before him, did not confess himself to be a Jesuit but Christina knew that he was a priest and got in touch with him. She told him of her wish to become a Catholic, even if it cost her her throne. Christina got the General to send two further Jesuits, disguised as Italian gentlemen. She had discussions with them as a result of which she was received into the Church, gladly paying the price of abandoning her throne. She left Sweden for Rome where she spent the rest of her life. She met Vieira in Rome and wished him to become her spiritual director, but Vieira after a time returned as an old man to his native Brazil, where he worked until his death.

SIX

The English battle

The principle of *cuius regio eius religio* was only formally pronounced in Germany, and not until the middle of the seventeenth century, but it was the principle by which English life was regulated all through the sixteenth century. In sixteenth-century England there were doubtless many people who preserved a general belief in the Christian promises. The number who felt any firm commitment to one particular denomination was clearly much less. The Wars of the Roses immediately before the century began had taught people the lesson that the first necessity was a strong prince, whose title was unchallenged and who could maintain order. This was far more important than any theological niceties. The disputes to the papal succession, the drain of money from England through commendation to fill the pockets of French Popes at Avignon at a time when France was their country's enemy, had meant that few Englishmen in the early years of the century thought of the papal headship as a very important or desirable part of the Catholic teaching. So when Henry VIII denied the papal headship, though the immediate cause of his repudiation – the desire to get rid of Katharine of Aragon and to marry Anne Boleyn – was not at all popular, yet the fact of it was almost universally accepted. Only a More and a Fisher and a handful of Carthusians stood out. The rest – the whole bench of bishops except Fisher – accepted without demur. Parliament obediently voted what it was asked to vote. So throughout the century Parliament and the great body of public opinion was always prepared to vote whatever the prince asked it to vote. Parliament was Catholic under Henry VII, accepted the king's headship of the Church under Henry VIII, became Protestant under Edward VI, Catholic again under Mary, Protestant again under Elizabeth. If a prince had arisen who had bidden Parliament to vote the nation Buddhist, who need doubt that it would have done so?

In the Catholic reaction under Mary Tudor the Jesuits had no part. Jesuits were not at that time popular with Philip II, Mary's husband, and Mary had no especial sympathy with new ways, nor on the other hand was the papacy in the early days of Elizabeth's reign prepared to go to any extremes against her. People had at that date no conception that there could be two religions or two churches in the same place. In every town or village there was one church. It was the duty of the ordinary Christian to go to it. It was the duty of those in authority to decide what might happen there, and thus, in the absence of any express condemnation from authority, people in the first thirteen years of Elizabeth's reign fell into the habit of going to the local church as they had done in previous reigns. Old priests continued to minister there undisturbed. To the great majority nothing drastic had happened.

This meant that when in 1570 Pius V was persuaded by Cardinal Allen that England was quietly slipping out of the Catholic Church and that drastic action must be taken to rescue it, the situation from the Catholic point of view was very much more difficult than it would have been had the Pope acted on the queen's accession. Whatever the rights and wrongs of a papal authority to depose heretical sovereigns, the Pope did not enjoy sufficient popularity or prestige in England for such a command to appear the more palatable for having come from Rome. Nor was there any practical way of deposing Elizabeth, if she was not to be murdered, except through civil war, and many Englishmen of the time, though they might not be quite sure whether or not they liked Elizabeth, were very certain that they disliked civil war. The Jesuits differed from other Catholic religious Orders in that they were especially vowed to the service of the Pope. This did not make them any more popular in the eyes of the average Englishman.

From the Jesuit point of view the invitation to the English mission was not one to be easily accepted. In the Ignatian plan the Jesuits should live in a Jesuit house, and one who went to England would not be able to live thus. He would have to live to all appearances as a layman. There were, it was felt, dangers in this. However the whole Catholic position would collapse into ridicule if the Pope should proclaim the deposition of Elizabeth and free Englishmen from their allegiance and then after that the life of England go on untroubled with no attempt at all made to enforce

the papal Bull. It must somehow be brought home to the average
Englishman that he was now under obligation to break with
Elizabeth and with the Elizabethan settlement. Who could do
this but the Jesuits? Father Mercurian, at Allen's urging, ordered
the Jesuits to the work. In 1580 Campion and Parsons and a few
companions crossed over to England. There is no purpose in re-
telling the very familiar story of their expedition and of Campion's
capture and execution. There is no one, of whatever belief, who
does not recognize the brilliant intellectual capacity of Campion,
which had caused him in his Oxford days to be hailed by Cecil as
'one of the diamonds of England' and to receive the favourable
notice of Queen Elizabeth. There is no one of whatever belief who
is under any temptation to withhold tribute for the heroic selfless-
ness which caused him to abandon a brilliant future and choose a
life that, it was clear from the first, was all too likely to lead him
to torture and the gallows. There is no one who is not horrified as
he reads the story of torture and ill-treatment in prison, of perversion of justice, of the unfairness of the staged debate, of the final
execution. We need not go to Catholic evidence. Hallam in his
History of England recorded that 'the trial was as unfairly conducted
and supported by as slender evidence as can be found in our
books'. While condemning this we must of course at the same
time record that torture was all too frequent in that brutal age;
in Mary Tudor's England just a few years before – and in many
other places at that time, Catholics had subjected their opponents
to equally cruel treatment. Those who actively supported
Elizabeth had, ever since her 'deposition' by the Pope, excellent
reason to fear that should her deposition be made effective, and a
Catholic regime instituted under Mary Stuart or some other
Catholic prince, their lives would be forfeited. They were fighting
for their lives.

Justice had to be perverted in order to bring Campion to the
gallows because he was not much interested in politics, and understood that, whatever the abstract rights of Pius' Bull of deposition,
in fact it was not possible for the Catholics to put Elizabeth off
the throne. The only effect of the Bull was to give Elizabeth an
excellent excuse for saying that all Catholics were traitors and for
punishing them. Therefore he had obtained leave to say that the
Bull was inoperative *rebus sic stantibus* and to assure Catholics that

they could properly give their allegiance to Elizabeth. When they asked him at his trial, 'Do you believe Elizabeth to be the lawful queen?' Campion was able to answer in good faith, 'I told it to herself in the castle of the Duke of Leicester.' A man can only be made treasonable by his own acts. He cannot be made a traitor by the words of the Pope or by any other man. There is no Bill of Rights to limit Parliament's power in the British Constitution and the queen in Parliament can make anything that she and the Parliament wish the law of the land. If Parliament had been content to pass an Act of Parliament which said that any Catholic priest would be liable to execution, then clearly Campion was a Catholic priest and that, so far as the legal argument went, would have been the end of the matter. But of course the government, whatever the law might allow it to do, was not content merely to execute Catholic priests for being Catholic priests. People remembered the days of Elizabeth's predecessor when all priests in England were Catholic priests. A good many of those were still officiating in English churches, having been ordained in Queen Mary's day, and, whatever their technical regularity or irregularity, were manifestly Catholic priests. It was Elizabeth's policy to pretend that as little as possible had been changed from England's traditional religion – that her religion was very much the same as that of her ancestors and that extravagant papal pretensions, backed by a new-fangled being called a Jesuit, were novelties that were a menace to the traditions of England. To achieve this purpose it was necessary to show that he was also a traitor – not merely in some technical sense which held all priests to be traitors but in the sense that he was actively working to compass the overthrow of the queen. This he was manifestly not doing and therefore lying and deceit had to be used to bring the verdict against him.

But at the same time the government could of course not unreasonably say that all the concession that Campion had been able to wrest was that *rebus sic stantibus* Catholics were not compelled to act on the papal Bull or to refuse their allegiance to Elizabeth. This was not a very satisfactory concession. It may be, the Elizabethan ministers could argue, that Campion is an apostolic man who genuinely wishes only to save souls and has no desire to dabble in politics. But supposing that Campion were successful and made many converts and as a result the Catholic body greatly increased? Is there any guarantee that this increased Catholic body, seeing now a greater hope of success, would not argue that things do not now stand as they had stood previously? It must be in candour confessed that there was little reason to doubt that that was how things would have turned out, as Bellarmine was going to prove in the following generation.

It cannot, then, be fairly claimed from Campion's career that the Jesuits were guilty, as they are frequently accused, of any unique wickedness in bringing religion into politics. Everybody in sixteenth-century England brought religion into politics. The two were thought of as indissolubly mixed and, if the Jesuits gained in the popular mind an especially bad name for treason, that was merely because they were unsuccessful.

> Treason doth never prosper. What's the reason?
> That if it prosper none dare call it treason.

Why was it a traitorous act to invite in a Spanish king in the sixteenth century and a patriotic act to invite in a Dutch king in the seventeenth century – except that the Spaniard failed and the Dutchman succeeded? It might be more cogently argued that it was Campion who did something wholly original in being the first in the sixteenth century who attempted to keep politics and religion separate from one another. Yet, if that was his attempt, it was of course an attempt in which he failed, and his death was taken by both sides as a declaration of war. The Elizabethan government took Campion's expedition as a sign that it must think of every Jesuit as its inveterate enemy to be hunted down and destroyed. The Jesuits took Campion's execution as a sign that they could not hope by abstaining from political action to escape persecution and drew the conclusion that the interests of religion therefore required the destruction of the Elizabethan government by any means, if necessary by revolution or by foreign invasion. Parsons, barely escaping from the country, retired abroad and gave up the rest of his life to plotting the invasion of the country. He was not alone in this. Even Cecil at one time plotted with Philip. But in view of the relations at that time between Philip II and the Society and indeed between Philip – 'the heretic' – and the Pope, Parsons' attempts unequivocally to

commit the Society to support of the Spanish cause were somewhat curious. The papacy was in fact as doubtful about Philip II's
cause in the sixteenth as it was about James II's in the seventeenth
century. Yet the consequence was that for the rest of Elizabeth's
life the Jesuit could expect no mercy from the hands of the
government and the years brought a steady stream of Jesuits to
the gallows, martyrs as they claimed, traitors as the government
claimed. The best known of them was the poet Robert Southwell.

This is no place for a recital of the martyrology, glorious as the
document is. The concern of this book is rather to tell the sad
story of the quarrels with which English Catholicism was at that
time distraught. In the Jesuit view after the execution of Campion,
if not before, the issue was clear. There was no freedom for the
Catholic religion under the Elizabethan government. Therefore
the Catholic had no duty except to overthrow the Elizabethan
government, nor during all the early years of Elizabeth's reign was
there any dispute about who should be her successor. Mary, Queen
of Scots, was the next in succession by blood, and Mary was a
Catholic. All that was required was that Elizabeth should die and
Mary would naturally succeed. Being the natural successor, she
would be accepted by all indifferent Englishmen who would have
been as ready to receive Catholicism from her as they had been to
receive any other religion from any other sovereign. It was as
simple as that, and had indeed about it the dangerous simplicity
that no more was required than the removal of one life for all this
to come about. Was it necessary to turn the country upside down
in civil war when the death of one woman would suffice?

On the other hand this reasoning, clear as it might appear to
the Jesuits, by no means appeared so clear to all English Catholics,
and particularly after Mary Stuart's execution in 1587 Catholic
opinion was bitterly divided over who should be supported for
the succession. The natural heir after Mary Stuart's death was her
son, James VI of Scotland, who did in fact succeed as James I of
England. But James was a Protestant and therefore on the principle that England ought to be a Catholic country and that
Catholic countries should be ruled by Catholic sovereigns, some
felt that he should be debarred from the throne. The extreme
papalists on the continent like Allen and Parsons took this view
and proclaimed that, if non-Catholics were debarred, then the

next heir to the throne was the King of Spain who was a distant
cousin of Queen Elizabeth. They gave their support to the
Spanish attempts to establish themselves by force which came to
such disastrous failure at the defeat of the Armada. But their
policies were so unrealistic as to be hardly sane. It was possible
that in the temper of the times England would have accepted a
Catholic sovereign who was the rightful heir and such a sovereign
might even with tact and time have been able to re-establish
Catholicism in the nation; but the notion that there was the
smallest chance that the nation would repudiate a Protestant who
was the natural heir in order to admit a Catholic foreigner who
was not the natural heir was fantastic. No one at all acquainted
with English opinion could possibly have held such a belief and
the advocacy of it created a schism between English Catholics;
some who were abroad supported the Spanish cause, but
Catholics resident in England were almost unanimously opposed
to it. The Jesuits, stationed abroad and coming into England only
on forays, were generally supporters of the Spanish cause, and
owing to Parsons' prominence got the reputation of being all of
that opinion. The reputation was not quite deserved. Father
Crichton, a Jesuit in Scotland, was a strong supporter of the
claims of James VI. Crichton held out hopes that James, owing to
his Catholic mother, would if he succeeded adopt a policy of
greater friendship towards the Catholics. Such hopes were wishful
thinking. Affections and loyalties did not play a large part in
shaping James' mind. Still no one can doubt that Crichton's
policy was the only sensible one and that the consequence of
Parsons' policy was to earn for the Catholics of England and for
the Jesuits in particular a reputation for lack of patriotism which
has not even to this day been wholly erased. English Catholics,
whatever may be true of Irish Catholics, have in fact throughout
all modern times always shown an almost pathetic anxiety to
support the establishment. Yet even today in certain circles the
Spanish Armada is an election issue hardly less inflammable than
birth control.

   The great curse of English Catholicism – the main reason why
England alone of the countries that had been part of the Roman
Empire lost her Catholicism at the time of the Reformation and
has shown no prospect of regaining it – is the inveterate quarrel-

someness of English Catholics. English Catholicism has been
ruined by internal squabbles. It would be beyond the purpose of
this book to attempt to tell the whole story, but the part that the
Jesuits played in it is relevant. In order to heal the divisions of the
English Catholics, Parsons presented a memorial to the Pope
drawn up in England asking for the appointment of two English
Bishops, one to have jurisdiction in England and one over the
English on the continent. The Commission of the Holy Office
however rejected the proposal and decided that England should
be put instead under an archpriest. A priest of the name of Blackwell was appointed. Blackwell strongly opposed the policies of
Parsons, and encouraged the distribution of pamphlets bitterly
denouncing the Jesuits. A Jesuit called Lister replied to them as
bitterly. One of Blackwell's supporters, Bluet, indiscreetly said
to the Anglican Bishop Bancroft that 'it was clearer than light
that Parsons had no other object except the conquest of England
by the Spaniards'. Bancroft reported this opinion to the queen
whose policy henceforth was astutely to destroy the Catholics'
influence by fomenting divisions between the Catholics. Elizabeth
issued a proclamation bidding all Jesuits to leave the country
within thirty days but remitting the case of all other Catholics to a
commission which would examine each particular one. In return
the Catholic opponents of the Spanish case, headed by a priest
called Perkins who had been a Jesuit but had left the Society,
drafted an instrument which stated that a Catholic owed the same
civil obedience to the queen that he would owe to any Catholic
sovereign, that they would inform her of any plots or threats of
rebellion to put a Catholic sovereign on the throne and that they
would regard any excommunication proclaimed against her and
calling on them to implement it as not binding. It might be
thought that this instrument, issued without any authority from
the Pope, was not only an act of loyalty towards the queen but
also an act of defiance towards the Pope. It was issued during the
closing year of Elizabeth's life, in 1603, and before it became
possible to discover Elizabeth's reaction towards it she was dead.

James I succeeded her, and his reign was opened by the Bye
plot. The plot was in the main a Protestant one, but two somewhat
obscure Catholic priests, Watson and Clarke, were somehow mixed
up in it – it is not very clear how – and executed. The incident

gave the Pope the opportunity of writing to James to express his regret at the action of these two priests and it looked as if the papacy, having discovered the ineffectiveness of Pius v's Bull of deposition against Elizabeth, was anxious to seize the opportunity of a new monarch to extricate itself from an impossible position. It looked as if the Pope would bid Catholics loyally to accept the new king and that the Jesuits, if they remained in obstinate rebellion, would be repudiated. On the other hand James showed himself in no mood to go half-way to meet the Pope. Had he done so the matter might have been settled and, had he been merely a politician, that is what he probably would have done. But James fancied himself as a theologian whose main doctrine was that of the divine right of kings. Therefore in the next year, 1604, he drew up for the Catholics an oath of allegiance by which they would be required not only to deny the Pope's power to depose sovereigns but even to stigmatize such a doctrine as heretical, impious and damnable. Heretical to whose authority? It was not easy for a Catholic to take such an oath without at any rate implicitly conceding the king's claim to the headship of the Church. Nevertheless Blackwell, the archpriest, took the oath and said that any Catholic could take it. Bellarmine and Parsons protested against Blackwell's pronouncement and he was deposed and a new archpriest, Birkhead, put in his place. Some Catholics followed Blackwell's advice but the majority, however little question there might be of any active attempt to depose James, were not willing directly to defy the Pope by taking the oath. But there was a small fanatical minority which not only refused the oath but considered itself under obligation to take drastic action to overthrow an anti-Catholic regime. This is not the place to enter into the enormous complexities of the Gunpowder Plot. Whatever the facts, we do know that it was a plot entirely of laymen and Jesuits had nothing to do with it. The Jesuits only became involved because Catesby, a leading conspirator, had proposed, in confession, to Father Garnet, the Jesuit Provincial, the hypothetical case whether, if he was a soldier in a properly constituted army and was asked to blow a mine whose explosion would be the cause of the death of innocent people, he would be justified in doing so. Garnet assured him that he would and the conspirators, somewhat illogically as they were not soldiers of a properly constituted army, took this as a resolution of their scruples and a justification if they should blow up the king and Parliament. Later Catesby in another confession revealed the details of their whole plan to another priest, not a Jesuit, Father Greenwell. Greenwell was horrified. When Greenwell refused to countenance it Catesby bade him consult under seal of confession Father Garnet, which he did. There was no reason to think that Garnet had in any way approved the plot nor that another Jesuit, Gerard, who had given the conspirators the sacrament, had in any way been privy to it. But the authorities were anxious to persuade public opinion that the plot was not merely a plot of a few irresponsible fanatics but the deliberate work of the wicked Jesuits. Gerard escaped to the continent but they had against Garnet the diabolical advantage that he could not say how he knew of it because he had learnt it in confession. Garnet was duly arrested, and after a trial of total injustice in which no shadow of evidence that he was the originator of the plot came to light, was condemned and executed. The opportunity was taken to bring into force a much more drastic anti-Catholic penal code.

In the early years of the seventeenth century, a certain young Dalmatian named Antonio de Dominis had joined the Society in Illyria. He was already, it seems, a priest before he joined. For a time his career was a brilliant success. He delivered lectures on sacred philosophy and won glittering encomiums. But he sighed for preferment and after a time got permission to leave the Jesuits and to become a secular priest. He soon rose to be a Bishop and then an Archbishop but his sympathies were with the Venetians in their protests against papal claims and eventually, not content to be a minimizing Catholic, he repudiated the Pope altogether and fled to England. He was welcomed there by King James I who made him Dean of Windsor. He has an importance in ecclesiastical history that far exceeds any personal merit, for, whatever may be true of any other Anglican Bishop, all de Dominis' orders were beyond question valid and James' ecclesiastics were careful to use him in their consecrations. Therefore in the controversy about the validity of Anglican orders the Anglican protagonist can say that, whatever may have happened at the time of Queen Elizabeth and even if it be conceded for the sake of argument that the chain of continuity was snapped then, it is certain that valid

orders came back again to the Church of England with de
Dominis. Furthermore, since Leo XIII asserted only that the continuity was broken in Elizabeth's time, the day may well come
when the precise details of de Dominis' action is a matter of
crucial importance. (Though of course, even if the continuity and
validity of Anglican orders were established with de Dominis'
help, through the seventeenth century, there would still remain
the further problems of carrying them through the eighteenth
century, and discovering the lineaments of a sacrificing priest in
the Whig functionaries who were created Bishops by the Duke of
Newcastle.)

In the third quarter of the century Father Claude de la
Colombière was sent to England to be confessor to Mary of
Modena, the wife of the Duke of York, afterwards James II.
Though de la Colombière was very careful to keep out of all
political intrigues, in which indeed he took no interest, that did
not prevent Titus Oates from making accusations against him and
against the whole Society when he launched his plot. Both at the
time of the Great Plague and at the time of the Great Fire the
Jesuits had been accused of responsibility for the catastrophe and
had been ordered out of the country. When Oates made his
charges his story was that among other things a Popish army was
to occupy England and put all Protestants to the sword. The Pope
and the Society of Jesus were then to send an Italian bishop to
England to proclaim the papal programme. Then either Father
White, the Provincial, or Father Oliva, the General – Oates was
not quite sure which – would issue commissions to Catholic naval
and military officers. The king, Charles II, would then be
murdered and his brother, James, put on the throne, and at the
same time the Jesuit Provincial would establish himself as Archbishop of Canterbury. The consequence of this absurdity was
that, among many others, seven wholly innocent Jesuits were
sent to the gallows.

In the next reign, that of James II, there was a more real Jesuit
influence. James, who was not a man of wisdom, was undoubtedly
indiscreet in his friendship with Father Petre, a Jesuit, and was
anxious to make him the Royal Almoner. James, though of course
fervent in his Catholicism, was owing to his close alliance with
Louis XIV by no means in high favour with Rome, and Oliva, the

General, was therefore insistent that Petre should not accept the position. Moderate English Catholics were equally alarmed to see him in high position. How much influence Petre really exercised is not clear, and has probably been exaggerated. But certainly he remained loyal to James and afterwards went into exile with him, and as certainly his name was to be much used in perpetuating the legend of Jesuits as evil men who gave themselves to dangerous political intrigue.

SEVEN

The second generation

The rapidity of the expansion of the Society in the first hundred years of its life is of course one of the marvels of history. Bohmer wrote his book on the Jesuits in German and it was translated into French and published under the title of *Les Jésuites* by Monod. It is commonly referred to as Bohmer-Monod and it is by no means particularly favourable to the Society. But Bohmer-Monod collected and set out the precise statistics of the Society's first hundred years. In 1540, they tell us:

The Order counted only ten regular members and had no fixed residence. In 1556 it had already twelve provinces, seventy-nine houses, and about a thousand members. In 1574 the figures went up to seventeen provinces, 125 colleges, eleven novitiates, thirty-five other establishments of various kinds and four hundred members. In 1608 there were thirty-one provinces, 306 colleges, forty novitiates, twenty-one professed houses, sixty-five residences and missions and 10,640 members. Eight years after the death of its illustrious General Aquaviva the Society had thirty-two provinces, three hundred and seventy-two colleges, forty-one novitiates, one hundred and twenty-three residences, 13,112 members. Three years later, namely in 1626, there were thirty-six provinces, two vice-provinces, 446 colleges, thirty-seven seminaries, forty novitiates, twenty-four professed houses, about two hundred and thirty missions and 16,060 members. Finally in 1640 the statistics showed thirty-five provinces, three vice-provinces, five hundred and twenty-one colleges, forty-nine seminaries, forty-four novitiates, twenty-four professed houses, about two hundred and eighty residences and missions and more than 16,000 members.

In Italy and Portugal the Society was predominant in the middle of the seventeenth century. In Spain it had its difficulties both with the government and among its own members. Yet there it had ninety-eight colleges and seminaries, three professed houses, five novitiates and four residences. In France, where it had also its problems, La Flèche College had 1,200 pupils and the Society had sixty-five colleges, two academies, two seminaries, nine boarding schools, seven novitiates, four professed houses, sixteen residences and 2,050 members. In Germany, where it had of course been the spearhead of the Catholic counter-attack, colleges under Canisius's inspiration were found everywhere – in Vienna, Ingolstadt, Munich. The German College flourished in Rome. The Upper Palatinate, Styria, Carinthia, Carniola had been turned from almost completely Protestant to almost completely Catholic lands. In Bohemia and Moravia the Jesuits had established their colleges, though they had no monopoly there. In Poland the Protestant movement had been completely conquered and by the middle of the seventeenth century all the higher education in the land was in Jesuit hands. And of course coincident with these achievements in Europe were the labours of Jesuits in India, the Far East, America and elsewhere of which we have spoken.

The first question that must obviously be answered is, What was the reason for this extraordinary success? The answer is to a large extent simply 'competence'. The Jesuits succeeded in imposing their education because they took the trouble to offer much better education than other people. 'There is no training beyond that', wrote Francis Bacon of Jesuit education; and he had no particular reason to look at them with favour, nor did he share their religion. It is quite true that in places they offered free education where those before them had charged fees – and incidentally acquired considerable unpopularity by doing so. It is equally true that when to avoid this charge of undercutting, they consented to ask for fees then the houses inevitably became rich because the individual Jesuits, with their vows of poverty, could not of course put the fees into their own pockets or spend the money on their own pleasures. The money all went to the house which therefore accumulated wealth, and all religious houses, unless they are from time to time attacked and despoiled, tend to become rich because they do not die and their fortunes are not therefore dissipated among a number of competing heirs as happens in the secular world. But no mere financial reasons could account for the success of the Jesuit schools. They succeeded because of their method of education. The new humanism had made its challenge to Catholic

Europe with the Renaissance. The Greek learning was redis-
covered. Very often, though not always – not of course by such
men as Thomas More or Pico della Mirandola – this new humanism was presented as an alternative to the Christian religion. Self-
sufficient man, it was said, no longer needed the Church – and in
reaction against this new heady gospel conservative Catholics
often thought it both safest and sufficient to denounce all novelty
and to think that man could do better without learning. Ignatius,
for all his military temper and love of discipline, had the wisdom
to see that ideas could not be killed by mere regulations. Ideas
could only be conquered by ideas. Since the new learning had
come in there was no alternative but to accept it, to teach it, and
to show how it could be turned to Christian purposes. The secret
of the success of the Jesuits was to be found in the *Ratio Studiorum*.

To the men of the Middle Ages education was on the whole only
thought to be necessary for those who were to become clerics.
The Renaissance brought in the notion that a layman should be
educated. But, though it brought in the notion, it did not effectively
supply the demand. There were few schools where boys who were
not proposing to become clerics could get their education. For the
most part they had to obtain it as best they could in private houses
and from private tutors. The Jesuits were almost the first to see
that there was a need for widespread free and good education for
the laity – such as could be obtained before them hardly anywhere
save at Winchester and Eton in England. They supplied the need
and it was that which was more than anything else the secret of
their success. They supplied for Europe what Eton and Winchester
were supplying for England.

The first question then to be asked is, What was the reason for
the extraordinary success of the Jesuits in their first hundred
years? The second question is, Why was that success not continued at the same pace over the next hundred years? We shall
come later to the merely political story of the campaign of the
monarchs against the Society in the eighteenth century and its
eventual suppression. Yet it has had now nearly a century and a
half of its second life since its restoration. Up to a point this second
period has been a period of success. The Society, like all religious
Orders, has at the moment its problem of vocations, but in general
the years have been years of steady growth. Refounded, the

IHS

.DMVNDVS CAMPIANVS Q PR E SOC·IESV LONDINI
O CAT "FIDE MARTYR" CONSVMAVIT P² DEC·1581·

14. Blessed Edmund Campion

15. Father Henry Garnet. From a Flemish engraving

16. (*Below, left*) Father Robert Parsons

17. Blessed Robert Southwell

P. ROBERTVS SOVTHVELL. Soc.
Londini pro Cath. fide suspensus et S
tus .3. mar. 1595.

18. St Robert
Bellarmine

19. Father Francisco
Suarez

20. The church of the Gesù, Rome

Society at once started to open new colleges in every quarter of
the world. Its numbers soon exceeded the numbers of its earlier
period. Yet it cannot be pretended that Jesuit education has ever
in its modern period regained the unquestioned predominance
that it enjoyed in the early years of the seventeenth century. It has
its defenders. There are those who argue that a Jesuit education is
superior to any other. But today the matter has to be argued. It
can no longer be taken for granted.

What has happened? One feels the temptation to make a very
cynical suggestion. Throughout the years the Jesuits have of
course often enough recruited members who were not themselves
educated at Jesuit schools. But the greater number of Jesuits all
through the years have been themselves Jesuit-trained. The
Society is on the whole an inbred Society. It is only of the first
Jesuits that in the nature of things this cannot have been true.
Would it be altogether too cynical to say that a part of the reason
for the success of the first Jesuit colleges was that they were staffed
by men who were not themselves educated at Jesuit colleges?

As a mere epigram this statement would of course be cheap and
absurd, and it must be carefully explained. One must understand
the world in which the Society was born. The early years of the
sixteenth century dawned on a Europe that was a Catholic society
but a society of bad Catholics. The Church was in an appalling
state. Its leaders from the Pope downwards made no attempt to
allow Christian principles to regulate their conduct. A few earnestly called for reform but the majority thought that things would
inevitably go on somehow and that there was no urgency in the
matter. Then came the Reformation and it looked for the moment
as if Protestantism might be established throughout Christendom.
Some welcomed its advent. Others – the greater number – were
appalled at its menace but could not think how it could be resisted,
very much as many people in the West in the years immediately
after the First World War and again immediately after the Second
World War talked of and trembled at the menace of Communism.
In such a crisis men were willing to accept the demand for discipline which Ignatius raised. The few heroic souls accepted it for
themselves, and became Jesuits. The majority at least welcomed
the appearance of a body which by its discipline might save them,
and were willing to accept the discipline for themselves at least

E

to the extent of sending their children to Jesuit schools. Of course even in those early days the Jesuits had their Catholic enemies, but it is noteworthy that these enemies were most vigorous in the country that was least threatened by Protestant invasion – in Spain.

A hundred years later the situation was very different. Large areas in Germany and Poland which had been captured for Protestantism had, owing mainly to the Jesuits, been recaptured for Catholicism. Protestantism far from threatening to overrun all Europe was itself on the retreat. Enthusiastic Catholics perhaps even promised themselves that the counter-offensive would be totally successful and Protestantism quite obliterated. This proved an exaggerated view and by the Treaty of Westphalia the matter was compromised and Germany divided into Protestant and Catholic on the formula of *cuius regio eius religio* and along lines which correspond with curious exactitude with the old provinces of the Roman Empire. What is even more curious is that these frontiers have remained definitive. Catholicism lost vast tracts of land to Protestantism. In a hundred years of counter-attack she regained vast tracts of land, but, since the middle of the seventeenth century, the lines have remained fixed. No country that was then Catholic has gone Protestant. No country that was then Protestant has gone Catholic. The battles of conversion have been fought out in strange, individual souls – some of them the rarest and most delicate of mankind – but the numbers of converts have only amounted to tens of thousands out of tens of millions. To the vast majority of inhabitants of European countries on either side of the line conversion has never appeared a serious question at all. They have been content to remain what they were born and the battle in both parts of Europe has not been a battle to convert from one faith to another but a battle to prevent a total shipwreck of faith.

The reason for this is of course that the formula of Westphalia under the appearance of conceding a limited form of toleration was in reality a declaration of scepticism. If one religion was to be reckoned as true in one country and another in another, that was merely a concealed way of asserting that nobody really knew the truth at all. If ministers of one country with one religion were to negotiate and make their treaties with ministers of another country with another religion it was hard for them not to conclude

that faith was little more than a geographical accident. The simple
who lived in their own country and never saw a foreigner might
still entertain old prejudices; they were no longer possible to the
cultivated.

It is debatable whether on balance this new mentality has been
better or worse than the old; but the fact is certain that in the new
age educated men no longer thought of a foreign faith as a
menace to all good living – as a threat so terrible that a man should
die sooner than submit to it. Catholics no longer thought of
Protestants as men thought of the Communists in the years immediately after the war. They thought of them much more as we
are now invited to think of Communists – or at least of Russians –
in the era of peaceful coexistence, and of course in such a changed
world a disciplined method of teaching which had suited the first
era did not necessarily suit its successors so well. Yet the Constitution of the Society is such that it does not easily change its rules
and it is perhaps to some extent true that it has continued to fight
the battles of subsequent centuries with the weapons of its first
hundred years, and that what was once the last word in progress
has sometimes become a little behind the times. The Danes in the
first decade of this century were the most up-to-date pig-breeders
in the world, but their very success has tempted them not to
bother to keep up with recent discovery and progress itself has
caused them to lag behind. Perhaps with the instruction of their
pupils the Jesuits have strayed a little bit along the same path.

Yet the phrase 'behind the times' is of course in itself a neutral
one. The present is not always necessarily better than the past and
there are some times which it is very good to be behind. Of all
titles for a religious movement the silliest is 'modernist' – the mere
worship of the topical – the passion at all costs to be 'with it'. The
Jesuits might well retort that if by the middle of the seventeenth
century people had come to persuade themselves that a new stability had been achieved and that Christendom no longer lived under
threat, the event was to prove the folly of their security. What
were the next hundred and odd years to show? They were to show
a society whose secular leaders were increasingly indifferent to
moral discipline, a steady decline in the influence of the Jesuits and
indeed of the Church, and a diminished confidence that the
Church's guidance was necessary for society's preservation. During

this period the Jesuits were attacked and eventually suppressed, and a few years later the monarchical system which had destroyed the Society collapsed. Out of the ruins of the Church the Society rose again, still powerful – according to Macaulay, straining perhaps a little for paradox, more powerful than it had ever been; not quite the dominant Order perhaps that it had been three hundred years before but, rising again in vigour, at least *primus inter pares* among religious Orders. On the other hand the monarchs, who had been their enemies, were restored, if at all, to very insecure thrones; some to fall almost immediately, others to keep their thrones for a time by compromises with parliamentary institutions which would have seemed to their predecessors acts of disgraceful surrender, and even then destined in the end to lose this simulacrum of a throne. The Church and the Jesuits continued.

Where the truth may lie in such analyses, how close in reality was the connection between the suppression of the Jesuits and the fall of the monarchies, are very complex questions on which opinions may differ. Our concern for the moment is simply to recount the facts, that for a hundred years people felt themselves as living under a threat of the overthrow of all Christian civilization and under that threat accepted the strict Jesuit discipline and its almost military organization of society, and that after that rightly or wrongly (largely as it proved, wrongly) they did not feel the threat to be so imminent and as a result became more restive of discipline.

Let us again make clear what we mean by speaking of Jesuit discipline. The discipline over the pupils of Jesuit schools was of course strict. So was all school discipline in those times. Notions of running schools without punishment and the like were then quite unknown. But the Jesuits reserved the extreme severity of discipline for their own members. They were of course under obedience, they were obliged to go where their superior sent them, and to accept the standard of living which was offered in the house in which they found themselves. All that goes without saying. What is more important is the discipline that was imposed on the mind. To what extent a scholar might choose his own subject for study depended on the superior whose leave and *imprimatur* had to be obtained. Most superiors were beyond question, as the records show, sensible people who saw that it was but common sense to let their members work on the subjects in which they were interested. But there was always the chance of having a wooden, stupid, unimaginative superior and when the Jesuit found himself under the rule of such a man he had of course to accept obedience. The strictness of the discipline also tended to make the Jesuits form to some extent an ecclesia within the ecclesia. There tended to be a special Jesuit point of view on certain matters – the doctrine of grace was the clearest example– and that in spite of the fact that the Church had not laid down a final definitive doctrine. A Jesuit tended before the world always to defend another Jesuit. It is true that things did not always happen like that, but they often did, and what was more important, that was how the world thought that they happened.

The enormous list of Jesuit publications on almost every subject is amply sufficient to prove that the Jesuit system did not discourage intellectual activity. Very much the reverse. The Jesuits led the Catholic world in philosophical, theological and apologetic literature. They were learned historians. They were astronomers and scientists. They were the founders of systematic anthropology. Their missionaries taught advanced methods of agriculture to those to whom they brought the Gospel and, having travelled to distant lands to which none others had ever penetrated, they brought back to Europe the news of strange languages, strange ways of life, strange people. But all was of course very directly for a purpose. They worked and they wrote most consciously To The Greater Glory of God. Their history was almost always ecclesiastical history, their philosophy had an apologetic purpose. They produced little in the way of imaginative literature, painting or music. Jesuits did not personally create the Jesuit – the baroque – architecture. But if the Jesuits were not the artists, they were responsible for what may be called the philosophy of the architecture. Baroque architecture made its first appearance in 1568 at the Gésu. Baroque architecture and painting came into general fashion in the first years of the next century. Renaissance churches were enormous buildings that might incidentally be used for a religious purpose. The Calvinists of course deliberately whitewashed their churches in order to emphasize the fact that they were not places of mystery. The baroque purpose in opposition to both these was to concentrate all attention on the central mystery – the altar. They multiplied ornaments, as it were, in defiance of those who muttered their Puritan objections.

It was a natural and proper consequence of the Jesuits' vocation that they eschewed romance. They had their poets, among whom the English Robert Southwell was the most notable, but their poetry was almost entirely devotional and even then as a rule devotional according to a particular pattern. The Jesuits were always a little suspicious of originality within their own ranks. It is noteworthy that Father Campbell, the learned American Jesuit who has written a full two-volume history of the Society, devotes a long chapter to Jesuits' literary achievements. Southwell is honourably mentioned, as is Frederick von Spee. Gresset is mentioned but in sorrow because his 'Epicureanism' of style led to his expulsion from the Order, but Gerard Manley Hopkins is not mentioned at all. In modern times the Society's treatment of Teilhard de Chardin has not shown it in a very favourable light. Jesuit superiors were of course under no obligation necessarily to accept every speculation of de Chardin, but they showed little sense that truth in such matters must necessarily be the product of what Newman called 'many minds acting together' – that the search for truth could only prosper if conducted through a free clash of opinions. They gave all too much evidence of the military mind which thinks it to be its business to give orders, to see truth as something already completely known, and believes that towards any new speculation authority has no duty but to look up the book and see if it is right or wrong. It is perhaps a fair criticism of the Jesuits that they have always tended to allow an insufficient importance to debate as the necessary means to discovery of the truth. If we look at the literary works published by Jesuits throughout the centuries, as recorded for instance in Sommervogel's *Bibliotheca*, the list is indeed a formidable one. The thousands of volumes divide themselves into a number of classes. There are the devotional and theological works. There are all the scientific works, accounts of the grammar, the languages, the customs of strange lands in every corner of the world to which Jesuits had penetrated at times when hardly any, if any, other white man had done so. There are a number of books of devotional verse – mainly in Latin. There is plenty of history and philosophy.

Jesuits as a general rule love composing dictionaries. There are also a large number of plays from the early years of the Society – Edmund Campion's *Sacrifice of Isaac*, the *Tragedy of Saul* and *Nectar et Ambrosia*, for instance. These were pre-eminently compositions for special occasions. The boys at boarding schools in those days did not go home for holidays. The custom of the Church required the celebration of holy days and in particular an intermission of their lessons at Christmas time. In order to keep them out of mischief it was necessary to devise something for their entertainment. The Catholic tradition always favoured play-acting. On the other hand the public drama of the sixteenth and seventeenth centuries was becoming increasingly secular and often to clerical eyes not very edifying. The particular problem of the modern school play for a wholly male school – that of either finding women actors or of finding plays without women in them – of course did not exist, as in those days boys played the women's parts in all plays. The Jesuits wrote plays – more often than not with plots derived from a biblical story or from the life of a saint – for the boys to act to one another over the Christmas holidays. There is also a curiously large number of ballets from these early years, written by Jesuits to be danced by their pupils among themselves. But, these apart, works of creative imagination are few. The Jesuits do not run to novel-writing, nor have they produced very many poets, as opposed to mere writers of pious verses. As I have mentioned, there are only two English Jesuit poets – though both of them important – Robert Southwell and Gerard Manley Hopkins.

One of the most considerable of all Jesuit productions is the Bollandist *Acta Sanctorum*. It has a long and curious history. In the early years of the seventeenth century a Belgian Jesuit, Father Rosweyde, conceived the notion of producing full accounts of the lives of all the saints. He began his work in a small garret with all his books piled on the floor. The first volumes appeared in 1643. Father Rosweyde on his death handed cn his work to a successor, Father Bolland, after whom the enterprise is now generally named. From that day the work has been carried on without interruption, each member when the days of his work are passed nominating a successor. In its early days the work met with obstacles. It was denounced and condemned by the Spanish Inquisition. The Carmelites were bitterly angry because one of the

Bollandists, Father Papebroch, denied that the Order was founded by Elias. When the Society was suppressed in 1773 the commissioners at first announced that the work of the Bollandists was both so harmless and so useful that it should be allowed to continue. They were moved to the Abbaye of Caudenberg in Brussels, given a small pension, and bidden to continue, and in 1778 produced three new volumes. In 1788 the pension was withdrawn and the Bollandists had to move to the Premonstratensian Abbey of Tongerloo. There they produced a further volume in 1794 but in that year the French Revolutionary troops invaded and overran Belgium. Both the monastery of Tongerloo and the Bollandist manuscripts were dispersed. What were left were deposited when peace returned in the Burgundian library in Brussels. Nothing was done with them until 1836 when a hagiographical society in France offered to buy them. The offer aroused Belgian patriotism and the Belgian government appointed four Belgian Fathers to continue to work on the manuscripts in order to justify their retention in Belgium. They paid them a small salary which was continued until 1868 when the liberal government of the day withdrew it. The work of the Bollandists continued and continues to this day and by now well over a hundred volumes have been produced.

Aquaviva died in 1615 and was succeeded as General by Vitelleschi, who ruled until 1645. His reign thus almost exactly coincided with the Thirty Years' War which raged from 1618 to 1648. Some historians – von Ranke and Bohmer-Monod for instance – have seen in the death of Aquaviva the end of the great period of the Jesuits and asserted that after it the Society went into a decline. It is of course true that in its first sixty years the Society produced a galaxy of talent that is almost beyond belief – the dominating work of Laynez and Salmeron at Trent, Canisius' reconquest of half Germany for Catholicism, the intellectual restatement of the Catholic position by Suarez and Bellarmine, the educational work of Nadal, to speak only of the most outstanding. This small band of a few thousand men took it on themselves to change the face of Europe and succeeded, while at the same time sending out their missionaries to the most distant corners of every other continent. History has no parallel to their extraordinary achievement.

It is true that this heroic period did not end exactly with

Aquaviva's death. Suarez survived him for a few years to die in 1617; Rodriguez, the author of *Christian Perfection*, in 1617; St John Berchmans in 1621. In the years after Aquaviva's death neither heroism nor sanctity perished from the Society, nor was there any abatement of the heroic exploits of Jesuit missionaries in Asia and America. Peter Claver lived till 1654. It was in 1624 that Andrada made the famous journey to Tibet and in 1630 that de Rhodes started off to walk from India to Paris. The missions in America were still vigorous. The Jesuits in Japan still awaited their martyrdom. Still, while it would be absurd to pretend that there was any sudden, immediate decline in the standards of the Society with the death of Aquaviva, it is as true as such generalizations can ever be that his death marked the end of a first heroic period. What was the reason for this? Can we say more than that Ignatius was a man who combined genius with luck in a degree that was almost supernatural; that he forged for Christian Europe exactly the weapon that it needed at that moment; that men were bewildered and dismayed at the sight of Europe falling into disruption, waiting for a call to its recapture and yet uncertain what to do and that Ignatius' call came at the moment when a response to it was ready; that he had a genius for attracting, inspiring, leading and ordering men exactly as was needed by the world of the moment; and that it was inevitable that, when the first Jesuits had passed away and when a new world with new problems had come into existence, things would not be the same again? The success was of a dimension to which the world has no parallel. But success of that order cannot be expected to be permanent; it must of its nature be ephemeral.

To put the point again and perhaps more generally, is it not the lesson of history that genius does not distribute itself evenly over the nations and over the ages, one to each country, one to each generation? On the contrary one crowded city – fifth-century Athens – produced more in the way of genius in one century than has been produced by the whole Greek world through all the rest of the centuries, and one century in Florence did the same for the Renaissance times. Is it not much the same with the Jesuits? The wind bloweth where it listeth, and in one short half-century it produced an extraordinary coruscation of genius that transformed the world. Of course such a high level, such a vast explosion of

E*

energy could not be maintained. Who was to suppose that it would be? Why seek explanations that such things did not happen twice? The wonder is that they happened once. Whether the answer lies in such generalizations or whether it was to some extent true that the Ignatian technique was in its nature a technique that could bring short, sharp, sudden, extreme results but could not expect continuing success at this higher level, who shall say? It is perhaps a failing of the Jesuits that they appeal too frequently to precedent, even when circumstances have changed too drastically to make such appeals valuable. It was the good fortune of the first Jesuits that they had no precedents to appeal to, and so had to make up their minds for themselves.

Whatever the answer to these more general questions, there was a simpler cause for the check in the Jesuits' advance during the years of Vitelleschi's generalship, namely, that this was the period of the Thirty Years' War. All Germany was devastated. Disease and famine stalked the land. The rural population was reduced to an almost animal existence. It was hardly surprising that in such an atmosphere intellectual programmes, the building of colleges, and missionary activity did not progress with so much vigour.

Vitelleschi, in this alone joining hands with James I and anticipating Pius XII, fought an uphill battle against smoking – particularly pipe smoking – *per tubulos sorbendi*. It involved a considerable waste of time and did not make for edification. 'Your reverence must take care to remove this abuse or so to moderate it,' he wrote to the English Provincial, 'that its use is merited only for some clear need on the advice of a doctor and with the approval of the Provincial.' *

Yet in one way at any rate the Jesuits were fortunate in the Thirty Years' War. The battle in Germany was between the Catholics and the Protestants. The Catholics owed their revival and consequently their hope of success mainly to the Jesuits. Therefore they and their leaders – the Emperor Ferdinand, Maximilian, Tilly the great captain, who had himself almost become a Jesuit, Wallenstein, Tilly's successor, who had been a Jesuit pupil – all favoured the Jesuits. But on the other side the Protestants were largely kept in the field by the support of Cardinal Richelieu, who had no wish to see France confronted by a

* Chadwick, *St. Omers to Stonyhurst*, London, Burns and Oates, 1962, p. 168.

politically united Germany and therefore took the side of the opponents of the Emperor. Yet Richelieu, though he had no objection to supporting Protestant princes, was himself a Jesuit pupil and was their champion on the religious field. He always included a clause in all treaties with Protestants that the Jesuits be protected in any territories that he handed over to them.

After Vitelleschi the Society had in rapid succession four Generals, none of whom lived long. The Jesuits are of course commonly accused of political ambition and of mixing too much in political affairs. We have spoken of such careers as that of Parsons in earlier years. In this period it was rather the monarchs who demanded the services of the Jesuits than the Jesuits who were anxious for positions of importance. Louis xiv had what was in some ways, for the Jesuits, a dangerous liking for the Society. He made his confessor, Father François Amat, a member of his council on religious affairs and François de Lachaise distributor of the royal patronage. This put them and the whole Society in a position of some difficulty when the king fell out with Pope Innocent xi.

In Portugal the king insisted on Father Fernandes being made a member of his council, but the king of Portugal was a man of a different kind from the king of France and the General was able peremptorily to order Fernandes to refuse the honour. In Spain the queen made her confessor, Father Nithard, regent, and in this case the Pope insisted on his accepting the post.

When de Noyelle, a Belgian, succeeded Oliva as General in 1682 he attempted to compose the quarrel between Louis xiv and Pope Innocent xi. It was predominantly concerned with the royal claim to administer the revenues of certain vacant abbeys and episcopacies; Louis xiv had revived claims that had been waived by Henry iv, and the Pope refused to accept them. Unfortunately a distinguished Jesuit, Father Louis Maimbourg, saw fit to publish a book in support of the king's contention. He was at once expelled from the Society. As almost all the French Bishops were on the king's side and would not receive the Pope's Bulls of excommunication against Louis, the Bulls were sent to the Jesuit Provincials for distribution. The Jesuits were clearly in some difficulty. If they obeyed the Pope's command they could expect little favour from the king. The task of actually bringing the Bulls to France was entrusted to a certain Father Dez who happened to be travelling from Rome to France. Father Dez, foreseeing the trouble and thinking the Pope's action a trifle precipitate, delayed his journey with the hope that before he reached Paris the Pope would change his mind and withdraw the Bulls. His hope proved to be justified, but the withdrawal did not do much to appease the king, who replied with the full Gallican Constitutions of 1682 which submitted the Church in France in all matters of patronage to the king. The Pope rejected them and refused to accept any nominations from the king for vacant bishoprics. Father Lachaise seems to have written to the Pope asking him to relent and to transmit the Bulls confirming Louis' nominations. The result was that the Pope's displeasure fell not only on the king but also on the Jesuits. It was the first occasion on which papal displeasure had been turned against the Society, which had been formed, and was generally considered, to be the Pope's especial militia, vowed whatever the difficulties to do his will without question. The Pope was not well pleased and it is often said that he intended to bring the Order to an end by refusing to allow it to admit any more novices. This story is a slight exaggeration. The relevant document of 1684 is not from the Pope but is a document of recommendations from the College of Propaganda of the Faith to the Pope. Still there was no question that by this controversy the Jesuits were manoeuvred into a seriously unpopular position at the Vatican.

In 1685 Louis revoked the Edict of Nantes and expelled the Huguenots from his dominions. The Revocation had little to do with the Jesuits, but since they were at the moment on better terms with the king than with the Pope they were freely blamed both by Catholics and Protestants, and the Dutch in particular threatened to retaliate by special laws of discrimination. The Jesuits had not played their hand with great adroitness.

In 1689 Innocent XI died and was succeeded by Alexander VIII and the opportunity was taken to patch up the quarrel between Pope and king. A compromise was found and the Articles of 1682 were withdrawn, though the Church in France preserved and continued to preserve right up to the Revolution its essentially Gallican Constitution. One result of the compromise was that it gave the Jesuits the opportunity to slip out of the controversy. It was Louis' ambition to make the French Jesuits independent of the General in Rome much as some hundred years before some of the Spanish Jesuits had wished to become independent of the General in their country. When Louis lost the Netherlands to Spain he insisted that the Jesuit houses in the Walloon districts should still be annexed to the French assistancy. When this was refused he ordered them all to return to France and eventually the matter was compromised by a promise that the superiors in the Walloon houses should be selected from men who had been superiors in houses in France. But Louis' major claim to independence for the French provinces was not of course conceded and in the following years the conflict between the king and the Pope over Gallicanism broke out again and irrepressibly. By then de Noyelle, who was a Walloon, was dead and had been succeeded as General by Gonzalez, a Spaniard, up till then mainly known for his opposition of 'Probabiliorism' to the more common doctrine of Probabilism. Whatever doubts there may have been about the Jesuits' attitude in earlier years, the Jesuits now threw themselves under Gonzalez' leadership unequivocally into opposition to Gallicanism. He proved himself, if anything, more papalist than the Pope and aroused the anxiety both of Pope Alexander and some of his own colleagues by the vigour of his combat. He everywhere championed the claims of the Pope against those of monarchs and when a dispute between King Pedro II of Portugal and the Papal Nuncio about the ownership of some estates was referred to him, he decided with such vigour in favour of the Nuncio that the king closed down all the novitiates in the country and banished some of the Fathers.

In Europe at that time France was the great power, and the situation there was complicated. There was the controversy between the Pope and the king over Gallicanism. There was also the controversy between the Jesuits and the Jansenists. Whatever the Jesuits might say about him over the first controversy, over the second Louis XIV was always on the Jesuits' side. When Louis XIV died and the Duke of Orleans became regent for his great-grandson the Jansenists hoped for better things, but, though the regent dissolved the Jesuit sodalities in the army, he refused to revoke their rights in the university.

In these early years of the eighteenth century the Society

apparently prospered, but to those who had the skill to read them there were signs of trouble. Perhaps the Society's greatest blow was the desertion in 1747 of the Abbé Raynal. He left the Society for the Sulpicians but after a short period with them abandoned the faith altogether and died as a confessed and scoffing unbeliever, the associate of Rousseau and Diderot. Priests have occasionally lost their faith both before and since, among the Jesuits and elsewhere; it is inevitable that such things should happen from time to time. But in previous generations the loss of faith carried with it a social stigma, was thought of as something disgraceful to be concealed by him who lost it and spoken of by others in shocked terms. It was a sign of the times that Raynal was not only readily accepted in society, but actually found apostasy to his social advantage. To some extent this was evidence of a decline in religious belief in general, but apart from this, the perspicacious both within and without the Society could not fail to notice that there was now much less anxiety to speak out in support of the Jesuits than there had been a few years before. The reigns of Louis XIV and Innocent XI were in fact turning points in the Jesuits' history. Up till then this Society, devoted to the service of the Pope, could feel confident that whoever might attack them the Pope would support them. In the quarrels between Louis and Innocent they had up to a point attempted to play a mediating role and had received what is so often the mediator's reward: they were in a measure suspect to both sides. Louis XIV supported them after a fashion but after Louis' death their devotion to the Pope meant that they were not greatly in favour with the secular-minded statesmen of the day, whether in France or in other countries, whereas their loyalty to Louis meant that after Innocent's time they no longer had quite the unquestioning, whole-hearted papal support that they had previously enjoyed.

In 1757 the Jesuit General Visconti died and there was elected to succeed him Lorenzo Ricci, a member of a noble Florentine family and a man of considerable intellectual attainments. He had been a professor of rhetoric at a number of Jesuit colleges in Italy and in 1755 had been appointed Secretary to the Society. He was a man of unblemished character, but he had never held any post as a religious superior.

EIGHT

The suppression

The victory in the Hundred Years' War between Catholics and Protestants had gone to neither party but to the *politiques* – to men who, whatever their private convictions, thought that the Reformation demonstrated that men could not really know the ultimate truths, that denominational conflict was sterile and brought with it unending misery and no final certainty, and that the greatest boon that government could give its subjects was peace. It should perhaps preserve some official national religion for the comfort of those who had a hankering after such things, but the state should see to it that religion was not allowed to get strong enough to threaten the state's tranquillity.

Side by side with this general view went the fact that during the first three-quarters of the eighteenth century, whether for this or for other reasons, Protestant states were gaining and Catholic states losing power. The seventeenth century had been the century of France and the Grand Monarque. By the Seven Years' War of 1756–63 Protestant England and Prussia had won the victory over Catholic France and Austria. Britain established herself over France as the imperial power in America and India. Prussia established herself as a rival to Austria in Germany. It was an age of little faith among the educated and the classes who obtained important posts of government. Filled by the Encyclopedists with the belief that all claims to knowledge of ultimate truth were of dubious validity, looking in the practical affairs of the day to Britain and observing that apparently a country which rejected Catholicism prospered more than the countries that accepted it, it was not surprising that the *rois philosophes* of the eighteenth century and their ministers, if they did not specifically repudiate Catholicism, at the least strongly objected to anyone who took its claims as important. In the temper of the times it was often not very difficult to find even priests who would agree with them in a refusal to take such claims seriously and would cooperate in undermining the position of the Church, little thinking that in doing so they would in the end destroy their own position. The major obstacle in the eyes of the philosophers to the success of their policy was the Jesuits' obstinately determined assertion that religion was something which must be the dominating force in life.

The attack on the Jesuits began with Pombal in Portugal. Pombal had been Portuguese ambassador in London and was an admirer of the English system by which the Church was reduced to no more than a department of the state. Why should not the Pope's authority be wholly repudiated and the Church in Portugal made as completely independent of him as the Church in England? Was there not reason to hope that if that were done, Portugal's prosperity would increase as rapidly as that of England? He was prepared to go a great deal further than Louis xiv had ever planned to go with his Gallican Constitutions. It is alleged that he had an absurd plan to marry George ii's son, the Duke of Cumberland, the butcher of Culloden, to the Princess Maria and to make him king of Portugal. The Maréchal de Belle Isle writes: 'It is known that the Duke of Cumberland looked forward to becoming the king of Portugal, and I doubt not that he would have succeeded if the Jesuit confessors of the royal family had not been opposed to it. This crime was never forgiven the Portuguese Jesuits.'* Of course, if any reform of such a nature was ever to be carried through, the first necessity was to get rid of the Jesuits, the dedicated sentinels of the Pope, and that was beyond doubt Pombal's intention from the first. But some of the Jesuits, when first he returned to Portugal from abroad, singularly misunderstood his character and intentions. King John v's Jesuit confessor, Carbone, urged the king to make Pombal a minister. The king, who distrusted Pombal, refused most obstinately, but the queen who ruled as regent after John's death was less hostile and largely on the recommendation of another Jesuit, Moreira, gave Pombal the appointment. Once installed in power, Pombal revealed his true nature. For all his admiration for England, Pombal, as so often

---

* *Testament Politique*, quoting *Vita di Pombal* and *Memoria Catholica Secunda*. See A. Weld, *Suppression of the Society of Jesus in the Portuguese Dominions*, London, 1877.

happens when a statesman seeks to introduce into one country the habits of another, did not fully understand the English. The regime which he introduced, far from being one of freedom, was much more nearly a reign of terror – totalitarian rather than libertarian. It resembled England only in that no great attention was paid to clergymen. By his ruthless policies he indeed brought about a certain economic development, but he was as indifferent as any modern dictator to the price in liberty that he extracted for it. He threw rivals ruthlessly into prison; he executed without pity; he suppressed all freedom of opinion; he turned out the Jesuits.

A certain Pereira had raised the cry that the Jesuits excluded white men from the Reductions in Paraguay because they had discovered valuable gold-mines which they were exploiting. Paraguay was, according to Pereira's accusation, a gigantic and profitable speculation. Whether Pombal ever seriously believed this – it was of course wholly untrue – or whether it was merely an excuse, is uncertain. It is perhaps more probable that his motive was one of mere hatred. In any event he determined to destroy the Reductions. The first necessity was to get control of them, since they were in Spanish territory. Therefore Pombal in 1750 signed a treaty with the Spaniards by which Spain received the rich colony of San Sacramento at the mouth of the Rio de la Plata and in exchange made the Reductions over to Pombal. He then ordered the immediate expulsion from the Reductions of the thirty thousand Indians who were resident there. They were to be turned out of their homes with no alternative accommodation provided for them, and the Jesuits were ordered by Pombal to announce to them that this was to be their fate. It was, says Southey in his *History of Brazil*, 'one of the most tyrannical commands that were ever issued in the recklessness of unfeeling power'.

The Jesuits in Paraguay of course appealed against Pombal's order but they received no support from their superiors in Rome, who played throughout the story a craven and discreditable part. Visconti, who was at that time the General, decided that in the vain hope of appeasing Pombal it was necessary to obey and to betray the Indians. He sent a Commissioner Altamiano who, not content with transmitting Visconti's orders, bluntly accused his fellow-Jesuits of being rebels when they protested. His conduct aroused such indignation among the Indians that they would have murdered him had he not fled. Some readers will remember the dramatization of the story in Herr Fritz Hochwaelder's *The Strong Are Lonely*. The Jesuits in Paraguay had their hands tied: deserted by their superiors, opposed by the Bishop of Paraguay who told them that if they did not obey they would be suspended, there was little that they could do to protect their own Indians. The whole story is a sad lesson in the dangers of an excessive insistence on obedience as an unqualified duty. After their Paraguay surrender the monarchs were always confident that whatever the Jesuits might do in the scattered corners of the world, their superiors in Rome no longer had sufficient confidence either in the Pope or in themselves to resist a frontal attack. Rome has a fatal capacity for sapping resolution. As it was, deserted by the Jesuits, some of the Indians accepted. Others resisted and maintained five years of guerrilla resistance until in 1755 the Portuguese concentrated artillery and broke that resistance by tactics of ruthless massacre. Such Indians as survived drifted back into total savagery.

Further north in Brazil, Pombal launched a similar campaign against the Jesuits in Maranhão. There had for years been a running conflict between the white slave-owners and the Jesuits who protected the Indians from slavery. As early as 1725 the then Portuguese governor of Maranhão had given this tribute to the Jesuits:

The Fathers of the Society in this state of Maranhão are objects of enmity and have always been hated for no other reason than for their strenuous defence of the liberty of the unfortunate Indians and also because they used all their power to oppose the tyrannical oppression of those who would reduce to a degraded and unjust slavery men whom nature had made free. . . . Whatever has been charged against the Fathers by wicked calumniators who through hatred and envy manufactured ridiculous lies about the wealth they derive from these missions, I solemnly declare to Your Majesty, and I speak of a matter with which I am thoroughly acquainted, that the Fathers of the Society are the only true missionaries of these regions. Whatever they receive from their labours among the Indians is applied to the good of the Indians themselves and to the decency and ornamentation of the churches, which in these missions are always very neat and very beautiful.

Shortly before Pombal came to power King John v's commis-sioner, dos Santos, had reported:

The execrable barbarity with which the Indians are reduced to slavery has become such a matter of custom that it is rather looked on as a virtue. All that is adduced against this inhuman custom is received with such repugnance and so quickly forgotten that the Fathers of the Society in whose charity these unfortunate creatures often find refuge and protection and who take compassion on their miserable lot, become, for this very reason, objects of hatred to these avaricious men.

Nevertheless Pombal when he came to power sent out his brother as Governor of Maranhão, supported by a fleet and troops and with orders to destroy the Jesuit missions and to transport the Fathers back to Lisbon. Unfortunately, as in Paraguay, the local Bishop cooperated with the government in hostility to the Jesuits. A consequence of Gallican Constitutions all over Europe and throughout all European colonies was naturally that bishoprics were held by men favourable to government policies and there-fore naturally hostile to Jesuit Ultramontanism. The French Revolution was to reveal how deep was the gulf between Bishops and the ordinary clergy. Pombal's brother obeyed his orders and sent the Jesuits back to Lisbon.

Two years after this, in 1755, Lisbon suffered its famous earth-quake, and when the learned and holy Malagrida preached a sermon saying that this was a punishment on the people of Lisbon for their sins, Pombal interpreted this as an attack on the govern-ment and put him into prison. A reign of terror was then un-loosed. By that time, at any rate, Pombal must almost certainly have been mad. Our parents would have said that the stories about him were incredible, but we who have lived through the age of Stalin and Goebbels have learnt from experience how limitless is the passion for atrocity of a tyrant drunk with sadistic madness, and how unbridled the language of denunciation of those who know that they have effectively silenced all who might answer back or who might ask for evidence. Pombal was deter-mined to endure no rival of any sort to his absolute power. He arrested and executed the leading aristocrats of the country on ridiculous and invented charges of plotting the assassination of the king, and in the case of Tavora was not content to murder the head but wiped out the whole family. There were, it is said, three hundred gibbets standing at the same time in various parts of Lisbon. Nine thousand prisoners from every grade of society rotted in its gaols, suffering every form of torture and degradation. One always wonders of this and similar reigns of terror how the public was induced to tolerate them. Government, we often tell ourselves, whatever its form, must command at least a certain measure of consent, otherwise it cannot continue, and it was true of Pombal's, as it is true of all such tyrannies, that in the end it destroyed itself. For a time terror deters; its subjects have not the courage to organize among themselves to dethrone the tyrant. They cringe in security. Perhaps they hope that the tyrant himself will grow tired of tyranny and that quieter times will return without the need of revolution. But in the end they come to prefer an end of terror to terror without end, and at whatever risk rise up and overthrow the tyranny. So it was with Pombal, but it must remain an indictment of the Portuguese nation that they tolerated him even for a period.

We are not here concerned with the details of his reign of terror, but it is necessary to note them, in order to understand that his campaign against the Jesuits was not a unique act but merely one item in a general campaign against everybody. Everybody was accused of plotting against the king, the Jesuits along with everybody else. The General, by then Centurioni, wrote to the king pleading the Fathers' innocence, but Pombal saw to it that the king never received the letter. He published a pamphlet entitled *A Brief Account of the Republic which the Jesuits have established in the Spanish and Portuguese Dominions of the New World and of the War which they have carried on against the armies of the two Crowns, all extracted from the Register of the Commissaries and Plenipotentiaries and from other Documents.* Acciajuoli, the Apostolic Nuncio in Lisbon, for a time believed the accusations but even belief did not save him from expulsion from the country. Other pamphlets followed. A certain Jesuit Plantico was accused of being connected with a plot to set himself up as Emperor Nicholas I of Paraguay. Pombal laid his accusations against the Jesuits before the Pope. They were accused of:

Seditious machinations against every government of Europe; scandals in their missions so horrible that they cannot be related without extreme indecency; rebellion against the sovereign Pontiff; the accumulation of vast wealth and the use of immense political power;

gross moral corruption of individual members of the Order; abandonment of even the externals of religion; the daily and public commission of enormous crimes; opposing the king with great armies; inculcating in the Indian mind an implacable hatred of all white men who are not Jesuits; starting insurrections in Uruguay so as to prevent the execution of the Treaty of Limits; atrociously calumniating the king; embroiling the courts of Spain and Portugal; creating sedition by preaching in the capital against the commercial companies of the Minister; taking advantage of the earthquake to attain their detestable ends; surpassing Machiavelli in their diabolical plots; inventing prophecies of new disasters, such as warnings of subterranean fires and invasions of the sea; calumniating the venerable Palafox; committing crimes worse than those of the Knights Templar, etc.

At Rome a certain Cardinal Passionei, under the influence of a fanatical ex-Capuchin called Norbert who had written a book called *Mémoires Historiques Sur Les Affaires Des Jésuites*, was violently opposed to the Society. He was able to work on the dying Benedict XIV to attend to this document. Benedict XIV was in many ways a very good Pope and had indeed in previous years spoken very warmly of the Society. But in his failing days he made a sad mess of this problem. Not only did he accept Pombal's demand for an inquiry into the doings of the Jesuits in Portugal, but he was tricked into appointing to head the inquiry Cardinal Saldanha who, though Benedict did not know it, was in fact a creature of Pombal. Ricci, by then the General, laid before the new Pope Clement XIII, who had succeeded Benedict, a protest against the Portuguese proceedings. But the day had passed when the Jesuits could look for any undivided support in Rome. Cardinal Passionei vigorously opposed Ricci's protest, saying that it was but a wicked plot to persuade the Pope to hand over the rest of his flock to those 'ferocious wolves', the Jesuits. Clement however took the Jesuits' side and backed by the report of a commission declared the Jesuits exonerated, writing a courteous letter to Pombal to that effect. But the Portuguese government was in no mood to accept such a defeat. Monsignor Bottari, a cleric in Portuguese pay, produced an anti-Jesuit work called *Reflections Of A Portuguese On The Memorial Presented To His Holiness Clement XIII By The Jesuits*, and when it was suggested, perhaps foolishly, that this book should be put on the Index, Almada, the Portuguese ambassador, declared that if that were done the Portuguese king would repudiate Rome altogether and declare himself Head of the Church on the model of the Anglican constitution.

Saldanha went on 31 May 1758 to the Jesuit Church of St Roch in Lisbon and there assured the Provincial that the Fathers would be treated with great clemency. It was not until later that it transpired that sixteen days before this on 15 May, before he had even begun to take any evidence, he had already signed a document to say that the Jesuits had been found guilty of indulging in worldly traffic. The Procurators were commanded to produce their books. The Cardinal Patriarch at Pombal's demand suspended the Jesuits from preaching or hearing confessions throughout the patriarchate. The Patriarch, it is true, was afterwards very contrite for what he had done, and a month later, when he was dying, made a public confession at the time of receiving the last sacraments of the injustice of his action. In these strange times the Society had its insensate enemies and its devoted friends, but there was an oddly large middle class, to which a great many of the most distinguished of the clergy belonged, who did not believe the accusations that were made against the Society and yet did not feel any impulse to fight for them. It was not a time when the faith of the faithful was very ardent.

The death of the Patriarch did the Jesuits no good, for Saldanha was appointed to succeed him. Saldanha commissioned the Bishop of Bahia in Brazil to inquire into the financial affairs of the Society in Maranhão. But the Bishop, who was for those times an unusually honest and courageous man, reported that 'it would be an offence against God and his conscience and against the king's Majesty to condemn the Fathers.' As a result Pombal confiscated all his property and deposed him from his see.

It was in 1759 that Pombal launched his attack on the Tavora family and other aristocrats for their alleged plot to assassinate the king. The Jesuits had no connection with the plot, if indeed it existed. Many of them were already in prison; 221 had already been there for many years, and 88 had died in chains. But Pombal saw fit to implicate them, committed some on specious evidence, and then blandly announced that 'even if the exuberant and conclusive proofs already adduced did not exist, the presumption of the law would suffice to condemn such monsters.' Therefore an edict was issued that:

These religious being corrupt and deplorably fallen away from their holy institute and rendered manifestly incapable by such abominable and inveterate vices to return to its observances, must be properly and effectually banished, denaturalized, proscribed and expelled from all His Majesty's dominions, as notorious rebels, traitors, adversaries and aggressors of his royal person and realm; as well as for the public peace and the common good of his subjects; and it is ordered under the irremissible pain of death that no person of whatever state or condition is to admit them into any of his possessions or hold any communication with them by word or writing, even though they should return into these states in a different garb or should have entered another Order, unless with the king's permission.

The Jesuits in their various houses were all rounded up. The younger Jesuits were sent to Evora. The professed were compelled, whatever their condition, to march to the Tagus, where they were put into open boats and taken to a vessel which was waiting for them. A first vessel sailed to Cività Vecchia in the Papal States, where the Fathers were deposited, in September, a second in October. It was Pombal's expectation that if the professed were taken away, the other Fathers would desert the Society. This did not happen and therefore a few months afterwards the younger Fathers were also deported and sent to follow the professed. With similar measures Pombal hunted out the Jesuits in all the colonies of the Portuguese Empire until the Society was finally cleared from all its territories.

Almost the only Jesuit remaining in Portugal was Malagrida, now over seventy years of age, who, as will be remembered, had been imprisoned because of his observations on the Lisbon earthquake. Pombal determined to use Malagrida to give the story of the Portuguese Jesuits their dramatic and, as he hoped, final end. A book was produced which was said to have been written by Malagrida in prison. The charge was manifest nonsense. Malagrida had no facilities to write such a book in prison even had he wished to do so, and the Inquisition refused to attend to the charge. Pombal then dismissed the inquisitional court and made his own brother Grand Inquisitor in their place. By him Malagrida was duly condemned. He was led through the streets with a rope round his neck to the square of Do Rocco where he was strangled by the public executioner and his body afterwards burnt.

The country of greatest importance in eighteenth-century

Europe was of course France, and there, owing to Jansenism and Gallicanism and the long battle with the Parlement of Paris, there was a vigorous tradition of hostility to the Jesuits, perhaps strengthened by the failure of the Society's enemies to get the support from the Regent Orleans that they had hoped for. Choiseul was France's Pombal. Yet there was a great difference between the two. The French prided themselves on being civilized; not even the bitterest of the Society's enemies wished to beat them down with Pombal's brutal weapons. 'He was a butcher with an axe', was their disgusted verdict on him. The ambition of the Jesuits' enemies in France was to prove a case against them and to defeat them by a verdict won in a court and before judges. Unfortunately for the Jesuits their enemies were given a chance to win such a verdict. In the Portuguese battles it had been a constant accusation against the Jesuits that behind a façade of religion they were really engaged in trade and making money, though every attempt of Pombal to prove this charge had met ridiculous and total failure. In France of course the accusation that the Jesuits condoned a lax morality, a remnant of the Jansenist controversy, still survived and was championed, not very convincingly, by Madame de Pompadour, when Jesuit confessors refused her absolution. Men of reason, whatever their opinions on religion in general, poured scorn on this charge against the Society. Voltaire for instance, so often, though not perhaps quite justly, spoken of as religion's prime antagonist, wrote to D'Alembert in 1746:

What did I see during the seven years that I lived in the Jesuits' college? The most laborious and frugal manner of life; every hour of which was spent in the care of us boys and in the exercises of their austere profession. For that I call to witness thousands of men who were brought up as I was. Hence it is that I cannot help being astounded at their being accused of teaching lax morality. They have had, like other religious in the dark ages, casuists who have treated the pro and con of questions that are evident today or have been relegated to oblivion. But *ma foi*, are we going to judge their morality by the satire of the *Lettres Provinciales*? It is assuredly by Father Bourdaloue and Father Cheminais and their other preachers and by their missionaries that we should measure them. Put in parallel columns the sermons of Bourdaloue and the *Lettres Provinciales* and you'll find in the latter the art of raillery pressed into service to make indifferent things appear criminal and to clothe insults in elegant language; but you will learn from Bourdaloue how to be severe to yourself and indulgent to others. I ask then which is the true morality and which of the two books is more useful to mankind? I make bold to say that there is nothing more contradictory; nothing more iniquitous; nothing more shameful in human nature than to accuse of lax morality the men who lead the austerest kind of life in Europe and who go to face death at the ends of Asia and America.

Yet shortly after this, unfortunately for the French Jesuits, in the West Indian island of Martinique a Jesuit Father La Valette was managing extensive plantations and selling the produce in France for the advantage of the Order. In the early years of the Seven Years' War the British fleet captured a number of French vessels carrying merchandise between the West Indies and France, among them one carrying considerable cargo from Father La Valette. In order to make good his losses he borrowed heavily and, having once got into debt, plunged more deeply. He was eventually sued by his creditors and, since he was unable to pay, a verdict of the Parlement's tribunal held the whole Society liable. They paid almost a third of the debt, but, when they were unable to pay the other two-thirds, the government seized all the Jesuits' property.

La Valette had acted in direct disobedience to the rules of the Society and in fact in direct disobedience to particular orders which forbade the contraction of debts on this scale, but with communications as they then were it was difficult to enforce rules upon distant authorities overseas, ecclesiastical or secular. It was not until 1762 that a Jesuit investigator was able to visit the island, which was by then in British hands. This investigator, Father de la Marche, reported that La Valette had acted in defiance of canon law and concealed what he was doing from his superiors. La Valette confessed his fault, was expelled from the Society and spent the rest of his life in England. But it was then too late to save the Society. The Parlements had already demanded a copy of the Constitutions of the Society and made their various reports upon it. Of those reports the most outstanding was that sent by La Chalotais, a Breton magistrate. La Chalotais reported that the Society taught 'every form of heresy, idolatry and superstition and inculcated suicide, regicide, sacrilege, robbery, impurity of every kind, usury, magic, murder, cruelty, hatred, vengeance, sedition, treachery.'

On receipt of this report the judges, on 8 May 1761, ordered the confiscation of all the Society's property in France. The professed Fathers were voted a small pension of thirty cents a day. Those Fathers who were not professed were turned loose with nothing. The works of twenty-seven world-famous Jesuits, including Bellarmine and Suarez, were to be burnt by the common hangman. Yet these verdicts were verdicts of laymen. The General Assembly of the clergy, although invited to do so by the king, refused to join in the condemnation of the Jesuits. The Archbishop of Paris, de Beaumont, very vigorously championed them, but the sole result was that he was expelled from his see. The government approached the Pope and asked him to appoint a special Jesuit Vicar for France, more or less independent of the General, much as the Spanish dissidents had asked for a special Jesuit Vicar for Spain in the days of Philip II. Clement XIII refused most curtly. '*Sint ut sunt aut non sint*', were his famous words. On 19 December 1761, a document was issued, allegedly signed by the Provincial of Paris, in which the Jesuits apparently conceded the point at issue, accepted the Gallican Constitution of 1682 and professed that they would be obedient to it even in despite of the commandments of their General.

On 6 August 1762, a decree was issued which declared that the Jesuits' doctrines 'contained the errors of Arius, Nestorius, Calvin, Luther, Wycliffe and Pelagius, that they were blasphemous, outrageous, and insulting to the Blessed Virgin and the saints, destructive of the divinity of Christ; favourable to the Epicureans and to the Deists; encouraged murder, patricide, usury, vengeance and cruelty; threatened the safety of princes and were contrary to the decisions of the Church, to the divine will, to peace and good order.' Louis XV, under pressure from Choiseul and Madame de Pompadour, agreed after some hesitation to expel the Jesuits from the French dominions by an edict of November 1764. In company with his fellow Bourbon monarchs in Naples and Parma he requested the Pope to suppress the Society altogether. This, Clement XIII indignantly refused to do and in his Bull *Apostolicum* of 9 January 1765 paid the Society a ringing tribute: 'Let no one dare be rash enough to set himself against this my present approbative and confirmative Constitution lest he incur the wrath of God.'

The Bourbons also reigned in Parma and Naples, and in both those countries, but particularly in Naples where the Minister was the vigorous anti-clerical Tanucci, strong campaigns were waged against the Jesuits ending in their expulsion which was enforced with a brutality more nearly resembling the tactics of Pombal than those of France. The king of Naples joined with the king of France in the final request to the Pope to suppress the Society.

The most important Bourbon-ruled country after France was of course Spain. Ever since the Bourbon Philip of Anjou had been established on its throne in the place of the Hapsburgs, on the conclusion of the War of the Spanish Succession, Spain had been linked with France in a *Pacte de Famille*. It was therefore of great interest to Choiseul that the Spaniards should be persuaded to follow the French example in their campaign against the Jesuits. The country was then in an extraordinary and disgraceful condition. The royal family had degenerated to a state where most of its members were almost mentally deficient. The Spanish people talked much of their national pride and affected to despise all foreigners, yet they allowed themselves to be governed by a series of incompetent adventurers of whom the majority were of dubious foreign origin – Dutch, Irish or Italian. Charles III, king during the middle years of the century, was the second son of Philip V. He had ruled first for twenty-four years in Naples and then on the death of his elder brother, Ferdinand VI, had moved to Spain in 1764. He was thought to be reasonably pious, had a Jesuit confessor and was not suspected of any prejudice against the Society. On the other hand he was not credited with being very intelligent and in Naples had appointed Tanucci as his Minister without apparently at all understanding the principles of Tanucci's policy.

To begin with, Choiseul's plot to embroil Charles with the Jesuits did not meet with much success. Choiseul tried to persuade Charles that a Father Ravago had been responsible for stirring up the Indians of Paraguay to revolt. But Charles knew Ravago and could not be persuaded. In the end Charles' suspicions of the Jesuits were aroused by a wholly ridiculous incident. Charles, who regarded himself as a reformer, looked on his subjects as children and believed himself possessed of a duty to correct them in the most absurd and petty details of their lives. His Minister, Squillace, as interfering as himself, was easily able to persuade him that the sombrero hats which the people of Madrid wore were too broad in the brim and not such as would be found among

progressive people like the French. He issued an edict forbidding
them. The people of Madrid, who had no great interest either in
the principles of democracy, the rights of clerics or the moral
doctrines of the Christian religion, had no mind to allow the
government to interfere with their hats. They rose in riot, stormed
Squillace's house shouting 'Down with Squillace', and compelled
him to flee. The next day they went to the royal palace and the king,
who was a man of little courage, also fled from Madrid. In the face
of the disturbances some of the Walloon guards at the royal palace
fired on the mob and a number of people were killed. The situation was now really ugly and peace was only preserved by a
number of Jesuits making their way among the crowds and quiet-
ing them. The Ministers were persuaded to grant all the people's
demands and a placard was affixed to the palace gates announcing
that all sumptuary regulations had been withdrawn. The crowd
then dispersed with loud cheers for the Jesuits who were rightly
thought to have fought a battle for the people's right to organize
their own lives, and to have won it.

Yet the episode did no good to the Jesuits in the eyes of King
Charles. There was no concealment of the fact that he had cut a
ridiculous figure and that the Jesuits had by comparison shown
themselves at least courageous and sensible. Nor was it very
difficult to persuade the king that the Jesuits had not so much
composed the riot as fomented it. Charles' mind thus effectually
poisoned, Aranda, the new Minister, and his friends proceeded to
produce before Charles a collection of fantastic documents pur-
porting to convict the Jesuits of almost every species of treachery.
In January 1767, when the ground was felt to have been sufficiently
prepared, Campomanes, another Minister, laid before Charles a
plan for the expulsion of the Jesuits from all the Spanish dominions. It was arranged that for the moment complete silence about
the plan should be preserved but that on 2 April a public announcement should be made that the Jesuits should be expelled from
Spain for 'just and necessary reasons' and their goods confiscated.
Those reasons were in no way specified. They were, it was said
in a curious phrase, to 'remain for ever buried in the royal heart'.
This announcement was to be handed to the Pope in Rome by the
Spanish ambassador who was then to withdraw without saying a
word. All Governors and military commanders received a copy

of the announcement enclosed in two envelopes, on the outside of which was written: 'Under pain of death, this package is not to be opened until 2 April 1767 at the setting of the sun.' It was found to contain instructions to descend at once with full military power on all Jesuit houses, to seize the Fathers and to take them within twenty-four hours to an indicated port, where they would be put on board ship. 'If after your embarkation there is left behind a single Jesuit either sick or dying in your department, you shall be punished with death', said the instruction.

Whether the secret in Charles' breast was the widely believed rumour that the Jesuits were casting doubts on his legitimacy, or whether the king meant something else, or, as is likely enough, he meant nothing at all, we cannot certainly say. The announcement was received with stunned horror by Clement XIII. He demanded some proof of the accusations and was shown a document alleged to have been written by a certain Italian Jesuit containing a libellous attack on the Spanish government. A young priest who was standing by – afterwards Pope Pius VI – pointed out that this document, pretendedly composed in Italy, was in fact written on paper of Spanish manufacture which contained as water mark a date of manufacture two years later than that at which the document was supposed to have been written.

The Pope wrote to the king a stinging letter: 'Of all the blows I have received during the nine unhappy years of my pontificate the worst is that of which Your Majesty informs me in your letter.' He bluntly threatened the king with hell for his conduct. This threat to such a man as Charles, coming as it did from the Pope, was not merely an exercise in abuse. Weak, foolish Charles, oscillating as weak and foolish people did at that time between a superstitious fear of hell and an encyclopaedist's belief that progress required that the state should be emancipated from the Church, had an uneasy feeling that if the Pope said that he would go to hell, then to hell he would go.

During the night soldiers in all the Spanish cities marched to the Jesuit houses, pulled the inmates out of their beds, sealed the doors and marched the Jesuits to the local gaols. They were not permitted to speak a word. They were then taken from the gaols to the nearest sea-port and herded on board ships so grossly overcrowded that they had to be piled on top of one another. They were

taken to Cività Vecchia, whither their Portuguese colleagues had
been taken before them. The Pope had been given no warning of
their coming and Cività Vecchia was so overcrowded with
refugees that there was no room to accommodate them. The ships
therefore had to make off to Corsica, at that time fighting under
Paoli for its independence from the Genoese. Paoli received them
well and they were allowed to bivouac or live in sheds for a time
in the town of Saint-Boniface. They then, when arrangements had
been made for them, proceeded to various places in the Papal
States, principally to Bologna and Ferrara.

Charles to his dismay found that there was a universal and
cynical disbelief in his possession of some mysterious secret which
justified him in his action. Even the scoffers at religion like
D'Alembert scoffed also at the king. The very ineptitude and
poltroonery of the Minister and the royal family in Spain made
the Jesuits there at least by comparison popular. When on 4
November 1768, the king in accordance with custom presented
himself on his balcony to receive the plaudits of his people he was
greeted with cries of 'Send us back the Jesuits'.

The Jesuits were soon afterwards brutally expelled from Naples
and Parma by methods similar to those employed in Spain. Parma
was the Pope's fief and the Pope therefore especially condemned
the actions taken there in the duke's name.

There only remained the final battle. The Bourbon monarchs,
not content with having expelled the Jesuits from their own
territories, were determined to suppress them utterly. They made
a succession of démarches on Pope Clement XIII with their
demands. First came the Spanish representative, then a few days
afterwards the Neapolitan, and finally Aubeterre, the French
ambassador. All received from Clement stinging rebukes. 'His
Holiness is horrified at the attitude of the king', Cardinal Torre-
giani wrote to the Papal Nuncio at Madrid. The Bourbon kings,
or at least their encyclopaedist Ministers, held strong cards. Things
had by now moved far beyond mere Gallicanism. Their threat was
that if the Pope should prove obdurate they would remove their
countries from the Roman Catholic Church altogether and establish a Church Constitution on the Anglican model. It was by no
means self-evident that they would not be able to do this with
concerted action, and if they succeeded the days of the Catholic

Church as the major religion of Europe were numbered. Whatever the validity of its claims before God, in the eyes of men it would be henceforth but an inconsiderable local band, overwhelmingly outnumbered even among Christians by those who repudiated its authority.

Events thirty years later were to show how gross an error it was to judge public opinion merely from the opinions of the upper classes and the intellectuals; there was a much stronger substratum of genuine faith among the poor and simple than the intellectuals had guessed. It may be that Clement, a very great and brave man, had some inkling of the truth, but who shall say? The Church,

> Though doomed to death, yet fated not to die,

has at many stages in its history looked as if its long term was at last ended. There have been many times when by every human calculation it seemed doomed to defeat, and no man could believe in its survival save through unshaken faith in its divine promises. There was never a time when the final destruction of the Church looked by any human calculation more probable than during the pontificate of Clement XIII. Yet he stood firm as a rock. He made no surrender. But firmness was only bought at the price of anguish. On 2 February 1768, ten days after he had heard the last threat from the French ambassador, he died of a stroke of apoplexy. No one can doubt the cause of that stroke.

Everything of course turned on the choice of his successor. The Catholic monarchs at that time were allowed to exercise a veto over papal elections. Among the Cardinals a majority were what were known as Zelanti, who were opposed to the suppression of the Society. The monarchs naturally saw to it that all these were excluded. Cardinal Bernis was instructed to see to it that any Cardinal who hoped to be elected Pope accepted certain terms of which the chief was that he annul Clement XIII's Bull against Parma and agree to the suppression of the Jesuits. By these tests it was finally agreed that only two Cardinals could be considered *papabili*, Ganganelli and Stoppani. Instructions from Madrid made it clear that the monarchs would recognize no Pope who did not accept these terms. They made no bones about it that if an election was made contrary to their wishes they would take their countries out of the Church. As Schoell, a Protestant historian, has put it, 'the formation of state Churches in the three kingdoms was clearly the avowed purpose of these plotters.'

There was some relic of self-respect among the Cardinals and they baulked at allowing the extraction from any candidate of a written promise. That would be simoniacal. Still, before they allowed Ganganelli to be elected as Clement xiv, the monarchs were reasonably confident that he would do their will. Clement xiv was probably the worst but he was by no means the wickedest of all the Popes. The event was to prove that he was both weak and foolish and possessed of an insufficient faith in God, but it would be unfair to suggest that he acted in this instance out of merely base motive or for personal gain. He accepted the monarchs' terms with reluctance and because he had convinced himself that opposition would mean the destruction of the Church. He had no wish either to agree with the monarchs or to oppose them. He hoped at first to evade a decision by procrastination. It was the custom to issue a brief of indulgence in favour of missionaries. The occasion presented Clement with a difficulty. It would have been too absurd to praise the Church's missionary endeavours without mentioning the Jesuits and Clement found within himself the courage to write:

We include among these fervent apostles the religious of the Society of Jesus and especially those whom our beloved son, Lorenzo Ricci, is to assign this year and afterwards in various provinces of the Society to that work; and we most certainly desire to promote and increase by these spiritual favours the piety and the active and enterprising zeal of those religious.

The result was an explosion. Choiseul, who up till then had conducted his campaign with an air of suave courtesy, boiled over. 'Who are going to win the fight?' he asked. 'The kings or the Jesuits?' Bernis attempted to calm him down. Of course the king would win, the Cardinal assured Choiseul. Of course the Jesuits would be destroyed, but it was necessary to recognize that the Pope must play his hand carefully. Catholic opinion all over the world must be considered. He must be given time. For the moment it would be wise to content oneself with extracting from the Pope a promise that it was his intention to destroy the Society. Louis xv in France was content with that and Clement wrote him a letter on 30 September, giving the assurance. But Charles iii in

MIRVM IN DÆMONES
EXERCET IMPERIV

21. A detail of the interior of the Gesù, Rome

22. A celebration at the birth of Louis XIII at the College of Clermont

24. (*Opposite*) Title page of the Bollandist *Acta Sanctorum*

23. A scene from the seventeenth-century Jesuit play *Pietas Victrix*

scientiam
Sanctorum. Sap. 8.

in plenitudine Sanctorum detentio mea.

ACTA SANCTORVM
Quotquot toto orbe coluntur, vel à Catholicis Scriptoribus celebrantur.
Quæ ex Latinis & Græcis, aliarúmque gentium antiquis monumentis
collegit, digeſſit, Notis illuſtrauit
IOANNES BOLLANDVS
SOCIETATIS IESV THEOLOGVS,
Seruatâ primigeniâ Scriptorum phraſi.
OPERAM ET STVDIVM CONTVLIT
GODEFRIDVS HENSCHENIVS
EIVSDEM SOCIET. THEOLOGVS.
Prodit nunc duobus Tomis
IANVARIVS,
In quo MCLXX. nominatorum Sanctorum,
& aliorum innumerabilium memoria
vel res geſtæ illuſtrantur.
Cæteri menſes ex ordine ſubſequentur

RVDITIO.

UÆKITAS

TIQVA REDVCO.

OBSCVRA REVELO.

Ær a Diependele dele. *Theod Ioz van Merlen fecit*

NTVERPIÆ, APVD IOANNEM MEVRSIVM. ANNO M. DC. XLIII

25. Blaise
Pascal

26. Nuns at
Port Royal

Spain had by now worked himself up to a frenzy that was hardly distinguishable from insanity. To quieten him Clement wrote to him on 30 November a letter in which for the first time he moved out of mere weakness and folly into positive dishonour. 'We have gathered all the documents,' he piteously pleaded, 'that are needed for writing the *motu proprio* agreed upon; so as to justify to the whole world the wise conduct of Your Majesty in expelling the Jesuits as troublesome and turbulent subjects.'

All that the Pope had achieved by writing this letter had been to render himself capable of blackmail. He was by now terrified and indeed in such a panic as to be hardly sane, let alone infallible. He was convinced that he would be poisoned, though whether by the Jesuits or by the monarchs he was not quite clear. Choiseul spoke of his fears as the contemptible panic of a fool. In a wild hope of appeasement Clement appointed Marefoschi, a bitter enemy of the Society, to prepare the Brief of Suppression. The matter proved more complicated, reported Marefoschi and his commission, than had been foreseen. It dragged on from year to year. In the hope of appeasing Charles III the Pope made the infamous proposal that he should canonize the insane megalo-maniac Palafox. But Charles would brook no delay and accept no alternative to the total suppression of the Society. He sent the intransigent Florida Blanca as his ambassador to Rome. Florida Blanca presented without ambiguity the blank alternative of suppression of the Society or Spain's secession from the Church. Had Clement been a man of a little more courage and wisdom he would have looked to the history of Spain and the public reaction to Charles' past treatment of the Jesuits, to Charles' own poltroonery and unpopularity, and asked how far Charles was really in a position to carry out the threats which he was uttering. The papacy had much more prestige than the monarchy in Spain if only the Pope had had the courage to use it, but Clement had no such courage. Clement pleaded to be allowed to wait till Ricci's death. Florida Blanca would make no such concession. He forced out of Clement the Brief of 1773. 'He did not obtain it, he tore it from the Pope's hand,' was the comment of a diplomat at the time. 'I will disgrace you by publishing the letter you wrote to the king,' Florida Blanca bluntly told Clement. The Pope sur-rendered to the blackmail.

F

While the Bourbons were unanimous in their opposition to the Pope, his one hope up till then had been in Austria and Maria Theresa. Maria Theresa had appeared for a time to be a friend of the Society, but her son, Joseph II, was as deeply imbued with encyclopaedist principles as any of the Western monarchs. Maria Theresa preferred that injustice should not be committed, but, as she showed over the Polish partition, believed that if injustice could not be prevented, then she must have her share in the benefits of it. '*Elle pleurait et prenait.*' It was much the same with her treatment of the Jesuits. She would not have suppressed the Jesuits at all had the matter been left to her, but, if they were to be suppressed, then her main concern was that she should have the right to dispose arbitrarily of their property.

On 16 August 1773, Macedonio, the Pope's nephew and secretary, afterwards to be prosecuted for peculation of the Jesuits' property, went to the Gésu and officially notified the General of the Brief. Seals were put on the archives. All the Jesuits, even the old and infirm, were collected there and told that they had been relieved of their functions. On the 17th Ricci was ordered to repair to the English College and was there put under house arrest, in which he was kept for a month. He was then transferred along with his leading comrades to the Castle of Saint Angelo, where he remained for the further two years of his life. He was closely and brutally questioned by Andretti, the Chief Inquisitor. As it was not possible to find any charge that could be brought against him, there was at one time a possibility that he might be released, but Florida Blanca intervened to prevent this and he died, still in prison, on 24 November 1775. Those of his companions who had survived him were then released but under the strict order that they should speak no word of their experiences in prison.

It is sometimes pleaded in support of Clement XIV that in his Brief *Dominus Ac Redemptor* he does not make any charge against the Jesuits. He merely records the fact that throughout history others have made charges against them. This is true enough, but he records them in such a way that any reader would imagine that he believed them. The gravamen of his charge is that wherever the Jesuits have been throughout their history there has always been discord. He does not even advert to the possibility that it may be

an explanation that the Pope had been steadily attacked for the last
two hundred years and that the Jesuits were attacked because they
supported the Pope. A Pope might at least in decency have mentioned that. The Brief is written in an exceptionally unattractive,
whining, Uriah Heap-like style. We read of 'our son in Christ, the
most faithful king of Portugal' – Pombal's king who had only
with humiliation and difficulty been bought off from apostatizing
from the Church. Clement claims, as he plunges in the dagger, to
have been 'aided, as we think, by the presence and inspiration of
the Holy Ghost'. As Cardinal Antonelli, Prefect of Propaganda,
reported to Pius VI when questioned after Clement's death:

In its form and execution all law is set aside, it is based on false accusations and shameful calumnies; it is self-contradictory in speaking of
vows both solemn and simple. Clement XIV claims powers such as
none of his predecessors claimed and on the other hand leaves doubt on
points that should have been more clearly determined. The motives
alleged by the Brief could be applied to any other Order and seem to
have been prepared for the destruction of all of them. Without specifying reasons it annuls many Bulls and Constitutions received and recognized by the Church; all of which goes to show that the Brief is null
and void.

It is not easy to see any mitigation of Clement's conduct. If the
charges were not proven it was surely even less justifiable to
punish them. Clement's conduct was in fact despicable, and no
apologist can pretend otherwise. Pius XI in this century has
roundly condemned it as 'a painful page of history'. In fact Clement
has been generally treated by historians with undeserved lenity.
If the historians were anti-Catholic they tended to feel that, though
the action may have been harsh in detail, yet the Jesuits were a
malevolent organization and their suppression was desirable. If the
historians were Jesuit, then the Society's special loyalty to the
papacy has made them reluctant to speak strongly even against
such a Pope as Clement.

Yet the verdict is surely beyond doubt. The upshot of the controversies of the Reformation was, as has been argued, that many
people had quite honestly reached the conclusion that ultimate
certainty on Christian differences was unattainable; that denominational controversies were futile; that while it was perhaps desirable that a nation should profess a religion, the prosperity of

England proved that it did better with a purely national religion. These were the beliefs of the monarchs and of the secular governments of Europe of those times. They were beliefs which, even if on a full analysis somewhat superficial, nevertheless might be held honourably. They could not of course excuse the cruel and dishonourable acts by which the suppression of the Society was accomplished but they could furnish an explanation of why a man might be honestly opposed to the Society. But the Pope's position was a different one. He could not from his profession believe that denominational differences were of secondary importance. He might of course have believed, in contrast to his predecessors, that the Catholic cause ought indeed to be defended but that the Jesuit method was not a good method of defending it. He might conceivably have argued that the Jesuits had performed a useful service in their day but that the day was now passed and they had better be suppressed. Such positions would not have been logically impossible, however difficult to defend in detail, but, though they might have justified the Pope in suppressing the Society, they could not have justified him in persecuting its members who had served during the years when the Pope still recognized and praised the Jesuits, who had committed no shadow of crime and raised no finger to defend themselves when the Society had been suppressed. The persecution of Ricci and his comrades marked Clement's name with indelible infamy. The upshot was of course peculiar and sardonic. The one thing that seemed secure of survival in the middle of the eighteenth century was the monarchical, secular state of the *rois philosophes*. The Jesuits could go. The papacy, many men thought, might well go. Even the Pope himself thought that he could only hope to survive by appeasing the monarchies. Yet before less than a quarter of a century had passed the head of the French king had fallen. All the monarchs who had persecuted the Jesuits had lost their thrones. The papacy survived and regained in persecution the authority that it had lost by appeasement, and in forty years the Society of Jesus which the monarchs thought that they had destroyed for ever had risen again and once more taken up its place in the Catholic world.

NINE

The interlude

Since Clement's action was essentially an action of surrender to the secular power, it naturally followed that the vigour of the application of the Brief depended very much on the wishes of the secular rulers. Indeed it was a curiosity, that was in the event of considerable importance, that the Society was suppressed not by a Bull, which would have had universal authority, but by a Brief that only had effect in countries where it was promulgated by the secular power. In Portugal the Brief was read out and celebrated by the firing of cannon. Tanucci in Naples and Charles III in Spain would not allow it to be read at all because of incidental phrases of compliment to the Jesuits which it contained. In France the government wished it to be read but the Archbishop of Paris, de Beaumont, the Jesuits' fiery defender, bluntly refused to have it read. But in all those countries it was of little practical moment whether it was read or not because the Jesuits had of course already been expelled from them, and it mattered little whether they were also technically suppressed or not. However the controversy in France was important because of the extraordinarily outspoken rebuke which, as a result of it, was issued by the Archbishop of Paris to the Pope – perhaps the most outspoken rebuke that any Archbishop has ever given to a Pope. The Brief, wrote Archbishop de Beaumont:

Is nothing else than a personal and private judgement. Among other things that are remarked in it by our clergy is the extraordinary, odious and immoderate characterization of the Bull *Pascendi Munus* of the saintly Clement XIII whose memory will be forever glorious and who had invested the Bull in question with all due and proper formalities of such documents. It is described by the Brief not only as being inexact but as having been 'extorted' rather than obtained; whereas it has all the authority of a General Council for it was not promulgated until almost the whole clergy of the Church and all the secular princes had been consulted by the Holy Father. The clergy with common accord and with one voice applauded the purpose of the Holy Father and earnestly begged him to carry it out. It was conceived and published in a manner as general as it was solemn.

He wrote quite bluntly calling the Pope a liar:

We abstract, Holy Father, from the individuals whom we might easily name, both secular and ecclesiastical, who have meddled with this affair. Their character, condition, doctrine, sentiment, not to say more of them, are so little worthy of respect as to justify us to expressing the formal and positive judgement that the Brief which destroys the Society of Jesus is nothing else than an isolated, private and pernicious judgement which does no honour to the Tiara and is prejudicial to the glory of the Church and the growth and conservation of the Orthodox Faith. Moreover, Holy Father, we have remarked with terror that this destructive Brief eulogizes in the highest way certain persons whose conduct never merited praise from Clement XIII of saintly memory. Far from doing so he regarded it always as his duty to set them aside and to act in their regard with the most absolute reserve.

In countries that were under Protestant government the Jesuits fared better than in Catholic countries. In America they were of course expelled from the Spanish and Portuguese colonies and from the French territory of Louisiana, but ten years before Canada had passed from French to British rule and the Catholics of Canada had been granted much greater religious freedom than Catholics at that time enjoyed in Great Britain. Monsignor Briand, the Bishop of Quebec, refused to promulgate the Brief and Governor Carleton, the British Governor, supported him. The American colonies were of course then still British and therefore there was no organized Jesuit province there. But there were nineteen Jesuits at that time in Maryland and Pennsylvania. Bishop Challoner, the apostolic Vicar in London, wrote them a rather cold letter, bidding them secularize themselves. But it would have been absurd for the Jesuits in Maryland to have dissolved themselves and abandoned all Catholic activity in the colony. In fact the Jesuits in Maryland dropped the habit of calling themselves SJ but otherwise went on much as before. It was much the same with the English Jesuits. Teaching Catholic priests, Jesuit or otherwise, were not at that time allowed in Britain by the penal laws. The English Jesuits therefore kept their school at St Omers

in France where English Catholics were invited to send their sons.
When the Jesuits were expelled from France these English Jesuits
had to leave the country along with the rest and they crossed the
frontier into Belgium, then the Austrian Netherlands, and established themselves at Bruges. Maria Theresa still at that time posed
as the protector and friend of the Jesuits. But when the Society
was suppressed she accepted the suppression in her dominions and
the English Jesuits had to leave Bruges. They were given refuge
by the Prince-Bishop of Liège who remained their friend even
after the suppression, and they continued their school there, con-
ducting it under the title of 'the Gentlemen from Liège'. When,
with the French Revolution, the French overran the Netherlands,
they had again to flee and, coming to England, which was by then
willing to admit them, they established themselves at Stonyhurst
in Lancashire where they have ever since remained.

Among other countries, Poland for a long time refused to accept
the Brief, as did the Catholic cantons of Switzerland, but the two
countries where the Jesuits received the warmest welcome and
where the Brief was most decisively rejected were Prussia under
Frederick the Great and Russia under the Empress Catherine.

It has become almost a truism of our day that appeasement of
foes does not bring peace and although there may be times when
it is wise to strike a compromise with an antagonist who shares
one's desire for peace, certainly to make concessions to those who
desire one's destruction and to show oneself a coward only invites
further attacks. Clement xiv's antagonists, whether they were
actually atheist or not, were certainly men who wished to see the
destruction of the Catholic Church in any form that it had traditionally held or in which it had been entrusted to Clement for
guardianship. To the Church's enemies the whole episode was
important not merely because it eliminated the inconvenient
Jesuits but because it showed Clement to be a coward and a
traitor. Whatever others might think, to Charles iii and Pombal
the compliments which Clement paid to them and the abuse which
he showered on the Jesuits were important precisely because they
knew them to be insincere. They were appeals for pity from a
frightened man, and all that these men without pity needed was the
certainty that they were feared so as to assure them that they need
show no mercy. As D'Alembert wrote of Clement's suppression of

the Jesuits, 'such a treaty would be very like that of the sheep and
the wolves, the first article of which was that the sheep should
deliver their dogs to the wolves.' The surrender did not bring to
Clement the peace for which he had hoped; exactly the reverse.
Knowing that he was a frightened man who would not dare
answer back, his enemies carried insolence to unheard-of lengths.
In Rome itself pamphlets against the Pope were hawked about in
the streets with impunity and men conducted buffoon parodies of
the Mass and other sacred ceremonies in public places. Joseph 11
in Austria, seeing the way the tide was flowing, joined the Bourbon
monarchs in the campaign against the Church and outdid them in
his demands for complete subordination of the Church in Austria
to the state, and a total repudiation of the authority of Rome. The
very curial officials at the Vatican treated Clement as a contemptible man and refused to speak to him. Clement himself lived on
for thirteen miserable months after the Brief and died on 22
September 1774.

Two stories were put about concerning his closing days. One
was that he was poisoned by the Jesuits. That, it need hardly be
said, was, and is indeed admitted even by the Jesuits' harshest
critics to be, wholly ridiculous. There is no possible way in which
it could have happened and no glimmer of evidence that it did
happen. The story is only of importance as showing the strength
of a spirit of insane hysteria which existed then, and perhaps
sometimes even exists now, by which some people almost in-
stinctively ascribe to the machinations of the Jesuits every catastrophe which happens in the world. The other story was that
during his last year and after the issue of the Brief, Clement's mind
became unhinged. Monarchs at that time more often than not
were somewhat mad and there is nothing inherently improbable
in the story. There is a certain amount of evidence in its favour, of
which the most important pieces are the testimony of his two
successors, Pius vi and Pius vii. It is not easy to say where
ineptitude verges into insanity.

Throughout the rest of Italy outside Rome the Jansenists were
greatly encouraged by the defeat of their enemies, the Jesuits.
Their great supporter in that country was Francis, the Grand Duke
of Tuscany and brother of the Emperor Joseph 11. The Jansenists
claimed that the four Gallican Articles should be promulgated in

Italy and all patronage taken out of ecclesiastical and transferred to secular hands. When their demands were formally promulgated by the Synod of Pistola twelve years later in 1788, they were condemned by Pius VI, but so long as Clement still lived there was no voice at Rome with courage enough to protest against them.

After a prolonged conclave lasting four months Cardinal Braschi of Cesena was elected to succeed Clement and took the name of Pius VI. His main concern in his anxiety to save something from the wreck of the Church which Clement had left was to prevent an overt break with Austria. With this purpose he made a personal visit to Vienna in 1782. He was received with courtesy by Joseph II but with brutal incivility by his minister, Kaunitz, and the mission met with no success. Joseph promised that nothing would be done against the rights of the Holy See or of the Church without consulting Rome, but then, after having accompanied the Pope as far as the monastery of Marianbrunn on his return journey, contemptuously suppressed the monastery no more than an hour after Pius had left it. At the same time the three ecclesiastical Electors, the Archbishops of Mainz, Trier and Cologne, imposed Febronian constitutions which repudiated all papal powers of patronage in their dioceses. By a strange paradox, what saved Catholicism in Germany was the French Revolution. Fear persuaded the German Catholics, as common sense should have persuaded them, that the greater danger was a danger of total revolution which would attack the wealth and privileges of the Archbishops, indifferent whether they were in communion with Rome or not. Before such a menace there were advantages, as they thought, in the preservation of unity.

In Portugal the tide turned before the general revolution broke out in France. In 1777 the king died, and Queen Maria who succeeded him discovered that Pombal had been involved in a plot to keep her off the throne. She dismissed him and as a consequence threw open his dungeons. Eight hundred men of all classes were found to have been immured in them. Many had been there for eighteen years and many had never had any charge preferred against them. They were in an almost sub-human condition. Among them were sixty Jesuits. The sight of these pitiable wrecks so moved public opinion that there was a violent outburst against Pombal who, had he not escaped to the country, would almost certainly have been torn to pieces. At the petition of Father de Guzman, the last Assistant of the Society, who had been in one of the dungeons and who was then eighty years old, the queen ordered an inquiry into the events of 1758 which had led to the Jesuits' incarceration. As a result of it the Jesuits were declared 'absolutely innocent' and Pombal was condemned to receive 'an exemplary punishment'. In fact nothing was done to him, it being wisely thought that to execute him or to put him in prison at his advanced age would cause a certain reaction of public sympathy in his favour. He died of leprosy in 1782.

According to the conditions of the suppression the Jesuits became secular priests. Some of them, like Ricci, as we have seen, suffered ill treatment. In some places, as in France, they were submitted to odious injustices. In France, although their vows as members of the Society had been nullified with the Society's abolition, yet the vows were invoked by the Parlement to make it illegal for them to receive legacies from their relatives. But in many places they fitted easily into the lives of secular priesthood and in many cases went on living lives not so greatly different from those which they had lived before. Now that they were secular priests there was of course nothing to debar them from receiving ecclesiastical honours. A number became Bishops. The first two rulers of the American hierarchy, for instance, Carroll and Neale, were both Jesuits. Crétineau-Joly tells us that in the closing years of the eighteenth century there were twenty-one ex-Jesuit Bishops in European sees. As scientists, astronomers, teachers, social workers and the like they were naturally as useful now as ex-Jesuits as they had been as Jesuits, and, had they all abandoned the work that they had been doing at the time of the suppression of the Society, both the education and the scientific work of Europe would have been in a sorry state. Many of them, particularly throughout the territories of the Empire and throughout Italy, continued running the colleges and observatories which they had run before, merely ceasing to call themselves Jesuits. Some of them played a part of considerable prominence in the life of their country. When the States General was summoned in France, at least four ex-Jesuits were among its members. Overseas, in China, Africa and India, since there was no apparent way of promulgating or enforcing the Brief and since withdrawal of the Jesuits would manifestly be a disaster with no compensating advantages to anyone, they simply went on with their work without regularizing the position, though naturally receiving no further recruits. Where there was a government which could enforce the Brief and create a vacuum the results were disastrous. Southey writes in his *History of Brazil*:* 'Centuries will not repair the evil done by their sudden expulsion. They had been protectors of a persecuted race; the advocates of mercy, the founders of civilization; and their patience under their unmerited sufferings forms not the least honourable part of their character.'

These were the years when Poland was being partitioned out among its neighbours. A natural consequence of this was that the Polish government was in no position to do much to help the Jesuits. When the Brief was first issued the Polish king refused to promulgate it, and thus for some time the Jesuits remained in their possessions, but in the long run this turned out to be a disadvantage to them rather than an advantage, for it meant that when the Society in Poland eventually was dissolved and its members promised pensions to compensate them, the Polish government no longer had the possessions out of which to pay them. Zalenski in his *Les Jésuites de la Russie Blanche* quotes a pitiable letter which a hundred and five of them sent to the last king of Poland:

Will Poland so long known for its humanity be cruel only to us? Will you permit us, the Lord's anointed, the old teachers of the youth of Poland, to go begging our bread on the streets with our garments in rags and exposed to insults? Will you permit that our tears and our cries which are forced from us by the grief and abandonment to which we are reduced should add to the affliction of our country? Will you permit that our country should be accused of inhumanity and insulted because it withholds our pension? It is sad enough for us to have lost the Society, the dearest and nearest thing to our heart in this life, without adding this new suffering. Should you not have pity on our lot and grant us a pension? Do not bring us down to the grave with this new sorrow.

The suppression of the Jesuits was certainly a turning point in the history of the Church. Catholics often tend to concentrate their attention on the attacks on the Church by its adversaries from outside. It is in the nature of the Church that it should

* London, Longmans, 1810–19, vol. x, p. 310.

always have vigorous adversaries. Ignatius and indeed Christ Himself warned His followers that they ought to be very disturbed if they should ever remain long unharassed by the enmity of the world. But the real matter for concern is not when Christianity is vigorously attacked from without but when it is imperfectly defended by its own authorities. The tragedy of the Jesuit suppression was not that the Bourbon monarchies attacked them but that so many high ecclesiastics – and finally the Pope himself – should desert them and desert them, primarily, whatever might be said of an isolated episode like that of La Valette, not because they had been false but because they had been true to their calling. Under Clement xiv the papacy came as near as it has ever come since St Peter and the cock-crow to denying Christ.

Disastrous in Europe, the suppression of the Jesuits was yet more disastrous outside Europe. As has been said, Christendom had been driven back into Europe. Then in the sixteenth century the European had begun to push his way out into the other continents. The emigrants were for the most part adventurers, interested only in exploiting the Asian and the African, indifferent to his welfare. The missionary almost alone went to those countries anxious to benefit their inhabitants, and of missionaries by far the greater number were Jesuits. Had the Jesuits been encouraged, the expansion of Europe might have been a real expansion of Christendom. With the Jesuits hampered and eventually suppressed it was inevitable that the non-European world should look on the European as his enemy and that instead of the brotherhood of man we should have the racial conflicts by which today our whole existence is threatened. That world-wide racial conflict is as much the consequence of the suppression of the Jesuits as of any other single factor.

Yet the two sovereigns who gave the most vigorous support to the Jesuits and to whom above any other they owed their survival through this period of suppression were, of course, Frederick the Great of Prussia and Catherine the Great of Russia. It is important first to understand what they did and then to try to understand why they did it.

First let us take Frederick. Prussia at his accession was an almost wholly Protestant state. Then as a result of the War of the Austrian Succession, Prussia had annexed Silesia, with a purely

Catholic population, from Austria. Then by the First Partition of Poland it had acquired a further substantial Catholic population. Frederick was himself a free thinker, indifferent in his religious opinions, but he had no mind to complicate the problems of consolidating his new dominions by indulging in policies of religious discrimination. The Silesian Catholics and the Silesian Jesuits had both taken the Austrian side in the war, and Frederick determined to take advantage of Joseph's anti-Catholic Febronianism to show that Catholics would get far better treatment from Prussians than from Austrians. Therefore, while others were expelling the Jesuits, he invited them to take care of the education of the Catholic youth of his dominions. His calculation was that, if he offered the Jesuits a refuge, then he could hope that they would bring up Frederick's Catholic subjects to be loyal to Prussia and to abandon any notions of looking for a return to Austrian rule. The Jesuits in their parlous state were very ready to accept the proposal. Indeed shortly before the full suppression of the Society one Jesuit, Father Pinto, even asked Frederick to declare himself the protector of the Society, but Father Ricci saw that, when the Society was being widely accused by its enemies of being un-Catholic, it would give a fatal lever to those enemies if at such a moment it should put itself under the official protection of a Protestant who was in personal conviction notoriously a free thinker, and Ricci sternly rebuked Pinto for his indiscretion.

Frederick saw the sense of this and it did not in any way dissuade him from his purpose of attracting the Jesuits. By its terms of proclamation the Brief, as has been said, was only effective in countries where it was promulgated. Frederick wrote bluntly to all the Catholic ecclesiastics in his kingdom: 'We graciously enjoin upon you to take all necessary measures to suppress the aforesaid Bull.' (It was not of course, strictly speaking, a Bull. It was a Brief which, as has been explained, was slightly different.) 'You are commanded to see carefully to the execution of this order and to inform us immediately in case any high foreigner ecclesiastics endeavour to introduce any Bulls of this kind into our kingdom surreptitiously.' He had already written to his ambassador in Rome on 13 September 1773, immediately after the issue of the Brief, bidding him tell Clement XIV that 'with regard to the affair of the Jesuits my resolution is taken to keep them in my states as they hitherto have been.' He maintained that by one of the conditions of the Treaty of Breslau by which Silesia had been ceded to him he had promised to maintain the *status quo* in religion and added a little slyly that it was his habit to keep his word – which in general was very far from being universally true – and that since he was a Protestant the Pope had not the power which he perhaps had over Catholics to prevent him from doing so.

In the next year Clement died and was succeeded by Pius VI. Pius, who was a man of a very different calibre from Clement, made no bones about it that Clement had been guilty of an egregious blunder and that he would be only too glad to find a way of resuscitating the Society. Its survival in Prussia was therefore to his mind an advantage, as such a nucleus might one day give an opportunity for a full re-establishment. After a few perfunctory queries Pius VI let it be known that he had no objection to the Jesuits remaining in Silesia and wrote to tell Frederick that he was well pleased with the arrangement. Frederick wrote to the superior at Breslau to confirm him in his status. A difficulty in all Jesuit provinces is of course that, since the Jesuits cannot themselves become Bishops, they need a friendly Bishop to ordain their new recruits. There was such a Bishop in the early days of Frederick's reign – Bishop Bayer of Culm – but, when he died, the new Bishop, Bishop Hohenzotten, was much less accommodating, advising the king to secularize the Jesuits and refuse admittance to any new novices. Frederick refused and was only prepared to go so far in meeting Hohenzotten as to bid the Jesuits to dress themselves like secular priests – to which they had no objection – and to be known technically as Priests of the Royal Institute. So things continued until Frederick's death in 1786 on the eve of the French Revolution. His nephew who succeeded him was an old-fashioned Prussian Protestant who had sympathy neither with the Jesuits nor with free thinkers and under him the Jesuit experiment was suppressed.

If we ask what was Frederick's motive in showing this strange tolerance, a large part of the answer was certainly that which has already been suggested – mere political convenience. He had no Protestant sympathies, no wish to impose Protestantism on his newly acquired subjects. His sole interest was to make Prussia as powerful as possible and, in order that Prussia should be powerful, it was desirable that her citizens be contented. Let those then that were Catholics be given as much freedom to live their lives as possible, and, if in the nominally Catholic countries of Europe the sovereigns at that time were interfering with the freedom of their Catholic subjects, it both pleased Frederick's sardonic humour and conduced to the security of his kingdom, that Catholics should be much better treated in his kingdom than in those of his Catholic cousins. He himself was contemptuous of and indifferent to all forms of religion, and tolerant through mere indifference. Joseph II in Austria, bothering himself about the number of candles to be allowed on an altar, seemed to him a figure of fun. 'My brother the sacristan', he called him. At the same time, while Frederick's scoffing spirit brought him to look with some sympathy on the encyclopaedist philosophers, yet he saw that there was a bigotry in free thought that was even more ridiculous than the bigotry of belief. What he would have thought, how he would have treated the Jesuits had he ruled over a country where the Catholics were in a majority or where there was any chance of the Jesuits challenging the omnipotence of the monarchy, who shall say? But the Catholics in his kingdom were not so numerous that there was any danger that they would threaten the state. It was therefore but common sense to humour them and, as for the Jesuits, he was impartial enough to judge them on their real merits. Some of them perhaps had their faults, but they gave a better education than any other schoolmasters. If that education had a certain authoritarian stamp about it, Frederick had no objection, and he was quite intelligent enough to see that most of the common accusations against them were quite childishly absurd. When this folly was found in the mouths of people who prided themselves on being intellectuals and the friends of free thinking, it was to his sardonic mood supremely ridiculous. Besides the intellectuals were Frenchmen and Frederick had a curious love-hate relationship with French intellectuals. He himself was French in his culture – spoke the French language and hardly ever spoke German – and despised his own subjects as illiterate bores. Yet at the same time he had a certain resentment against the French because he felt that they despised him for being German and was ready enough on occasion to convict them of narrow prejudice at times when they themselves thought that they were being particularly broadminded. 'Remember Father Tourmentine,' he wrote to Voltaire 'who was your nurse and made you suck the sweet milk of the Muses. Reconcile yourself with the Order which in the last century gave to France its greatest men.'

Stranger and more important for the Jesuits was the friendship shown them by the Empress Catherine of Russia. It is a curiosity that the Jesuits were befriended by the two monarchs of Europe who were not only themselves not Catholics but also, of all the European monarchs, those who ruled over territories which were most dubiously part of Europe – territories which had formed no part of the Roman Empire or of the Empire of Charlemagne. Was it that these doubtfully European monarchs were anxious to stake their claims to be European by championing an incontestably European Society? Or was it rather that the Society itself had shown more forthrightly than any other Catholic body that it was not content to allow the Church to be an exclusively European institution?

Catherine, like Frederick, was a monarch on whom the claims of denominational religion and of conventional morality sat loosely. It was generally believed that she had murdered her husband in order to make more secure her accession to the throne. By origin a German and a Lutheran, she had not jibbed at joining the Orthodox Church when such a step was helpful to her career. Like Frederick, she had ascended to the throne of a country in which Catholics were only a small minority and had then acquired a considerable Catholic population – in her case in the eastern Polish territories, which she had acquired by the First Partition of Poland. Like Frederick, she had no mind to create for herself unnecessary difficulties in her new territories by attempting to discriminate against the religion of its inhabitants, and had no objection to showing herself before the monarchs of Catholic and western Europe as more liberally minded than they and more ready than they to tolerate the practitioners of their own religion. Had there been any danger in Catherine's dominions of the Catholics gaining a majority or attempting to dictate the nation's policy, who can say how she, any more than Frederick, would have treated them? But she was faced with no such threat and therefore could afford to be tolerant.

There were of course those who criticized the Jesuits for allowing themselves to be patronized by such monarchs, but as those critics would have criticized the Jesuits whatever they had done the Jesuits had no great reason to pay much attention to them. They sacrificed no principle in accepting what they were offered. If one prescinds from a few phrases of perhaps excessive compliment in certain letters, demanded almost by the customs of the day, they in no way gave any approval to their patrons' misdeeds.

Frederick brought the Jesuits into Silesia. Catherine's position was somewhat different. At the time of her annexation of Polish territory she found the Jesuits already established there. The partition was imposed upon the Polish kingdom without war, and the Jesuits who by that time were not on good terms with the Polish king (who was preparing like other Catholic monarchs to accept the suppression of the Society) greeted the Russian annexation quite readily. Catherine therefore at once announced that she would permit no promulgation of the Brief of the Suppression in her dominions. She established the Catholic diocese of White Russia, of which a Russified Polish collaborator of the name of Siestrzenciewicz was made Bishop, and announced that the Jesuits were to keep their four colleges of Potolsk, Vitebsk, Orscha and Dunaberg in that area. Refusing to accept the papal suppression, she at the same time announced the repeal of the Russian decree of Peter the Great banning Jesuits from the Russian Empire. The Jesuits, comically enough, were at first very doubtful of the propriety of going on living as Jesuits in what they thought of as defiance of the Pope's will and simply in obedience to Catherine's refusal to promulgate the Brief. But it soon became apparent that Catherine was not merely prepared to allow the Jesuits to remain as Jesuits. She was prepared to compel them to remain as Jesuits. The Jesuits acquiesced. The Orthodox Church was not at that time in any very healthy condition. The Jesuits were enormously the superior of the Orthodox clergy in scholarship and culture and it soon became a fashion, much as it had been a hundred years before in western Europe, for dignitaries of the Empire without any sort of religious intentions to cultivate social relations with the Jesuits, to exchange intellectual notes with them and even to visit their colleges. In May, 1780, Catherine even visited Potolsk herself, accompanied by her Minister Potemkin and a very special retinue. The college was illuminated in her honour and she was splendidly entertained that evening. The next morning she insisted on attending Mass and then went on to Mohilev, where she met the Emperor Joseph II, and at another Jesuit college she took the opportunity of showing Joseph how very much more generously Catholics were treated in her dominions than they were in those of the Holy Roman Empire, or indeed than they were at that time in any Catholic country.

Whatever first reluctance the Jesuits may have had in continuing the Society in Russia in spite of Clement XIV's apparent wishes, the reluctance quite vanished when with Clement's death it was soon seen that Pius VI had no wish at all that the Jesuits in Russia should close down. If they were to form themselves into a body which was to keep the Society alive until such time as it might be formally reconstructed throughout the world – as was fairly obviously Pius VI's wish – then it was clearly not sufficient that a few old men should be allowed to live together until such time as they had all died off. A novitiate was necessary and in 1780 Father Czerniewicz, the Vice-Provincial, established one at Potolsk. The Bourbon ambassadors at Rome protested to Pius VI but the Pope refused to take any step to prevent it.

'On the contrary,' says the historian Zalenski:

Pius VI knew very well, as did everyone else in Rome, that Clement XIV had published the Brief of Suppression in spite of himself and only after four years of hesitation and conflict with the diplomats. Moreover Cardinals Antonelli and Calini, eye-witnesses of what had happened, represented to Pius VI in personal memorials that the suppression was invalid. Pius himself had belonged to that section of Cardinals which disapproved of the destruction and, as has been already said, when he was Pope, he set free the prisoners of the Castle of Saint Angelo, rehabilitated their memory and ordered Father Ricci to be buried with the honours due to the General of an Order. In brief Pius VI, as both Frederick II and Tchernichef, was really glad that the Society had been preserved and his silence was an approbation of it.*

In 1782 the Empress in response to a petition from the Fathers gave them permission to elect a Vicar General. The Archbishop Siestrzenciewicz, who wished to have the Jesuits under his full episcopal control, protested but the Empress overruled him and granted the Jesuits' petition. As a result they met at Potolsk on

* Zalenski, Les Jésuites de la Russie Blanche, French translation, Paris, 1886, vol. I, p. 330.

10 October 1782, and elected Father Czerniewicz, who had been their Vice-Provincial, to be Vicar General of the Society. Potemkin, the Empress' chief Minister, compelled the Archbishop to withdraw his opposition.

Although Pope Pius VI had made it substantially clear that he had no objection to the Society of Jesuits remaining in existence and its members living according to their rule in Russia, the election of a Vicar General was a very much more definite assertion of their continuance and a more important matter. It was necessary, if it was going to be valuable at some future date as an evidence of the Society's essential survival, that the Pope's approval be obtained to this further step. The task was not altogether easy. As Archetti, the Papal Nuncio in St Petersburg, was opposed to what the Jesuits had done, and indeed even a few of the Jesuits themselves were not altogether happy about this bold step, Catherine asserted that she would settle everything. There was an ex-Jesuit priest, Benislawski, who had left the Society at the time of its suppression but who, though he had not returned to it at the time of its full restitution in Russia, had remained very friendly towards it. Catherine created him an ambassador and bade him go as quickly as possible to Rome. He was instructed not to linger at all in Warsaw but to make contact in Vienna with Garampi, the Nuncio there, and Galitzen, the Russian ambassador, and get them to prepare the ground for him at Rome. He was then to press on with all speed to Rome, and, arrived there, to have an interview with the Pope without having previously seen any Cardinal. He was to demand of the Pope his own recognition as a coadjutor Bishop to Siestrzenciewicz and the approbation of the Jesuits in Russia and of all their acts. If these demands were refused he was instructed to announce a breach of diplomatic relations.

On 21 February 1783, the very day of his arrival, Benislawski saw the Pope. Pius made no difficulty about accepting Benislawski as a coadjutor Bishop but maintained that the opening of the novitiate had been without authority. 'That was done by the order of the Empress,' said Benislawski. 'Since that is the case I shall forget the injury done me by the Bishop,' said the Pope. He then asked whether the election of a Vicar General had been by the express orders of the Empress. When Benislawski assured him that it was, he replied, 'I do not object'. So far things seemed to be going very well for Benislawski's mission, but the Bourbon ambassadors were naturally furious at what seemed a direct humiliation of their masters. They demanded interviews with the Pope and made their protest. As a result, when Benislawski appeared for his second interview he found the Pope considerably more frigid. He at once threw himself on his knees and asked the Pope's blessing. The Pope asked the meaning of this gesture and Benislawski explained that it was his instruction in the event of a refusal to break off relations and he was therefore taking his leave. Pius had no wish that the matter be ended thus abruptly. He therefore bade Benislawski retire and set out his whole case in writing. Benislawski returned to his lodgings and sat up all night composing an elaborate and even somewhat sophistical treatise. Its argument was that the Jesuits had done what they had done at the express wish of the Empress and argued that they had no alternative as the Empress had made it clear that it was a question of either the Jesuits or no Catholics at all within the Empire. If the Jesuits were refused then Catherine would launch a persecution to compel all the Catholics in her Empire to become Orthodox. At the same time Catherine according to Benislawski 'had made a solemn promise not to harm her Catholic subjects but she was convinced that she could not inflict a greater injury on them than to deprive their churches of priests and their schools of teachers who in her opinion were invaluable.'

Whether Catherine would have launched a persecution had the Jesuits been withdrawn is very uncertain. Her position, as Benislawski reported it, of at one and the same time threatening persecution and parading her promise to protect her Catholic subjects sounds slightly confused and disingenuous, but at least Benislawski's arguments put the Pope, as they were intended to, into an impossible position. Whatever he might think or wish about the Jesuits, he could hardly be expected to condemn all the Catholics in Russia to persecution, and if it was demanded by the Bourbon monarchs that he should do so, there was no honourable answer except to defy them. 'Your arguments are irrefutable,' said the Pope to Benislawski, and before a meeting of Cardinals he solemnly pronounced, *Approbo Societatem Jesu in Alba Russia degentem. Approbo, approbo.* When Father Pignatelli asked the Pope for leave to go to Russia and join the Society 'if it exists there', the Pope assured him, 'Yes, it exists and, if it were possible, I would have it extended everywhere throughout the world'. With the definite recognition of the Society in Russia a large number of ex-Jesuits in different countries of the world applied to it for enrolment. Some of them actually went to Russia. Others were enrolled as members '*extra provinciam*' and lived a Jesuit life in houses in various countries.

Catherine ruled until 1796 and as long as she was on the throne she continued her favour to the Society. Paul, her half idiot son, who succeeded her, was equally favourable. When Pius VI died and Pius VII succeeded him, Father Gruber, who had been Paul's guardian, persuaded Paul to ask Pius VII for formal recognition of the Society in Russia, which Pius VII in spite of the opposition of some Cardinals in Rome gave by the Bull of 7 March 1801, *Catholicae Fidei*. Eighteen days later Paul was assassinated but his successor, Alexander, continued his favour to the Society. Alexander was eager to colonize the uninhabited parts of his vast Empire and thought that the Jesuits would be useful in civilizing the German colonists whom he was introducing. He established Jesuit missions both around Riga on the Baltic in Esthonia and around Astrakhan on the Caspian in the south.

It was thus by the Russian province that the continuity of the Society was preserved but the Bull *Catholicae Fidei* re-established the Society 'only within the limits of the Russian Empire'. It is beyond the concern of such a book as this to describe the general treatment of the Church by the French Revolutionaries and Napoleon, since the Jesuits were not involved in those struggles. But in the western countries there were of course to be found those who felt a vocation to the Jesuit way of life – or to something as near to it as might be possible – who, once they had received the encouragement of the news from Russia, had the ambition to keep the structure of some such discipline against the day when the Society might be fully re-established. The superior of the seminary of Paris, Jacques André Emery, founded at the outbreak of the Revolution the Fathers of the Sacred Heart, of whom Varin and de Broglie were the leaders. These Fathers after various adventures established themselves at Augsburg, where they lived together a life that was substantially in accordance with the Jesuit rule. In

1798 the Pope gave his blessing to their enterprise. In Italy a somewhat less disciplined attempt to revive the Jesuits was made by that bizarre figure, Nicholas Paccinari. Paccinari was a travelling salesman of no education who formed a Society of his own which he called the Society of the Fathers of the Faith of Jesus. He wrote to the Fathers of the Sacred Heart in Germany announcing that he was their superior 'in virtue of an express wish of the Pope to have the two communities united', and that he would soon arrive at their house in order to take over. His arrival was in fact delayed by the misfortune that he was put in prison but eventually he arrived. The Society of the Fathers of the Sacred Heart obediently surrendered to him their independence but his conduct of a religious house was very peculiar. The discipline consisted mainly of inordinate athletic exercises. Paccinari announced that his main purpose was to incorporate the house 'in the Jesuit province of Russia', but it soon became apparent that he had no intention of doing anything of the sort. Eventually the Fathers of the Sacred Heart left him at Augsburg, and Varin, who had been their superior, went back to Paris where he took up work in the city's hospitals.

At first the Fathers of the Sacred Heart received the support of the government but before long there was an attempt to assassinate Napoleon. Mademoiselle de Cice, the pious niece of the Archbishop of Bordeaux, was alleged to have been in some way associated with the plot and Father Varin to have been associated with Mademoiselle de Cice. It looked for a time as if he and his companions might meet at the very least with suppression, but Father Varin made so favourable an impression in court with his explanation that his Society had no concern with politics or violence but was solely interested in religion and charity that not only was he acquitted but no obstacle was put in the way of the Society's religious work. Varin was in one way at any rate a man before his time. He formed the opinion that a main reason for the instability of society was the lack of education for its women. He was not so greatly interested in women's rights as an immediate programme as he was in women's education, an extension of which would doubtless in the end make essential an extension of their rights. Napoleon believed in education for girls up to a point. But in his view girls' education must be essentially military – even more so than that of boys – and religion was mainly useful as an excuse for discipline. 'What are the girls at Ecouen going to be taught?' he asked. 'You must begin with religion in all its strictness, with religion in all its saintliness. Don't allow any compromise on this point. Religion is an all-important matter in a public school for girls. It is the mother's surest safeguard and the husband's. What we ask of education is not that girls should think but that they should believe.'

This was of course almost a parody of the worst excesses which malice ascribed to the Jesuits and it was natural enough that Varin, so steeped in the Jesuit spirit, should react against it and wish in its place to introduce a true and humanely disciplined education for girls. He found two great collaborators – Marie-Sophie Barat, the foundress of the Ladies of the Sacred Heart, and Julie Billart, the foundress of the Sisters of Notre Dame de Namur. Both Orders are today of course widely known throughout the world. By no means every Jesuit approved of Varin's interest in communities of nuns. In America the development was particularly suspect. 'In one point,' wrote Bishop Carroll, the ex-Jesuit Bishop there, 'they seem to have departed from St Ignatius by engrafting on their Institutions a new order of nuns.'

In 1803 matters between the Fathers of the Sacred Heart and Paccinari came to a final breach. The Fathers were now quite convinced that Paccinari for all his protestations of intending to apply for admission to the Russian Jesuits had no intention of doing anything about it. Varin from Paris, together with his colleague Rozaven who had settled in London, decided to go to Rome to ask the Pope to free them from all dependence on Paccinari. The Pope who had by this time lost faith in Paccinari as completely as had the Fathers was entirely agreeable, indeed assured them that Paccinari never had the papal authority to which he pretended. But Rozaven on his return to London with the news found that his journey had really not been necessary, for his colleagues there, wearying of the delay, had applied to Father Gruber, the Provincial in Russia, for admission into the Society without waiting for the Pope's ruling or for Rozaven's return. Father Gruber had agreed and as a result twenty-five Fathers in western Europe – in England, Holland and Germany – were admitted into the Society. For the moment this left Varin and the Fathers in France still outside the Society. They were under the protection of Cardinal

Fesch, Napoleon's uncle; this patronage had its inconveniences as it made it difficult for them to act in defiance of the government, and Napoleon was not anxious to see the Jesuits once more an organized power in the land. However the very deterioration of relations between the Emperor and the Church gave them in the end the courage to act and in 1807 the French Fathers followed those in England and were incorporated into the Society.

Meanwhile the Bourbon monarchs – such of them as had survived – had no wish to maintain the family's quarrel with the Jesuits. They saw that that quarrel had a quarter of a century before played a disastrously important part in weakening their own thrones, and they were now anxious to annex to themselves any force of order which might help to rally opinion to their side against Napoleon and the terrible French. The Jesuits were such a force. The Duke of Parma, the son of Charles III of Spain, invited the Jesuits back to his duchy. King Ferdinand IV in Naples, another of Charles' sons, also invited the Jesuits back to his country and received them with a great display of piety, going to Communion with all his family at their first Mass after their return. The Jesuits were formally re-established in the Kingdom of Naples and Sicily by the Bull *Per Alias*. The Jesuits did not derive much gain from these death-bed repentances of the Bourbons because of course in a very few years the Napoleonic troops had driven them from their thrones and, expelling the Bourbons, expelled the Jesuits along with them.

These years were very far from being inactive years in Jesuit history, though the Order was most active in non-Catholic countries. Not content with establishing themselves in Russia, some of the Jesuits were anxious to push on and reopen their missions in China. Father Grassi, an Italian from Bergamo, was Rector of the College of Nobles in Russia. At the time of the suppression of the Society a certain old Jesuit, Louis Poirot, who was a skilled musician and whose skill had won him the favour of the Chinese Emperor, had remained behind in that country. Hearing of the re-establishment of the Jesuits in Russia, he wrote to Father Gruber, the Provincial there, asking that some Jesuit recruits be sent out to China. It so happened that a Russian ambassador, Golowkin, was just about to leave St Petersburg for the Chinese court and it was suggested that he take three Jesuits in his train. Father Grassi and two others were selected for the mission. It was decided that it would be better for them to travel by the ordinary sea-route rather than in the ambassador's train. They set off and by stages travelled to Sweden, Denmark, England, Ireland and finally to Lisbon. After two months' delay there they found a ship that would take them to China but learnt at the same time that the legal position of the Society in China was so uncertain that it was best not to attempt the journey until they had first been to Rome and clarified the position with the Pope. Before they had the chance to do anything about this they heard that some unidentified missionaries in China had been discovered to have made a map, and as a consequence the Emperor had expelled all missionaries from his Empire. After another year's delay in Lisbon they had no alternative but to abandon the project and return to England, whence Father Grassi went to America where he became the President of Georgetown University in Washington.

In some ways the years of the suppression were the most fruitful years of the Society's history. Because of the war, and the relations with Catholic monarchs, the Society was not able to establish itself satisfactorily in Catholic countries, but on the whole the Jesuit is better suited for activity in a non-Catholic than in a Catholic country. Where there is no opposition from other elements in society the Jesuit rule, critics have said, is apt to prove too rigid and stifling and the products of Jesuit education to be perhaps too often either rebellious in after life or else lacking in initiative. The Jesuit system, with its maxim of *agere contra*, thrives best among pupils who are destined to go into a society that lives in disregard of its principles. The pupil brought up on Jesuit principles and then thrown into this so very different society grows up under a condition of healthy tension. Of the life of Jesuits in these years in Prussia and Russia we have already spoken. The years also brought great good fortune to them in England. Eighteenth-century England lived under the penal laws and no Catholic Order, Jesuit or any other, was allowed to establish itself in England. The English Catholic colleges had to find their homes abroad and the boys to go overseas for their education. Then, when the French Revolutionaries both persecuted the Church and also went to war with Britain, Catholic priests were given a welcome in England that they had not known for a hundred years. The greater number of these priests who came to England were of course French. Along with the French priests came the English priests who had been teaching in the English Catholic colleges overseas, bringing their pupils with them. In the new atmosphere they were allowed to settle down and establish their schools in England, though at first it was thought both by them and by the English authorities that they would be there only for a few years until peace returned and they went back to their continental homes. In fact as the wars dragged on they were kept in England at Stonyhurst till 1815. By that time only a few Fathers were left who had been at Liège. A more tolerant English public opinion was content to leave them in their isolated home in Lancashire. There seemed no point in taking back an English school to the continent and they have remained at Stonyhurst to this day.

In America no regularly organized province of the Society had been permitted in the English days and before the United States had established their independence the Society had already been suppressed. Yet a few Jesuits had in fact set themselves up in Maryland under the English rule, and the independent states were committed, even though they did not all immediately in all respects fully practise it, to a policy of separation of Church and state and religious freedom. The consequence of this policy was that the state would no longer interfere with the Catholic Church or indeed with any other Church in its introduction of whatever religious Orders that it wished to help it to manage its own business. If over the years Catholics in the United States have on occasion suffered some disabilities – for instance, for long periods it has not been possible in fact for a Catholic to be elected to the presidency or to other high offices – it has not been any formal provision of the Constitution which has forbidden them, and if the Catholic schools have not been able to obtain financial support from federal funds, those funds have not been denied to them on the ground that they were Catholic but on the ground that it was alleged to be unconstitutional and in violation of the principle of a separation of Chuch and state that support should be given to any denominational school. There has never been on the American statute book any provision discriminating against Jesuits as such. But the curiosity of the Jesuit position in America in the eighteenth century was that, whereas in the English days the

Church encouraged them but the state forbade them, after independence they were accepted by the state but suppressed by the
Church. However, in America as in other non-Catholic countries
the Brief was not promulgated. The Catholic Bishop of the times
was Bishop Carroll, an ex-Jesuit and brother of one of the signa-
tories of the Declaration of Independence. Catholics were few and
could not be thought of as a menace to American institutions. The
day of massive Irish immigration and further massive immigration
from continental countries was still in the far future and in fact,
as in England, there was no objection to a few Jesuits quietly
getting on with their work. At the time of the Bull of Re-
establishment it was discovered that there were nineteen Jesuits
at work in the United States.

In 1805 there was a fire in the house in St Petersburg in which
Father Gruber was living, and he was burnt to death. Father
Thaddeus Brzozowski was elected to succeed him as General and
held the office during all the remaining years of the Napoleonic
Wars and up till the restoration of the Society. The Emperor
Alexander was full of idealistic plans for the educational development of his country, in which the Jesuits would have played a
prominent part, but the years were so filled with war, culminating
in Napoleon's march to Moscow in 1812, that nothing much
could be done about these projects. As we have seen they were
years during which the Jesuits were, so to speak, creeping back
into existence in various other countries. These developments
were by no means wholly welcome to the czar who would have
liked the Jesuits to have become a predominantly Russian Society,
so that Russia might pose before the Catholic world as an
Orthodox power which treated Catholics more generously than
they were treated by Catholic monarchs, and doubtless so that on
occasion he might use them to intrigue in Catholic countries into
which it might suit him to throw confusion. The ambition of Pope
Pius VII was quite different. The Pope bitterly regretted what
seemed to him the disastrous error of Clement XIV in suppressing
the Society. This decision, as he interpreted it, had proved unfortunate in every way. Clement had agreed to the suppression
against his better judgement in the vain hope of appeasing the
Bourbon monarchs. He had thus deprived the papacy of its main
support against the pretensions of the monarchs. Nor had the

monarchs gained from the surrender. On the contrary they were brutally taught the lesson which they had been very foolish from the first to overlook – that a habit of suppression was a habit that might easily spread to them and that, if they started by suppressing the Jesuits, their subjects were likely soon to follow suit by suppressing them. Pius VII was of course kept by Napoleon for eighteen months in virtual captivity at Fontainebleau and was only released when Napoleon's defeat was certain. Pius afterwards generously recognized how great were the incidental services which Napoleon had rendered to the Church by his concordat and by stopping the persecution of the clergy, when he first assumed power, and the Pope bade Catholics always remember these and to set them against his subsequent outrages. But it was natural enough that the ordinary Catholic in the street, who was not well enough informed to strike a balance of merit and demerit, said that an Emperor who took a Pope into captivity was an enemy of the Church. Therefore in these closing years Catholic opinion was opposed to Napoleon and, understandably though not very reasonably, thought that if it opposed the Napoleonic regime it must necessarily support the restitution of the old monarchs who were clamouring to return to their thrones.

Pius VII however at his first return showed himself possessed of some astuteness – of more astuteness than he was to display four years later. He was determined to restore the Society. He saw that in the years to come the Society would have an essential role to play as the defender of the independence of the papacy against the encroaching demands of secular governments. He had indeed had to meet such demands in a most offensive form from Napoleon. But he knew enough of history to be well aware that there was every likelihood that he would receive demands all but as offensive from the restored monarchs. There were some among the Cardinals who greeted him on his return to Rome who, while not opposed to the restoration of the Jesuits, advised the Pope to go slowly and to do nothing until he had first reached agreement with the monarchs on exact conditions. Consalvi, the Secretary of State, who was always cool in his enthusiasm for the Jesuits and much more concerned with good relations with the monarchs, and who was a few years later to acquire so predominant an influence over Vatican policies, seems to have inclined to this policy. Pius' opinion was the exact opposite. He was determined to take the bull by the horns and restore the Society immediately and thus to present the monarchs with a *fait accompli* precisely in order that he might not become bogged down in negotiations with them about conditions of restoration. He saw that he was for the moment in a stronger position than they and had no need to make concessions to them. Public opinion throughout Europe had been enormously moved and shocked by the sufferings of Pius VII and of Pius VI before him. His return from Fontainebleau to Rome was a triumphal procession. He was greeted in Rome with tumultuous enthusiasm. As always the Church had gained from persecution. On the other hand there was no enthusiasm at all for the returning monarchs who had played no part in the defeat of Napoleon and who travelled back to their capitals in the luggage trains of the Allied armies. Why should Pius make any concessions to them? It was not even certain how long they would succeed in occupying their thrones.

Pius therefore announced that the Society would not only be restored but restored in its old form. In June 1814 the Italian Provincial presented to him in the name of Father Brzozowski, the General, who was not permitted by the czar to leave Russia, a petition begging him to restore the Society throughout the world. Pius agreed and answered that he would issue the Bull of Restoration on St Ignatius' day six weeks ahead. Many were astonished at the speed, so unlike the general habit of Rome. Rumours were put about that Pius' intention was not to restore the old Society but to approve a new congregation which would lack some of those features of the old Society which had caused difficulties. Pius denied it. 'On the contrary,' he said, 'it is the same Society which existed for two hundred years.'

Pius had entrusted the destiny of the Bull in the first place to Cardinal Litta who as ablegate in St Petersburg had had the task of asking for the confirmation of the Society in Russia. Litta's wish was to make the Bull entirely outspoken. 'The suppression had been granted by Clement XIV,' he wished to say, and 'it was to be ascribed to the wicked devices, the atrocious calumnies and the impious principles of false political sciences and philosophy which, by the destruction of the Order, foolishly imagined that the Church would be destroyed.'

This was thought to be too strong. After all the monarchs were on their thrones again. It was necessary to live with them. No purpose could be served by abusively underlining the shortcomings of their predecessors. Cardinal Litta's draft was therefore rejected. The task of drawing up a new one was entrusted to Cardinal Pacca. He contented himself with speaking of 'the Pope's deep conviction of the Society's usefulness to the Church', and with bewailing 'the calamities which we shudder even to recall', skilfully leaving it uncertain whether the phrase applied to what had happened under Napoleon, under the French Revolutionaries or under the Bourbon monarchs of the *ancien régime*. Saying nothing about past monarchs, he made the Pope instead drop a broad hint to the existing monarchs to behave themselves decently:

Finally we earnestly recommend in the Lord this Society and its members to the illustrious kings and princes and temporal lords of the various nations, as well as to our venerable brothers, the Archbishops and Bishops and whosoever may occupy positions of honour and authority. We exhort them, nay we conjure them, not only not to suffer that these religious should be molested in any manner, but to see that they should be treated with the benevolence and the charity which they deserve.

There was a practical problem. To whom was this Bull to be formally delivered? The natural plan would of course have been to deliver it to the General, Father Brzozowski, but he was in Russia. The czar had no liking for these new policies which would move the headquarters of the Society from St Petersburg to Rome, and indeed it was fairly obvious – as in fact happened – that as soon as the General ceased to be a Russian the czar would suppress the Society in his dominions. In any event he had no mind to allow Father Brzozowski to leave Russia in order to take part in such a ceremony. Therefore after some discussion it was decided to deliver the Bull to Father Panizzoni, the Italian Provincial.

The ceremony was an impressive one. The Cardinals paraded in full pontificals before the Pope and behind them were marshalled Spanish, Italian, and Portuguese Jesuits, survivors of their expulsion forty years before – men who had been living for forty years or more in the hope of one day seeing the definitive resurrection of their Society. The youngest of them were more than sixty years old. Some were certainly ninety or so. Crétineau-Joly tells us that there was among them a certain Father Montalto who was born in 1689, was therefore eighty-four at the time of the Society's suppression and a hundred and twenty-six at the time of its restoration, but there is no record of any Father of such a name in Albers' *Liber Secularis* in the catalogue of 1773 or in Viviers' *Catalogus Mortuorum Societatis Jesu* and there can be little doubt that this is a story without basis which has grown out of some confusion. The Pope seated on his throne handed the Bull to an attendant Cardinal who read it out in a loud voice. Each of the Fathers then hobbled up in turn and knelt before the Pope, who spoke to each of them words of consolation. Cardinal Pacca handed to Father Panizzoni a document appointing him acting head of the Roman house until official confirmation of his appointment came through from the General. The Jesuits were given leave immediately to reoccupy their house at the Gésu.

TEN

The restoration

It is a general lesson of history that restoration never exactly restores. A Charles II or Louis XVIII may return to his throne, and those who in past years have suffered for their support of his line may hope that everything that they lost will be restored to them. But it never happens like that. The years of exile or repression cannot be merely wiped out. The institution, whatever it may be, which under the *ancien régime* had been merely taken for granted now returns as a result of a decision or a debate, and institutions which have been chosen are necessarily very different from institutions that have been simply taken for granted. So the restored Society of Jesus of the last hundred and fifty years, for all its reiterated appeals back to St Ignatius, has never been quite the same as the old confident Society.

As has been said, the restoration of the Society found it with a General in Russia. The General was ordered to come to Rome to receive the Bull of Restoration, but Czar Alexander refused leave. It was Alexander's desire to keep the Society as a private Russian Society, to be operated from Russia. He had no mind that it should become a world-wide Society operated from Rome. The reasons for his ambition were twofold. It was partly a matter simply of power politics; with the Jesuits under his thumb he would have always at hand a ready weapon with which to embarrass the Catholic powers. Partly his reason was a stranger one. Alexander was a power politician, but he was by no means merely a power politician. He had also a strange ecumenical ambition of uniting the whole world in one supra-denominational Christian body of which he would be the head. A certain Baroness Julia de Krudner travelled through Europe preaching this gospel and proclaiming Alexander as the White Angel of God in opposition to Napoleon who was the Dark Angel of hell. The great powers who had

conquered Napoleon were compelled at Vienna to proclaim their
Holy Alliance in which each recognized himself as one of the
branches of the great family of nations of which Jesus Christ, the
'Omnipotent Word', was the Sovereign. At the suggestion of his
Minister Golitzin the czar not only embarked on an extreme
course of Bible reading for himself but attempted to impose such
a course on his subjects and, in so far as he could, on all the
peoples of the world. In spite of the somewhat bizarre trappings
of the business it was on the whole to be encouraged. The Bible
was far less well known at that time in either Catholic or Orthodox
countries than it was in Britain, where religion was so largely
built on the reading of it. The slight difference between one translation and another was really of secondary and superable importance, and the Catholic Archbishop of Mohilev and his secular
clergy supported the project. The Jesuits unwisely refused to do
so on the plea that it was a danger to souls if Catholics were
allowed to read an unauthorized version. It was a stupid objection
and aroused the hostility of the czar and Golitzin towards the
Society. The hostility was greatly strengthened when Golitzin's
nephew insisted on becoming a Catholic. The czar concluded,
rightly enough from his point of view, that he could not rely on
the Jesuits to support either his political or his ecumenical ambitions and, far from giving permission to Father Brzozowski to go
to Rome to receive the Brief of Restoration, eighteen months after
the restoration of the Society on 25 December 1815, the czar
expelled all Jesuits from his dominions. To do him justice, he
expelled them with courtesy. There were none of the scenes of ill
treatment with which they had been greeted in Spain and
Portugal, and in fact the Jesuits were not altogether sorry to be
expelled. Expulsion solved for them the difficult problem of
transferring their headquarters from St Petersburg to Rome. They
were glad enough to base themselves in St Petersburg when they
had no home elsewhere. But with full restoration it would have
been absurd to have remained there and at the same time difficult
to have made the change without offending the czar, had he
remained benevolent. The expulsion of the Jesuits from Russia had
also from the Society's point of view a further advantage. Many
able men of many nationalities had collected in Russia and with
the foundation of so many new colleges and new houses in other

countries it was a considerable convenience to have this man-power at hand to stock those colleges.

Father Brzozowski lived until 1820. It was not therefore until that date that it was necessary to elect a new General for the now fully restored Society. Father Brzozowski on his deathbed had appointed Father Petrucci, the Master of Novices at Genoa, as his Vicar. It was not a happy appointment, as Father Petrucci was himself sick and ill. The election was fixed for 14 September, but Cardinal della Genga, who was later to succeed Pius VII as Pope Leo XII, and who was at that time at any rate a vigorous opponent of the Jesuits, wrote to Petrucci announcing that it was the Pope's wish that the election be postponed in order to make sure that the Polish Fathers would be able to attend it. As there was no difficulty in the Polish Fathers getting there by the original date of 14 September, it was not easy to understand the letter. However Petrucci, obediently but somewhat foolishly, wrote off to all the Provincials postponing the election.

Della Genga then wrote a letter to all the Assistants alleging that it was the strong wish of the Pope that there should be no irregularities in the constituted organization of the restored Society and that therefore a committee of five under his chairmanship would inquire into the Constitutions of the Society and, when the time came, preside over the election of the new General. It was of course quite unheard of that the Fathers should not be allowed to conduct their elections themselves but should have to hold them under the supervision of an extern. It betrayed the clear ambition which della Genga shared with a number of others at Rome to see to it that the restored Society did not recover the full independence of the old Society, whose strength in their opinion had proved a danger to the Church, involving it in con-flicts from which in more tactful hands it might have remained free. The other Fathers were by no means so complaisant as Petrucci and had no mind to take such interference lying down. They appealed direct to the Pope. There were many Cardinals around the throne who took della Genga's side, and it might well have proved that they were influential enough to prevent the Pope from changing his ruling. However by far the most influen-tial adviser of the Pope was Consalvi, the Secretary of State. Consalvi was fresh from his triumphs at the Congress of Vienna

where he had won the highest praise from the secular diplomats
for his ability – Castlereagh thought that he was the ablest man
there – and had succeeded in obtaining for the Pope the restoration
of his temporal dominions. Whether Consalvi and the Pope were
wise to ask for these territories back, whether it would not have
been far more sensible for them to have taken the opportunity to
free themselves from this encumbrance and to throw on the
powers the responsibility for finding a secular prince to rule Rome
and the Marches, is a very debatable question to which we shall
have occasion to return later. But of the brilliance with which
Consalvi argued his case there was no dispute. He was at the time
beyond challenge the first man in Rome after the Pope – indeed
in all but official position in many ways a more powerful man than
the Pope. Consalvi had in the past not been particularly friendly
to the Jesuits but he had by now become convinced of the necessity of their restoration and had no mind that they should be
restored in diminished condition and unable to play their traditional part in the Church's life – a part which he foresaw would be
increasingly important throughout the nineteenth century. As a
result of Consalvi's intervention the Pope rejected della Genga's
petition and ordered that the Jesuits be allowed to hold an
unsupervised election of their General as early as possible. As a
result of these negotiations it was not quite possible to meet the
original date of 14 September, but they held it on 9 October, and
Father Aloysius Fortis, who was Pius VII's *Examinator Epis-
coporum*, was elected.

The Society owes a deep debt to Consalvi, but it had to pay a
price for the benefit that it received from him. Very difficult
decisions had to be taken by those who were responsible for the
Church's policy immediately after 1815. As I have mentioned,
simple men and those with short memories were naturally only
mindful of the injuries that the Popes had received at the hands of
the French Revolutionaries and of Napoleon and took it for
granted that the cause of the Church was the cause of the returning
monarchs. Consalvi took that line and persuaded Pius VII to take
it. He threw the support of the Church behind the absolute
monarchs and looked on Parliaments and democracy as atheistical.
Catholics throughout the Church's history have felt, perhaps more
than other people, the foolish temptation to look on some current

movement as a devil-movement; we have seen in our time many
Catholics adopt this attitude towards Communism. Today it is
fashionable to favour democracy, but a hundred and fifty years
ago it was democracy which was the devil-movement. Consalvi
therefore committed the Church and – what is here our more
immediate concern – thus committed the Jesuits, to the support of
absolute monarchs, to the alliance of throne and altar and to the
policies of Metternich. It was an unfortunate commitment.
Neither the monarchs nor their Ministers were particularly
Christian. Louis XVIII, who had returned to the French throne,
was almost a confessed unbeliever. Metternich looked at problems
as entirely secular matters for the solution of which the influence
of the Church might be useful. There was of course no reason why
a Catholic should not reach the conclusion that on balance and in
the circumstances of the day the monarchical was the least bad
form of government, but in view of the record of the pre-
Revolutionary monarchs it was almost cynical to profess, or to
allow people to believe that you were professing, that the system
of absolute monarchy was in any way a divinely ordered form of
government or that the principle of authority in the Church
committed the Catholic as so many were inclined to believe that
it did, to a belief in absolutist secular government. The Jesuits who
on the whole had been on the progressive side in earlier centuries,
who in China had fought a battle for what Newman would have
recognized as a doctrine of development, turned with the nineteenth century and became conservative and the champions of an
extravagantly static theology. The very moment when the world
was in motion was the moment that they chose to stand still.

It is difficult to resist the conclusion that the early nineteenth-
century Jesuits would have been better employed if they had spent
more of their time in reading Suarez and less of it in reading de
Maistre. It is easy of course to use hindsight, but today at any rate
it is self-evident that the great fault of the Metternichians was their
failure to recognize that any government that endures must, whatever its form, be based on at least a negative consent of the
governed. If it has not that consent, then, whether it be theoretically a good government or a bad, it in fact collapses. Europeans
were weary of the excesses of the Revolutionaries and of the cease-
less warfare of Napoleon. In so far as the powers offered them as an

alternative a system of traditional and ordered government, they were offering something for which there was a solid demand. But to react from extreme to extreme was an error. As always truth lay in the middle course. Public opinion wanted order but within the system of order, if it was to be permanently acceptable, it was necessary to allow a place for liberty. Violent change could only be permanently avoided if some method of achieving peaceful change was allowed. The Metternichians in their exaggerations overlooked such political platitudes and thus built on an edifice which was certain eventually to collapse in violence. It was a tragedy that Consalvi should have allowed the Church, and by consequence the Jesuits, to be involved in the defence of such a system.

Napoleon had of course annexed Rome to his Empire and, as has been argued, after his fall the Pope would have been well advised to refuse to receive back the temporal power and to throw on to the statesmen of Vienna the obligation of finding a secular ruler for his former dominions. Under Consalvi's influence he did not do so, and the Jesuits not only supported the Pope's claims to temporal power but, as we shall see, later in the century some of them went to quite extravagantly ultramontane lengths in their support of it, even arguing that belief in it was a matter of faith and would probably soon be formally declared as such. In fact the rights and wrongs of papal temporal power could only be sanely argued on a much more pedestrian level. If it had been true that Constantine had made a donation of these territories to the Pope it would have had little bearing on the problem of the nineteenth century. In fact, as historians bear witness, Constantine was quite signally indifferent to papal claims to territory or to anything else. When the territories of the greater part of Europe were divided out between the great powers who were in conflict with one another, there was obviously a great deal to be said for establishing the Pope on a little corner of his own territory on which he could live independent and uncommitted to the rivalries of the powers. The experience of Avignon adequately demonstrated the importance of such independence. But the conditions of its success are clearly that the Pope's rule should be generally accepted by his subjects and that he should be able to maintain it without the use of violence. In the general indifference to the importance of consent in the post-Napoleonic world the necessity for this condition was strangely overlooked in settling the fate of the papal dominions. The depth of the enthusiasm shown for Pius VII on his return to Rome from Napoleon's captivity was probably exaggerated. But, even if it was true that Pius VII's rule and papal rule in Rome were in a manner accepted, that acceptance was by no means extended to Pius' successors, who had about them none of the glamour of having suffered for the faith, nor did it extend to Romagna and the Marches across the hills. Popes have never been popular in Bologna and the fact that they lived in Rome has not added to their popularity in the territories outside the Patrimony of St Peter. Therefore under Pius' three successors, Leo XII, Pius VIII and Gregory XVI, the condition of the Papal States became an open scandal. Such order as existed was only preserved by the enlistment under the title of Sanfedisti of what were virtually papal brigands to terrorize the populace. The Papal States obtained the name – and not unjustly – of being the worst governed territories in Europe, and in the end the Popes were only able to save themselves from expulsion by calling in foreign garrisons to protect them, first the Austrians into Ancona and afterwards the French into Rome. As Odo Russell, the British representative in Rome, afterwards argued with Pius IX, there was something to be said for a Pope who reigned in genuine freedom over loyal subjects of a small dominion, thus holding himself aloof from the secular controversies of the day, but there was no advantage in a papal temporal power if the Pope could only preserve himself on such a throne by calling in foreign troops to protect him. Such a situation, apart from its inherent scandal, negated the one advantage of independence which the system professed to offer. The pity was that the Jesuits should have allowed themselves to be manoeuvred into the defence of such a ramshackle arrangement.

It was a pity not merely because their activities got the Jesuits a bad name as the defenders of political arrangements that were alike reactionary and from the first doomed to overthrow. What was worse than that was that their political standpoint inevitably stultified their intellectual criticism. If we look at the history of the Jesuits in the last hundred and fifty years since the Society's restoration it tells us indeed a tale of remarkable expansion – perhaps not quite so rapid and extraordinary as that of the

Society's first fifty years, but still very remarkable. It may be that just at present the Jesuits' numbers are for a variety of reasons a little reduced, but the general record had been one of a steady expansion. Yet on the other hand the Society has not perhaps produced the leadership and the originality of its earlier years.

In the sixteenth century the Jesuits wherever they went led the world. The new age had produced its new problems and the Jesuits had been the first in the field with their solutions of those problems. In education the Jesuits set the pace, while others followed in their footsteps or lagged behind as the case might be. In the nineteenth and twentieth centuries the Jesuits have indeed built their schools and colleges and have earned for them an honourable name. But there has been little in the way of development of the Jesuit system in the sense in which Newman would have used the word, of a 'development from within' of the system along its own lines. 'The Society,' Leo xii informed the Fathers shortly after the restoration in 1824, 'was restored for the purpose above all that it might instruct youth in learning and virtue.' The commission was accepted. But at that time there were only thirteen Jesuit schools in the world – five in Russia; four in the Two Sicilies; Stonyhurst in England; Georgetown in the United States; Clongowes in Ireland; Brig in Switzerland. It is not surprising if in the vast expansion of a hundred and fifty years the Fathers have not always been able to wait for an assurance of absolute pre-eminence before they commit themselves to an enterprise. They have been much more consciously in competition with other schools and colleges – secular or of other religious Orders. The changes that have been introduced have been adjustments towards what others around them are doing and sometimes the Society has been a little slow in introducing these changes. It is true that Father Roothan, the second General of the restored Society, in 1832 produced a Revised Order of Studies, professing to bring the *Ratio Studiorum* up to date in accordance with modern needs, but the revision was not a very wide one. The Society has been much more consciously a Society under challenge than it was in its earlier years. Their ambition has been much more to keep up with the times than to set the pace.

One of the most distinguished of the Jesuits of this period immediately after 1815 was Rozaven – a learned, pious and wholly honourable man. A Breton, born in 1772, he lived the years of the Revolution abroad in England, Germany and Belgium and then, when the Society was restored in Russia, he joined it there in 1804 and became Prefect of Studies at the College of Nobles in St Petersburg. At the end of the Napoleonic Wars he went to Rome and remained there till his death in 1851. He there joined issue with Lamennais and his major work, *Examen of Certain Philosophical Doctrines in Criticism of the French Liberal Catholics of the Day*, appeared in 1831. It would take us far afield were we here to attempt a full verdict on Lamennais' principles. No one can of course deny that by the end of his life he was advocating doctrines wholly incompatible with any possible form of Catholicism. Just as certainly, in his youth he at least thought of himself as fervently orthodox. Was Gregory XVI, the Pope who condemned him in the violently-worded encyclical *Mirari Vos*, a percipient man who saw beneath the façade of orthodoxy a deep challenge to the faith? or was Lamennais rather driven out of the Church by the harsh treatment that he met with? And might a little more courtesy, consideration and gentle language have kept him in it? Who shall say? But at least it is interesting to contrast Rozaven's approaches to these challenges of his own day with those of Suarez two hundred years before? Suarez, faced with the problem of defining the nature of sovereignty, recognized that a new situation had arisen since St Thomas' day, when it was possible to assume a society that accepted Catholic authority. He saw that it was therefore to no purpose to appeal merely to traditions which were no longer relevant, and sought out an answer for his problem on a basis of reason. In the nineteenth century we find indeed a similar radical approach in, say, the writings of Newman, but we find it singularly absent in such early nineteenth-century Jesuits as Rozaven. Events cannot be ignored. It is quite possible to argue that the French Revolution was a great misfortune – that it would have been much better had stronger and wiser rulers in the years of the *ancien régime* made the necessary adjustments in time so that the Revolution was not necessary. In the same way it is more than arguable that the Reformation two hundred years before was a great misfortune and that it would have been much better had the necessary reforms been made in time to prevent the revolt. But when events have happened they have changed the situation. The kind of restoration that attempts merely to ignore the facts is futile. As long as a traditional system survives people obey it because they have never thought to challenge it and therefore it can rule without violence. When a traditional system has collapsed and then after a time been restored it must accept the fact that it is now in power only as the result of a challenge, that men are continually contrasting it with that which it has overthrown, that it cannot again hope merely to be taken for granted, and that it has continually to demonstrate its superiority to its rivals. The great defect in Rozaven's reasoning was that he seemed to have so little sense that the French Revolution, for better or worse, had happened. Before the Revolution rulers had not felt the need to consult public opinion and public opinion had not expected to be consulted. But the Revolution had familiarized the people with the slogans of popular sovereignty. An appeal to Suarez was all that was required to teach a Catholic – and in particular a Jesuit – that there was nothing un-Catholic in such an appeal in itself, however extravagant might have been some of the things that had been done in its name. In any event, good or bad as the appeal might be, the fact remained that never again could any government hope to survive unless it was built upon the consent of the governed.

In the same way, St Thomas Aquinas wrote for a public that took the existence of God for granted, that believed in His existence, irrespective of the proofs that St Thomas advanced for it. Those proofs were therefore of secondary importance. But in a world that had read the Encyclopaedists and Hume and Kant and knew that they challenged those proofs, it was to little purpose merely to repeat the proofs and to cry 'stinking fish' at philosophers who rejected them. It was necessary to prove the existence of God by arguments that were convincing to the modern man and to refute the philosophers. It is useless to assert that a proposition is absolutely demonstrated if in fact a large number of competent and educated persons do not accept it. In modern times the two Jesuits who have won for themselves the greatest names in the world at large have been Gerard Manley Hopkins and Teilhard de Chardin. It is notable that neither of them, unimpeachably loyal to the Society though they were, received encouragement in their labours from their Jesuit superiors. How different from the story of the sixteenth-century Society!

Thus in the earlier years of the century it was foolish to shut one's eyes to the fact that the Revolution had happened. The only sensible approach for the Catholic was that of the great Bishop of Orleans, Dupanloup, when he said: 'We accept, we invoke the principles and the liberties proclaimed in '89. . . . You made the Revolution of 1789 without us and against us but for us, God wishing it so in spite of you.' Lamennais, along with wiser and more balanced Catholics like Lacordaire and Montalembert, rightly recognized this. But there was depressingly little recognition of it either at the Vatican or among the Jesuits. Rozaven sought to refute Lamennais not, as Suarez would have refuted him, by an appeal to reason, but by a mere appeal to precedents. It was not very cogent, partly because he was appealing back to pre-revolutionary writers who were writing in very different circumstances from those of Rozaven's own day and partly because, as Newman found when he went to Rome after his reception in the 1840s, the method of argumentation then in favour at Rome was singularly unconvincing. They did not appeal back to the real meaning of their authorities. Their method was rather to pick out stock sentences with little regard to their context and use them as weapons. Perhaps it was not possible in a so largely secularized society that a cleric should dominate the public mind in the way that Bellarmine dominated it three hundred years before.

It is true that when he went to Rome after his reception Newman found the Jesuits there of a higher calibre than the other clerics; he compared them to 'Oxford dons', and praised the intelligence of Perrone even when Perrone quarrelled with his theory of development. Yet the Jesuits in Gregory XVI's Rome were to him little more than the one-eyed men in the country of the blind. He found the general level appallingly low. The Jesuits of the early nineteenth century at Rome were indeed more sophisticated than the other clerics but they were a great deal less sophisticated than had been their predecessors of two hundred years before. The concentration on the preservation of the Pope's temporal power at a time when the world was alive with so many more important problems had the inevitable consequence that Roman ecclesiastics remained unfledged and never truly matured. They were like children.

It is difficult not to feel that throughout all these years of ultra-

montane controversy the Jesuits who two hundred years before
had been in the van of Catholic thinking had now sunk back somewhat. All too many of their energies were employed on fighting a
hopeless battle in which they could not possibly conquer and did
not deserve to conquer, and they have never quite recovered the
intellectual pre-eminence which they then lost.

The Jesuits are by their profession in challenge to the secular
world and it is to be expected that they should arouse its hostility.
The words of Our Lord in the Gospels bid them think that they
themselves must be amiss if they do not, and St Ignatius reinforced
this warning of Our Lord in his own words, begging that the
Society might never 'for long remain unharassed by the enmity of
the world'. So there is no cause for surprise that at every period of
its history the Society should have been the victim of most violent
demonstrations. Not only have these denunciations been violent
but in every age a good proportion of them have been frankly
idiotic. The Jesuits have a peculiar capacity for attracting to themselves charges that are manifestly nonsensical. We have in previous
pages come across plenty of instances of it, but there was perhaps
no period that was more rampant with absurd charges against
them than the first half of the nineteenth century. Of course it is
right to reject them, but they carry with them a certain danger.
The Jesuits, one cannot but feel, are sometimes almost in danger
of a certain masochistic self-pity. Because so many of the charges
brought against them are ridiculous they tend without proper
examination to dismiss all charges as ridiculous. Of course his
strict examination of conscience makes the Jesuit very rigorous –
perhaps sometimes too rigorous – in his judgement on himself for
his personal failings. But his strong *esprit de corps* makes him too
little critical of the policies of the Society. He thinks it a kind of
disloyalty to meditate on such matters. Now in the first half of the
nineteenth century, as at every other period of their history, the
Jesuits would certainly have been attacked whatever they had
done. But the policy that their authorities pursued certainly
rendered them unnecessarily open to attack. In those times the
great social problems of the day were the problems of the new
industrialism, the need of the day was for the Church to define
its teaching on these problems. Yet in these early years and up till
the pontificate of Leo XIII the Church had nothing to say on them.

The Jesuits in their position of great influence at the Vatican had a great opportunity to direct the minds of the not very well educated Popes of the period towards these matters, but they made little use of their opportunity. In those years, as Newman was to discover, intellectual life at the Vatican was at its nadir.

The nineteenth century was a century of the growth of journalism. Religious, including Catholic, newspapers appeared regularly for the first time, and, as was only to be expected, in almost every country the Jesuits produced their organs, most of which still survive. The nineteenth century saw the *Civiltà Catolica* in Rome, *Etudes* in France, the *Stimmer aus Maria Lach* in Germany, *The Month* in England, followed in the early years of this century by *Razon y Fe* in Spain, *Studies* in Ireland and *America* in the United States. Of these journals those published in Protestant countries could not expect to win much circulation outside the Catholic body and therefore could not of their nature influence general public opinion. They kept themselves for the most part to purely Catholic issues and were moderately and discreetly conducted. The writing of the continental journals was somewhat different. *Civiltà Catolica*, the senior of them, was founded in 1850 at the express wish of Pius ix. Pius had then just returned from his exile after the disturbances of 1848, as had also the Jesuits. He proposed wholly to abandon the constitutional policies upon which he had embarked and wished to have a competent journal to defend him before the world. Up to a point this was well enough. No one could complain of a Catholic journal for defending the Pope, but the trouble was that defence of the Pope at such a date inevitably meant more frequently than anything else a defence of the government of the Papal States, and that government was far from a perfect one. Incompetence, disorder and corruption were widespread. The task of a Catholic journalist who set himself to write about it was almost impossible. Were he to tell the truth, his paper would certainly have been suppressed in Rome and he would have been accused of disloyalty. Such a paper could only be continued at the price of suppressing a good deal of inconvenient truth and that, whether out of policy or out of loyalty, *Civiltà Catolica* in these years unfortunately did. It would have been a disastrous policy for any journalist. It was particularly disastrous for a Jesuit journalist – for a member of an Order which had been so widely and libellously accused of teaching that the end justifies the means. It was a peculiarly unfortunate moment to give to the world an example of a few Jesuits so manifestly practising that maxim, and the Jesuits throughout the world suffered, and perhaps still suffer, from the policies of *Civiltà Catolica* in these last years of papal Rome.

Most unfortunately, in later years *Civiltà Catolica* allowed Father Ballerina and Father Tonotini to propagate in its columns absurd stories about Jewish conspiracies against the world, which helped to prepare the ground for the later insanities of the Protocol of the Elders of Zion. Jesuits had so often been the victims of paranoiac and ridiculous denunciations of themselves that it is surprising and depressing that some of them should have played a part in propagating a very similar absurdity about the Jews. The surrender of those nineteenth-century Jesuits is in sad contrast to their predecessor of two hundred and fifty years before, von Spe, who argued from the hysterical tales that he heard about Jesuits in his day and knew to be baseless, that tales of a similar sort about witches were likely to be as wholly without foundation, and on the strength of his disbelief destroyed a bestial persecution and freed mankind.

Etudes in France followed the same sort of policy as *Civiltà Catolica* but at a distance, and was not under a direct curial eye: it therefore was not then or later so wholly obsessed by the fluctuations of merely Roman politics. The fortunes of the Church in France have not, whether for better or worse, depended to more than a limited extent on what has been happening at Rome.

More unfortunate perhaps was the German *Stimmer aus Maria Lach*, founded in 1865 specifically to defend Pius IX's *Syllabus Errorum* which had been issued in the previous year. The Syllabus was a collection of so-called liberal propositions which the Pope pronounced anathema. At first sight at any rate it looked as if he was roundly proclaiming the impossibility that 'the Roman pontiff' could 'accommodate himself to liberty, progress or modern civilization', and was indeed declaring unqualified war on every aspect of the world. As such it naturally caused difficulties and indeed consternation to Catholics in such countries as Britain, America, France or Germany, who had to live and work in the company of non-Catholic fellow-citizens. If this was really

Catholic teaching, how could non-Catholics be expected to tolerate Catholics in places where they had the opportunity to express it? Bishop Dupanloup explained that the teaching was not quite as bad as it seemed at first sight. These propositions which were condemned, he was able to show, were not unconditional propositions. They were all quotations from previous papal pronouncements, each one directed against a particular target – in fact against activities either of the Spanish liberals of 1812 or against the Piedmontese who had introduced anti-clerical legislation and suppressed monasteries and convents in the territories of which they had made themselves masters and, in particular, in the territories of Romagna and the Marches which they had seized from the papacy in 1859. Pius, Dupanloup argued, condemning liberty and progress and modern civilization, was not condemning everything that was done anywhere in those names. He was not necessarily condemning anything that was happening in England or America. He was merely condemning what the Piedmontese called liberty or progress or modern civilization. English and American opinion was immensely relieved to hear Dupanloup's explanation but naturally it could not be expected that it would forbear to ask 'If that was all the Pope meant, why could he not have said so in the first place?' There was no answer to this. Dupanloup was merely making the best of a bad job, and not surprisingly he received no thanks from Rome. There was no getting over it that the matter was handled in Rome with abominable incompetence, only to be explained by the fact that Roman minds were so dominated by the problem of the Papal States that it had not occurred to them that there were people in other parts of the world who were interested in other matters.

Unfortunately the Jesuits were among those to whom this reflection did not occur, and, while Dupanloup in France was doing what he could to smooth the matter over, the Jesuits of *Stimmer aus Maria Lach* in Germany saw fit to launch a bullheadedly total defence of the Syllabus. Their defence came out just as Ward in England, to Newman's great disgust, was arguing that the Syllabus was infallible. Germany was not a happy country in which to launch such a campaign. Dollinger had popularized among German Catholics the thesis – which was in general probably quite true – that German scholarship was greatly the superior of Italian scholarship and – quite a different matter – that it was something of a pious condescension when Germans submitted themselves to an Italian headship. Two years before, in 1863, a Congress under the leadership of Dollinger and Acton to encourage free Catholic historical inquiry had been arranged to take place at Munich. It had opened by sending messages of loyal filial duty to the Pope, to which Pius had replied by summarily dissolving it. German Catholic opinion was therefore very attuned to the notion that Roman scholarship did not treat the evidence honestly. Therefore the editors of the *Stimmer* when they rushed to the defence of this indefensible syllabus only strengthened the widespread German belief in the lack of clerical candour. Five years later Bismarck was to establish the Second Reich in the hour of French defeat and Dollinger was to leave the Church on the declaration of papal infallibility. The establishment of the Second Reich was at once followed by the violently anti-Catholic Kulturkampf. It would be absurd of course to assert dogmatically that had it not been for the *Stimmer*'s campaign Dollinger would not have left the Church or Bismarck would not have launched the Kulturkampf, and, if there was to be an attack on the Church, it was only to be expected that as always, the attack would fall with particular severity on the Jesuits. Yet certainly the *Stimmer* by putting it on an untenable ground rendered the Catholic cause a disservice.

The Jesuits along with the offices of the *Stimmer* had to go into exile. But, like most people, the Jesuits benefited from mild persecution. The *Stimmer* established itself first at Tervuren in Belgium and then at Bijenbek and Valkenburg in Holland, where it remained up till the First World War. Freed by exile from involvement in immediate politics, the paper greatly improved.

Whereas the Italian Jesuits in general rallied to the support of the extreme conservative cause of the alliance of throne and altar in the years immediately after 1815, and to the defence of the papal temporal power when that came to be threatened, it would have been surprising if even in a restored Society a policy so radically different from that of the earlier Society could have been carried through without arousing some doubts among some of its members. Of course it did not, and in these years the Society suffered its casualties – surprisingly few indeed but some of them notable. Carlo Passaglia was thought of in 1850 as one of the outstanding

professors at the Gregorian. He played a leading part in helping
to prepare the definition of the Immaculate Conception. But
after the Piedmontese had seized Romagna and the Marches in
1859, Passaglia thought it inevitable that they would eventually
enter Rome, that it was absurd to expect a united Italy for long to
deny itself this prize, and that the Vatican had better take what
opportunity there was to make a friendly arrangement. He wrote
a book advocating such a solution, called *Pro Causa Italica*. He had
already left the Jesuits before he wrote this book which was placed
on the Index. He left Rome and went to Turin where he started a
weekly paper called *Il Medicatore*. He argued that he had been condemned for advocating a political programme that was in no way
in violation of revealed religion and that therefore the condemnation was illegitimate. He dressed as a layman and got other dis-
contented priests to contribute to the paper, and extended his
criticism of the temporal power to criticisms of the *Syllabus
Errorum*. Carlo Maria Curci had been one of the original contributors to the *Civiltà Catolica* and at that time had been a vigorous
critic of the liberal principles with which Pius IX was then assailed;
but after a time he became disillusioned with purely obstructionist
policies and began advocating liberal opinions of a sort himself.
He left both the Society and the Church and remained estranged
throughout Pius' life. After Leo XIII's accession he saw hope of
better things and was reconciled towards the end of his life. These
were however exceptions. The very great majority of the Fathers
obediently accepted the line of their superiors.

   Thus in these years the Church allowed itself to be manoeuvred
into an almost absolute and dogmatic defence of the unconditional rights of property, very different from the traditional teaching of St Thomas. The Church, somewhat impotently facing a
hostile and godless world, had almost abdicated from any attempt
to proclaim the wickedness of war. The cautious admission of
traditional teaching that ownership of private property and war
must not under all circumstances be inevitably condemned was
twisted almost into a belief that the main purpose of the Christian
revelation was to protect property-owners in their property and
to encourage Christians with a good conscience to take part in any
wars that might take place, and the Jesuits said little to correct
these exaggerations.

27. Charles III of Spain

28. Clement XIV pro-
nouncing the suppression
of the Society

29. Cardinal Consalvi. By Sir Thomas Lawrence

30. Father Philip
Roothan, General of
the restored Society

31. Pope Pius IX as an
old man

32. Stonyhurst College, Lancashire

33 . The First Vatican Council

34. The expulsion of the Jesuits from the rue de Sèvres, Paris

35. Father Gerard Manley Hopkins

36. Father
Teilhard de
Chardin

37. Cardinal Bea

38. Paul III confirming the Society. From a painting in the sacristy of the Gesù

39. Paul VI blessing Father Arrupe, the General of the Society

No protest came from them in later years against the Church's extraordinary refusal to recognize a right of conscientious objection to conscription. When the Kingdom of Italy was established, it was in Catholic eyes a State so wicked that no Catholic might collaborate with its politics. Catholics were forbidden to be either electors or elected to its Parliaments. Any wars in which it was engaged would be almost by definition unjust wars, and yet at the same time the Catholic was told by the Church not to refuse to serve in its army.

By accepting the policy of alliance of throne and altar the Jesuits put themselves into the position of being thought the main defenders of those not very edifying and not very stable secular regimes and were held to blame for all their failures and injustices. They allowed themselves in most of these countries to be identified with a party, and therefore their story in those countries throughout the nineteenth century was the monotonous and tiresome one of going in and out with the rise and fall of governments. The insecurity of their life made it impossible for them to achieve any great development or continuity of educational policy.

The support which the Vatican offered to all established governments after 1815 was carried to so extraordinary a pitch that in three countries, Ireland, Belgium and Poland, the Vatican actually interfered to prevent persecuted Catholics from demanding the freedom of their religion from non-Catholic monarchs – from the king of England, the king of Holland and the czar. By the settlement of 1815 it was decided to unite Belgium and Holland under the king of Holland. The Protestant king of Holland had no mind to grant freedom to his Belgian Catholic subjects. Among other measures against the Church the king of Holland made it his first business to expel the Jesuits. In 1816 he sent a band of soldiers to drive them out and the Dutch province had to establish itself in Germany and Switzerland. However in 1830 the union of Holland and Belgium came to an end. The Belgians revolted against the Dutch – largely because of the king's anti-Catholic policies – and established their independence under Leopold of Saxe-Coburg, a not very pious German princeling, the uncle of Queen Victoria. One result of the change was that the Jesuits were able to return to Belgium, though not until some time later to Holland.

The Jesuits soon ran into trouble in Switzerland also. In Friburg there was a quarrel over methods of teaching in primary schools, which at first sight had little to do with religion, and the quarrel grew so bitter that the town council at the Bishop's request closed down all the schools in the town. This strange policy does not seem in any way to have emanated directly from Jesuit prompting, but public opinion was easily persuaded that it did, and on 9 March 1823 a mob attacked the Jesuit college and clamoured for its destruction. The Bishop was eventually able to quieten down the clamour but the story was ominous. In its earlier life the Society had always been, and had always been thought to be, the protagonists of education, introducing schools and colleges into districts previously without them, confident that it was by the weapon of education that the Church would win its victories. The alliance of the Jesuits with the absolutist monarchs of the continent in those years after 1815 meant an alliance with forces to whom democracy was the most dangerous of all threats and to whom popular education was suspect as likely to lead to popular demands for the vote. Even if the suspicion was not altogether justified, it was an ominous day – a sign of the difference between the old Society and the new – when the Jesuits were attacked as the enemies of popular education. In Switzerland in the 1840s there was a civil war between the Catholic and the Protestant cantons. The Protestants who were in the majority wished to impose a stronger central authority and to restrict the local autonomy of the cantons. Vatican policy with its natural sympathy at that time for authoritarian government was hesitant and uncertain. The Catholic cause was very vigorously championed by Montalembert but he championed it by an invocation of liberal principles and of the right of a people to choose their own form of government – a form of apologetic which was dangerously temerarious to Vatican ears. *Non tali auxilio* they were inclined to exclaim. The Jesuits had been accepted in the Catholic cantons of Uri, Schwyz and Unterwalden but were proscribed elsewhere in Switzerland. Palmerston, then British Foreign Secretary, did not greatly care whether the Jesuits remained or not, but he was alarmed at the danger to European stability if the Swiss Confederation should dissolve, a not unreasonable anxiety. In any event as a result of Palmerston's insistence that no external power interfere in Swiss domestic affairs the stronger Protestant cantons were able to defeat the less numerous Catholic, who had banded themselves together into the Sonderbund, and, as an incidental consequence of the Protestant victory, the Jesuits were expelled from Switzerland and the College of Friburg looted.

The Popes, Pius VI and Pius VII, had been shamefully illtreated by the French Revolutionaries and by Napoleon and it was natural that Catholics should remember these outrages. It was a pity that they should so wholly have forgotten the equally gross outrages that they – and the Jesuits among them in particular – had suffered from the monarchs of the *ancien régime*. The Catholic authorities had certainly no reason to commit themselves to the support of every extravagance that was preached in the name of liberalism. But they should have been as careful not to commit themselves to every extravagance that was preached in the name of absolutism. They should have repudiated the alliance of throne and altar and recognized that, in so far as they took a political attitude at all, their place was with the support of liberty, justice and government by consent.

Throughout their history the Jesuits have constantly been accused by their enemies of excessive wealth. In so far as the suggestion has been that individual Jesuits have lived luxurious lives, the accusation has of course at all times been merely ridiculous. The individual Jesuit, like the individual of other religious Orders, takes a vow of poverty and, whatever the wealth of his house or his Order, he only eats, drinks and wears what his superior provides for him. If there have been over the centuries individual Jesuits who have found means of evading their obligations and indulging in secret luxuries, their names have not been recorded and they must have been very few. It is of course true that, though absurd stories about secret American gold mines and the like can be dismissed, the very fact that the religious does not receive for himself any personal income means that a religious Order which takes any fees for its services, educational, agricultural or economic, tends to accumulate for itself considerable wealth over the years and it has already been mentioned that since the religious house does not die its wealth is not periodically distributed among a number of heirs as is a private fortune. It is certainly true that, had the Jesuit houses in every country enjoyed an uninterrupted prosperity over the last four hundred years, the houses – though not the individual Jesuits – would by now have been the possessors of considerable wealth. But of course that has by no means happened. Their history has, as we have seen, been one of constant expulsion and readmission. When they have been expelled their property has been confiscated. When they have been readmitted into a country it has not been restored to them. Secularists clamour for the wealth of the Jesuits. They do not understand that other secularists have been before them – as of course they have also with the property of other religious Orders. But would it be quite unfair of the Jesuits of the first half of the nineteenth century to say that they gave their political support too freely to the possessors of power?

In education, the first Jesuits were successful because they applied new policies to a new situation – offered education far more fully than it had been offered before to the new laity. Their successors should have seen that in their new age what was required was a policy for the problems of that age, not a mere adherence to the system of three hundred years before. They should have been with Newman in the van of the movement for associating the laity more closely with the teaching and for a relaxation of discipline among the pupils. Instead they tended to adhere more obstinately to the old ways and to change, when eventually they did change, not as the earlier Jesuits had done because they were in the van of progress, but because as the last laggards they did grudgingly and under complaint what all the world had done before them. In their writings they overlooked the fact that in every age certain beliefs can be taken for granted and certain beliefs are under challenge. In the world of the sixteenth century, Catholicism was under challenge from the Protestants, but it was possible to a large extent to take for granted the existence of God and the divinity of Christ. In the modern world the debate between Catholics and Protestants only arouses interest in out-of-the-way corners like Belfast, but the fundamentals of faith are everywhere challenged. The argument must be restated so as to make it cogent to the readers of the present age.

In the world after 1815 the most important social developments of industrialism were taking place in non-Catholic countries – in England and the United States. The papacy had until Leo XIII's time nothing to say about Catholic teaching on these problems.

Retreating into what Newman called its Novatian sulks in its Roman catacombs, it was content to think that the only important question in the world was whether the Pope could keep his temporal power and to denounce the rest of the world as a wicked and impious place. It cannot be pretended that the Jesuits at Rome did much to remedy this papal folly. All the real vigour of Jesuit life in the nineteenth century was found in Protestant countries – England and America – and the Jesuits there were a great deal more sensible than the Jesuits in Latin countries. But even they, important as was the work that they did, were compelled to live a hobbled life. Their sense of loyalty and their rules compelled them to pay an attention to the discipline imposed upon them from Rome, which Rome, as it then was, did not really deserve, and their minds were inhibited by the need constantly to express a respect to it which they could not truly feel. Jesuits in Protestant countries and Jesuits in Catholic countries are really quite different sorts of beings, though it is not convenient for either of them to say so.

ELEVEN

The restored Society: I

Some time elapsed before the Society was reconstituted in Spain and Portugal. In Spain the formal decree of reconstitution was not proclaimed until 25 May 1825. A hundred and fifteen Spanish Jesuits then returned to the country from their various homes abroad to reform the Spanish province. In Portugal the Jesuits had to wait even longer. The suppression of Protestantism in Spain and Portugal did not convert the inhabitants of those countries into pious Catholics. It merely meant that all too often those who held positions of ecclesiastical power used those positions for their own advantage and that those who were shocked by their antics collapsed into a total hostility to all religion. It was the custom of the militant Catholics – Jesuits and others – to talk of themselves as the defenders of righteousness against the forces of unbridled evil. The picture was no doubt up to a point true, but they would have been well advised to have meditated a little more on what must have been the quality of a Catholicism that had ruled for centuries over such a country and left it at the end so full of murderous hatred of class against class, of man against man and of district against district. In any event the upshot was that the Jesuits in those countries in the nineteenth century allowed themselves to become the mere creatures of the conservative party and monotonously went in and out with the success or failure of that party. In Spain, Ferdinand VII when he returned to the throne on the expulsion of Joseph Bonaparte in 1815 called back the Jesuits and made over to them the Imperial College. The liberal risings of 1820 took an anti-Jesuit form. Just as Ferdinand was besieged in his palace, so were the Jesuits pulled out of their beds and thrown into prison. A Jesuit, Father Urigolia, was murdered near Ignatius' cave at Manresa. Then the French troops came in and restored Ferdinand and brought back the Jesuits with them.

In the riots of 1820 in Spain twenty-five Jesuits were murdered. When in 1823 civil war broke out between the liberals under Queen Isabella and the conservatives under her uncle, Don Carlos, the Jesuits took the Carlist side and as a result there were attacks on them wherever the liberals were predominant. The liberals held Madrid and there were threats to murder all the Jesuits there on the ground that they had poisoned the wells and were responsible for the city's cholera epidemic. On 17 July 1834, troops stormed the Imperial College during dinner-time. Three Jesuits were killed inside the college. Four more disguised themselves and fled out into the streets but were caught there and murdered. Five others were captured and killed on the roof. The rest had fled to the chapel where an officer who was a brother of one of them led them out to a place of safety, but the college was entirely destroyed. The attack of that day was not on the Jesuits alone. Seventy-three members of other religious Orders were also killed. The liberal government ordered the expulsion of the Jesuits from all Spain and the decree was obeyed in the parts of the country over which their writ ran. In the parts of the country that were in Carlist occupation the Jesuits remained.

The Jesuits returned again to Spain after their dispersion in 1854, but a further revolution in 1868 led to attacks on all their houses. They were again expelled but returned again and remained there in spite of some threats until their expulsion at the time of the fall of the monarchy in 1931. In the civil war they, like other Catholics, were divided in their sympathies. Catholics, including the Jesuits, throughout the greater part of Spain, supported General Franco, but those from the Basque countries were on the other side, In the world of today Jesuits in Spain as elsewhere have been divided. The older ones have for the most part adhered to the support of the traditional ways. Many of the younger Jesuits have been prominent, as have other younger priests, in their advocacy of more liberal social policies and of the implementation of the decrees of the Second Vatican Council.

The Jesuits were not allowed back into Portugal immediately at the time of the Society's restoration. It was only in 1829 that the king, Dom Miguel, allowed them to return. Even then it was for only a brief reign. In 1833 Dom Pedro supplanted Dom Miguel and a liberal regime was installed. It at once decreed the expulsion of the Jesuits but the decree was superfluous as in the preceding riots the Jesuit colleges in Lisbon had already been sacked and their inmates expelled. In the next year the largest Jesuit college of Coimbra was also suppressed and the Jesuits there also expelled.

Soon afterwards they returned and the monarchy and a professedly conservative regime lasted on in the country until 1910 when a violent revolution expelled King Manuel and declared a republic. The Jesuits, as was to be expected, suffered in the disturbances. The story has been recorded by Cabral, the Portuguese Provincial of those days. It is a story of depressing familiarity – absurd tales about plots and secret arsenals, the Fathers marched out between files of soldiers, filthy food, beatings, threats and finally expulsion – scenes so similar to the scenes of a hundred and fifty years before. One can only wonder at the double folly of human nature – at the folly of those who could be so childish as to believe such nonsense and at the folly of the Jesuits in having lived a life so guarded from contacts with ordinary people that it was possible for anyone to believe such stories about them.

In South America, the history of the Jesuits in the years after those countries' revolt from their European rulers was curiously ambivalent. On the one hand, while circumstances had made it impossible for the Catholics in North America to look to any support from the state and compelled them to accept its formula of the complete separation of Church and state, in South America the traditional policy had been one of alliance of throne and altar and of the recognition of the Church as an official state Church. This inevitably meant that when those countries revolted against Spain their revolt took an anti-clerical form. The Church was looked upon as the upholder of the tyranny which they were bent on overthrowing. On the other hand, as we have seen, that traditional government, whatever its general attitude towards the Church, had been bitterly hostile to the Jesuits, and the Indian inhabitants justly looked on the Jesuits as their supporters against oppression. As a consequence, one of the first demands of the liberals in such countries as Mexico, in sharp contrast to the behaviour of liberals on the continent of Europe, was that the Jesuits should be brought back, and indeed even later in the century in Brazil the Jesuits received much more generous treatment from the republic when it was established than they had ever received from the Portuguese royal family so long as the house of Braganza still ruled as Emperors there. But in Spanish America the paradox of liberal Jesuits proved too violent to be tolerable either to the Jesuits or to the liberals and, as the century went on and the wars of liberation were forgotten, the traditional pattern of Europe tended to reproduce itself, the Jesuits to be denounced as the enemies of liberty and to go in and out with the rise and fall of governments on the wearisome European pattern. When in the years between the two wars a violent persecution of the Church broke out in Mexico, that persecution fell with especial violence on the Jesuits, two of whom, Father Pro and Father Vertiz, suffered martyrdom. In the years since the Second World War, in South America as elsewhere, young Jesuits have been vigorous in the advocacy of policies of social reform that are far removed from those of old-fashioned, unqualified conservativism which in so many eyes passed for Catholicism in the past.

The life of the Jesuits after 1815 was not comfortable in Italy. Even in the Papal States there were riots on the death of Pius VIII in 1830. Five Jesuit colleges throughout the Papal States – at Spoleto, Fano, Modena, Forli and Ferrara – were attacked and the Fathers and their pupils bundled out into the streets. Peace was maintained in Rome itself but nowhere outside the city, and all the Jesuit houses outside Rome were invaded and searched in the belief that the Sanfedisti were being allowed to use them as armouries.

In Italy in general in these years there was little of the intellectual criticism of Catholicism that was to be found in France, and little of the almost insanely violent hatred of it that was to be found in Spain and Portugal. The charge that Catholicism was a religion managed by foreigners was not relevant in Italy, but Italy had its peculiar problem: as the feeling for national unity grew, men inevitably asked themselves how the Pope could fit into such a scheme. Could the Pope in some way take the leadership of the movement for unity? Must he inevitably oppose it? There was clearly no intrinsic contradiction between Catholic principles and Italian unity. But how could Italy be unified without an interference with the rights of some established rulers – without the dethronement of the monarchs of the petty Italian principalities and without the expulsion of the Austrians from their territories in

Lombardy and Venetia, which the treaties had assigned to them?

As long as Gregory XVI was on the throne, papal policy was resolutely opposed to any concessions in the Papal States. There must be no parliaments and all power must be kept in clerical hands. Pius IX succeeded him in 1846, full of notions of reform. There should be lay ministers and a parliament in Rome. The trouble was that 1848 was a year of revolution in Europe and it was very difficult in such a year to inaugurate reforms that would not be at once captured by extremists. There was little reason to think that in Rome, any more than elsewhere, the great majority of the population cared very deeply about constitutional reform, but the few that did care were as strongly opposed to clerical as to political authoritarianism. Besides, to any patriotic Italian the Austrian domination of the Italian peninsula was naturally hateful, to be tolerated, if to be tolerated at all, only because it was successful and Austria appeared invincible. When news came through of revolution in Vienna and the overthrow of Metternich it was natural that the first use that the Italians in Rome and elsewhere should make of their recently granted political freedom should be to demand Italian unity. When Pius hesitated to put himself at the head of such a movement, feeling that a Pope could not lead a campaign against the Catholic country of Austria on a purely political issue, the nationalists turned against Pius. His Prime Minister, Rossi, was stabbed to death while mounting the steps of the Cancellaria. Pius himself was besieged in the Quirinal. A Bishop, Palma, was shot dead there when standing at a window and finally Pius had to flee and take refuge at Gaeta in Naples.

The Jesuits were thought, on the whole justly, to exert influence in support of the alliance of throne and altar, and against constitutional reform. Gioberti's *Il Gesuita Moderno*, exposing them as the alleged enemies of Italian unity, was a popular work. Therefore the fury of the liberal Roman mob turned naturally against them, and Father Roothan, the General, and his associates had to flee from the city. They escaped to Genoa, where they got on board a ship, but as it put out to sea loud cries of 'You have Jesuits on board; throw them overboard', were raised. Their supposed opposition to Italian unity earned unpopularity for the Jesuits elsewhere in Italy and there were riots against them also in

Naples, Venice and Turin. The Piedmontese government, which had up till then supported them, turned against them. Likewise in Austria, where their policy had been identified with that of Metternich, they suffered with his fall and were expelled.

The excitements of 1848 for the moment died down. The petty rulers succeeded in holding their thrones. The Austrians remained in Lombardy and Venetia. Pius was able to return to Rome, and for the moment the Jesuits re-established themselves. But their position was insecure. They were not willing to make any concession to the nationalists, and their refusal was partly the cause and partly the effect of the nationalist movement's increased violence in its hostility towards them. The leadership of the movement for unity was passing increasingly to the House of Savoy, and as a result Piedmontese legislation became increasingly anti-clerical. When, following the Franco-Austrian war of 1859 and Garibaldi's invasion of Naples, an Italian kingdom including all Italy except only Rome and Venice was established, the Jesuits were excluded from it. They remained for the moment in Venice, where they had been restored with the restoration of absolute rule in the Austrian Empire of which Venice was still a part, but when Venetia passed to the Italians in 1866 the Jesuits were expelled from there also. After that date there were no Jesuits anywhere in Italy except in the Papal States.

A consequence of the capture of Rome by the Piedmontese in 1870 was the expulsion of the headquarters of the Jesuits from Rome. Father Peter Beck, who was then General, had to leave the city and was given a home in the private house of the Count of Ricasole at Fiesole. He remained there until his death in 1884, as did his immediate successor. But the Italian government, even though the fact was not universally recognized in Catholic circles, was, in an unstable position, uncertain of the loyalty of its subjects or of its own permanence, very anxious not to give any unnecessary insults to Catholic feeling so long as the central fact of its possession of Rome was not challenged, and indeed treated Catholics after 1870 very much better than they had been treated in the Italian kingdom before the capture of Rome. It therefore made no objection to Father Martin, who was elected General in 1893, when he proposed to return to Rome and to exercise his functions from there.

In those days France was the only Latin country where there was an intellectual life of much vigour. In France the great Jesuit who kept the continuity of the Society was the remarkable Father de Clorivière. De Clorivière was a Breton, born at St Malo in 1735. He entered the Society in 1756 and was teaching a class at Compiègne when the Jesuits were expelled from France. He joined the English province and went to their Liège headquarters, where he was professed. When the English Jesuits returned to England after the French troops had overrun the Netherlands, de Clorivière returned to France as a secular priest, and when the Revolution came was the director of the diocesan college of Dinan. He refused to take the constitutional oath when that was preferred to all priests, and as a consequence was barred from all ecclesiastical positions. The times of the terror were not comfortable for him. His brother and niece were both guillotined, and his sister, a Visitation nun, was put in prison and was only saved from the guillotine by Robespierre's fall. He, like the Abbé Sièyes, was content to live through those times but with the coming of the Consulate he got into trouble in 1801 when a relation of his, Liomellan, was implicated in a plot to assassinate the First Consul and as a result de Clorivière was put in prison. He remained there for seven years, passing the time by writing a voluminous commentary on the Bible. He persuaded one of his fellow-prisoners, an ex-Calvinist, whom he had converted to the Church and who was released in 1805, to go to Russia, carrying a letter requesting the General there to readmit him into the Society. The request was granted. On his release from prison in 1809 he put himself under the orders of the General, saying that he was willing to go wherever he was sent and suggesting a mission in America. The General however ordered him to remain in France. When attempts were made to restart the Society in various western countries, Father Varin, the superior of the Fathers of the Faith, begged Father de Clorivière as a surviving Jesuit to receive them into the Society, as a number of Fathers in similar circumstances had been received in Holland. Father de Clorivière was at first hesitant but in 1814 received express permission from the General Brzozowski to admit suitable clerics. Therefore on St Ignatius' Day of 1814 Father de Clorivière received Varin and nine associates, in the chapel of the Abbaye des Carmes, where in 1792 twelve Jesuits had been martyred, admitted them into the Society and reconstituted the French province.

Louis XVIII was not particularly favourable to the Jesuits. They were able in the first years of the restoration to work quietly in country districts but found it unwise to call ostentatious attention to themselves. They established themselves in *petits séminaires* where they gave instruction both to lay and to clerical students but without advertising themselves as Jesuits. There was criticism of this arrangement from the enemies of the Jesuits and in 1828 an investigation was ordered to see which of these *petits séminaires* was really under Jesuit control. The Jesuits' main critic was the Count de Montlosier who about this time published his *Memoire* in which he listed 'the Four Calamities which were going to subvert the Throne' as the sodalities, the Jesuits, the Ultramontanes and the clerical encroachments. Of these four calamities the Jesuits were not only evil in themselves but also the organizers of the sodalities and the cause of Ultramontanism and clerical encroachment. The truth was that Louis XVIII had been a cautious and moderate leader who had no illusion about his own unpopularity and if he ever had such illusions they had been dissipated by the experience of the Hundred Days. Like England's Charles II, his main ambition was not to go on his travels again. He was neither anxious to quarrel with the Jesuits nor to be dominated by them and was content with an arrangement by which the Jesuits were allowed to remain in the country provided that they did not call attention to themselves. He died in 1824 and was succeeded by his brother, Charles X, who had strong views about the divine right of kings and denied any authority to the people to interfere with their sovereign. He unfortunately did not understand how times had changed and how, whatever might be desirable, it was not possible to maintain himself on his very insecure throne unless he had some regard to public opinion. In five years he had succeeded in talking himself out of his kingdom. He had embraced in full the doctrine of the alliance of throne and altar and put himself without reserve into the hands of the Jesuits. It was a pity that the Jesuits were so foolish as to accept his invitation, for the result of it was of course, as usually happened in nineteenth-century Europe, that the Jesuits were blamed for the mistakes of the government. Montlosier's attacks unloosed a furious campaign in the popular *Journal des Débats*. 'The name Jesuit,' wrote the *Journal*, 'is on every tongue but it is there to be cursed; it is repeated in every newspaper of the land with fear and alarm; it is carried throughout the whole of France on the wings of terror that it inspires.'

Such writers as Thiers, Béranger and Casimir Périer joined with less distinguished pamphleteers in their attacks on the Society. As a result when Charles' Minister, Polignac, was driven from office and Charles was driven out of the country in 1830, there were widespread attacks on Jesuit houses. The novitiate of Montrouge was attacked and pillaged as were other Jesuit houses throughout the land. At St Acheul, a mob assembled shouting 'Down with the Jesuits'. Father de Ravignan attempted to reason with the mob but he was shouted down and struck in the face by a stave. The house was wrecked and the Jesuits had to flee the land. In the reign of Charles x's successor, Louis Philippe, many of them dribbled back, but they had to live and work as individuals. It was not possible at first for them to live together in Jesuit houses.

When Louis Philippe in his turn ran into difficulties his supporters put about rumours that the Jesuits were plotting his overthrow. The *Journal des Débats* published an article of violent attack on de Ravignan. It was its argument that de Ravignan was himself a virtuous man but that the principles of Jesuitry were intrinsically evil, incompatible with, and intolerable in, a liberal society. 'What matters his virtue?' asked the *Journal*, 'if he brings us the pest?' and the word 'pest' caught on and became usual in anti-clerical circles as a term of description of Jesuits. De Ravignan replied to the *Journal* with a temperate and well-written description of Jesuit history and principles, entitled *De l'Histoire et de l'Institut des Jésuites*. The crucial point of controversy was that of the control of education. To religious opinion at that date, Protestant or Catholic, the notion of a religiously indifferent university was unthinkable. The first business of a university was to teach religious truth. Without that it had no excuse for existence. All other disciplines were subordinate to this supreme discipline. The dominant religion must necessarily be master of the nation's universities. Oxford and Cambridge for instance were at that date still closed Anglican monopolies and the notions of

Newman's *Idea of a University* still lay in the very distant future. In France alone under Louis Philippe were universities allowed to be indifferent in their religious teaching, and many among the Bishops, in some cases out of mere ignorance, idleness and lack of interest, in other cases out of a wiser and more far-seeing appreciation of the value of tolerance, were willing to accept that it should be so. The philosophical teaching at the University of Paris was under the control of the positive Cousin. It was the Jesuit Father Delvaux who raised the first Catholic cries of alarm against the dangers of this complacency. A battle of the books broke out with distinguished names on both sides – Veuillot and Montalembert in favour of Catholic education, to name only two, Michelet, Quinet and Sainte-Beuve against it.

Prudent controversialists should perhaps have learnt the lesson that the list of opposed writers was such as to show that, for better or for worse, the day when the opponents of the faith could be dismissed as cranks and fanatics was past – that there were honourable and learned men who were unable to accept the Christian claims and that, whatever treatment might be suited to the simple, it was no longer possible to expect an educated young man to preserve his faith unless he was allowed to feel that he had been left free to study both sides of the question and to make a decision for himself.

In any event, and with the prevailing opinion in Louis Philippe's France, the attacks were not powerful enough to dislodge Cousin. Instead he counter-attacked. He put the *Lettres Provinciales* into the university syllabus. Villemain, the Minister for Public Instruction, denounced 'the turbulent and infamous Society which the spirit of liberty and the spirit of our government repudiated'. Quinet and Michelet attacked the historical record of the Society, Michelet reviving Pasquier's hoary old Jansenist *Plaidoyer* with its secret Jesuits and secret code of Jesuit morals. Eugène Sue in his *Juif Errant* made popular a highly unflattering and ludicrously absurd picture of the typical Jesuit. Yet the Jesuits, though they had their assailants, had also their defenders – Veuillot in a somewhat unbalanced form, Montalembert with wise moderation. De La Riche Arnault, who had been expelled from the Society when he was a scholastic a quarter of a century before and had devoted his life to fighting it, repudiated his attacks on his death-bed. The

Jesuits might have weathered the storm had they not been the victims of an unexpected and dangerous blow when Affre, the Archbishop of Paris, declared against them. Guéranger, the famous Benedictine, rallied to the Jesuits' support against Affre, but it was by then obvious that the detailed merits of the case were rapidly ceasing to command attention. Affre's démarche was evidence of the revival of the old Gallican spirit in the French episcopacy and there was grave fear at Rome that there might soon come from Louis Philippe's France murmurs of a revival of the old claims to a quasi-Anglican Church almost completely free from Rome. The Pope of the time, Gregory XVI, wrote to Affre in stern rebuke of his 'very inconsiderate ruling'.

In 1844 Villemain presented a bill to the French Parlement which declared the total independence from any ecclesiastical interference of the University of Paris and excluded all religious of any sort from teaching in it. Dupin proclaimed in the debates on the bill that 'France did not want that famous Society which owes allegiance to a foreign superior and whose instruction is diametrically opposed to what all lovers of the country desire'. But it proved that Villemain, by extending the prohibition on clerical teaching to all religious, had overplayed his hand. Had he confined himself to prohibiting the Jesuits, he would at least have divided the clergy and would certainly have had some of them on his side, for the Jesuits were not universally popular. But the clergy were not willing to abdicate from their own functions. Affre, whether because Gregory XVI's rebuke had changed his mind or merely because Villemain's bill had opened it, greatly to the Government's surprise came out vigorously against Villemain's bill. He denounced the ministry as 'a centre of irreligion', and to those who argued that to oppose the bill was to oppose the king, he argued that those who destroyed the traditional bulwarks of order, though they might destroy in the name of the king, were in fact undermining the king's authority and it would be he who in the end would infallibly suffer. Affre had no difficulty in pointing to examples from recent French history to support his thesis. 'We may embarrass the throne for the moment,' he argued, 'but in the ministry are to be found all the perils of the future.' The debate raged furiously with strong speeches on both sides and a good deal of absurd rhetoric about the 'detested congregation' and 'the poisoners of the pious Ganganelli'. Eventually on the division the bill was passed in the Upper House by eighty-five votes to fifty-one. It was a majority, but not from the point of view of the administration a comfortably sufficient majority. Guizot conceived that it might be more convenient for the government if the Pope could be persuaded to withdraw the Society from France himself. He sent a special ambassador, Rossi, to Rome to request that this might be done. Rossi arrived in Rome on 11 April, but only three days later a petition was presented to the Upper House, emanating from Marseilles, and requesting the suppression of the books of Michelet and Quinet. Dupin's *Manual of Ecclesiastical Law* and Cousin's *History of Philosophy* were put on the Index. This was interpreted by the anti-clericals as an unabashed counter-attack. It was taken as evidence, as indeed proved to be the case, that the Pope had no intention of listening to Rossi's request that he expel the Society from France. The most that the General of the Jesuits would consent to do was to reduce their number. This concession Guizot brazenly and falsely announced as a papal surrender, but the only effect of his doing so was to bring down on his own head the denunciation of the militant Catholics. Guizot, a Protestant and a moderate man, who did not greatly care how the Catholics organized their education, withdrew, dismissed Villemain from the Ministry of Public Instruction and rebuked Michelet and Quinet. The only result was that he and his king lost the support both of the men of the right and of the men of the left, and his incompetence and timidity contributed substantially to the fall of the regime a few years later.

The story of France up till 1848 had been different from that of the other continental countries. Whereas the other countries had up till that date had absolutist governments, and it was against such governments that the revolutionaries rose in that year, France under Louis Philippe had already had a government which professed to hold liberal ideas on, at any rate, the theological plane, and in France it was liberal government which was overthrown. The Government of the Second Republic which succeeded to it was less opposed to religious education in the schools and universities than its predecessor. As a result the Jesuits' policy there of lying low and hoping that there would be a turn to better times proved successful. In 1850 the new Falloux law was passed, permitting freedom of education, and the Jesuits were able without interference to establish their colleges.

The position alike of the Church and of the Jesuits under Napoleon III was not to a superficial judgement unsatisfactory. Those who looked a little below the surface were disturbed at the readiness of ecclesiastics to allow themselves to be used as the supporters of Napoleon's policies. They feared that a day might come when they would have to pay dearly for this complacency and so it proved when Napoleon abdicated and fled the country after the defeat of Sedan. The Commune which for the moment seized power in Paris was bitterly anti-religious and particularly anti-Jesuit. The Archbishop of Paris, Darboy, was killed, as were fifty-seven other priests, of whom five were Jesuits. Eventually, government troops marched in and overthrew the Commune. They established what was for the moment a comparatively conservative government and what for a time looked like being a monarchist government. It ended the persecution of religion, but the freedom of religion appeared to be dependent to a dangerous extent on the survival of one particular and not very stable regime. The monarchies missed their opportunity owing to their divisions between Bourbons and Orleanists. The Third Republic established itself and showed every sign of becoming increasingly anti-clerical.

A number of Catholics – and indeed a number of Jesuits – foolishly insisted on identifying the Catholic cause with the monarchical cause, a foolish policy in any event, and doubly foolish as it became increasingly self-evident that the monarchical cause was not likely to succeed. Leo XIII on his accession attempted to rescue the French Catholics from the consequence of their own folly by proclaiming that there was no especial Catholic form of secular government and that it was the duty of Catholics to accept and respect in their country whatever form of government they found established, so long only as it was not condemned by religious authority for acting in flagrant violation of the moral law. The Third Republic, he insisted, could not be so condemned. It was the duty of Catholics to accept it. Yet this Papal démarche came too late and was too widely disregarded by French monarchists of the *Action Française* movement to check the steady growth of anti-clericalism among the politicians of the Third Republic.

This anti-clericalism was of course particularly directed against the Jesuits and against clerical interference in education – the bugbear of all French lay-clerical controversies. In 1880 Jules Ferry issued a decree which commanded the dispersion of the clerical staffs of all Jesuit colleges and the substitution for them of lay teachers. But it was not exactly obeyed. The Jesuits, through all their experiences in Catholic countries throughout the nineteenth century, had developed a technique of their own. When their expulsion was ordered by a government decree, they obeyed for the moment, and then, when the excitement died down, crept unostentatiously back and reoccupied the posts from which they had been evicted. This was what they did at this time, but soon afterwards the scandals of the Dreyfus case raised anti-Catholic feeling in France to a white heat. It appeared that men of distinguished Catholic families had not scrupled to defend perjury and to procure the terrible punishment of an innocent man because he championed a cause other than the Catholic cause. What, it was asked, must be a system of education that could inculcate such wickedness? So there was a renewed outbreak of demands for the suppression of denominational education and for the expulsion of the Jesuits in particular, though in fact the Jesuits had not been especially implicated in the campaign against Dreyfus. By Waldeck-Rousseau's law of 1901 the houses of all religious congregations, unless they had applied for and received authorization from the state, had to be vacated and their inmates expelled. The Jesuits knew that it would be pointless for them even to apply for such authorization and they left the country. Soon afterwards the Concordat between the Church and the French State was repudiated.

The German nation, as is known, is divided in rough equality between Catholics and Protestants. In the southern and Catholic half, where Austria was the leading power, the Jesuits had not been treated with favour in the years before the Revolution under Joseph II and it was only with some reluctance that they were allowed back into the country after 1815. Metternich, trained in the Josephist tradition of the *ancien régime*, was at first suspicious of them as men likely to preach an independence of the secular government. He persuaded himself that, whatever might have been true of the earlier Society, there was no danger of that in their restored form. The Jesuits could be safely trusted to support the Metternichian system. He therefore in 1836 gave them permission to establish their independent colleges anywhere within the Austrian Empire and especially encouraged them to set themselves up in Austria's Italian provinces of Lombardy and Venetia. This they did, and threw their influence against the Italian nationalist cause, thus in the long run doing themselves great harm.

On the other hand in Protestant Prussia, as has been said, under Frederick the Great the Jesuits had been hospitably received, even though that policy was reversed under Frederick's somewhat uncoordinated successor. After 1815 Prussia received as her reward what had previously been the prince-bishoprics of Mainz, Trier and Cologne, carrying an almost solidly Catholic population, in the Rhineland. As a result the Catholic proportion of the Prussian population after 1815 was much greater than before, and the Prussian government was careful in these first years to treat their new Catholic subjects very satisfactorily. The Prussian policy was to grant complete toleration to subjects of every denomination and to support them with a subsidy raised by taxation. In this way it was hoped to be assured of their loyalty. The result was that in these first years Catholics were in many ways better treated in Protestant Prussia than in Catholic Austria. In spite of this, the smaller Catholic countries of southern Germany generally preferred Austria to Prussia and took the Austrian side in the war of 1866. But after Austria's defeat in that war they acquiesced in that country's expulsion from Germany and accepted the fact that German unity could only be achieved under Prussia. They joined with Prussia in the French War of 1870 and afterwards became members of the Second Reich under Prussian leadership. Owing to the expulsion of Austria the proportions as between Catholics and Protestants in the Second Reich were different from those of the Holy Roman Empire or of the Confederation. In place of an equality, the Protestants outnumbered the Catholics by about two to one. Coincidentally with the Franco-Prussian War Italian troops entered Rome and – what was of more interest to Bismarck – the Pope proclaimed the First Vatican Council's qualified assertion of papal infallibility. German Catholics – Dollinger, Ketteler and others, for instance – had been fairly prominent among the Inopportunists who regretted the definition, and there were a number of people in Germany, as elsewhere, who thought mistakenly that the Pope's claim to infallibility somehow committed Catholics to a disloyalty to their secular rulers. Bismarck, a member of an old Protestant junker family, thought that with his Empire established and now no longer threatened from abroad, this might be a good opportunity to establish definitely the total superiority of the state over the Church in Germany. He launched the Kulturkampf. The most obstinate of the opponents of these Bismarckian claims were of course the Jesuits, and therefore it was only natural that one of the consequences of the campaign should be their expulsion. By a decree of 19 June 1872, the Emperor William I expelled the Jesuits, along with members of a number of other religious Orders, from the German Empire. After a time Bismarck found that his campaign was creating division rather than unity among the German people. Windhorst, the leader of the Catholic Centre party, maintained a vigorous resistance, and therefore Bismarck took advantage of Leo XIII's succession to Pius IX to open negotiations and bring the conflict to an end. By the settlement other Orders were allowed to return to Germany but not the Jesuits.

Among the terms of peace Leo agreed to procure, somewhat against his better judgement, that the Centre party would vote in the Reichstag for the government's military programme. What with good relations in Germany, the continuing breach between Church and state in Italy, and the violent anti-clerical government in France, Vatican opinion during the First World War on the whole favoured the German side.

TWELVE

The restored Society: II

It can be seen that the Pope's act of restoration was given a mixed reception in Catholic countries and in non-Catholic countries where the Jesuits had been allowed to establish themselves during the Napoleonic days. In England, as has been said, they had been allowed to settle at Stonyhurst under the title of the Gentlemen from Liège. The fact that they were not any longer Jesuits and that the Society no longer existed lessened, in English Protestant eyes, the danger of allowing them into the country. Thus the danger of their being attacked was increased by the formal reconstitution of the Society. It might well be argued, and indeed was argued, by people of some sense, that, Jesuits or non-Jesuits, the number of Catholics in England at that time was so minute that no sane man could suppose that they could subvert the realm, even if he supposed that they wanted to do so. In so far as there was any modicum of sense in the popular opposition to Catholic Emancipation, that sense could only be found by looking to Ireland with a population that was both Catholic and of doubtful loyalty to the British crown. It might be argued that there was a danger from the Irish Catholics. It could not be argued that there was a danger from the English Catholics and in fact, in spite of excitement and the turmoil of the times, there was never any serious question, even after the restoration, of the Jesuits being expelled from Stonyhurst.

The difficulty of the Jesuits in England in those years was not so much the hostility of Protestants as the hostility of other Catholics who feared that the presence of Jesuits in the country would arouse the hostility of Protestants against all Catholics. As has been said, the life of the Catholic minority in England ever since Queen Elizabeth's time had been bedevilled by the most bitter internal quarrels and these quarrels had been concerned with the question how far it was right for the Catholic to accept the nation's anti-Catholic political regime. After the final defeat of the Stuarts in the second rebellion of 1745 there was no longer any serious question of expelling the Hanoverians. The English Catholics were as loyal as any other subjects to the British throne, and indeed rather more anxious than others to proclaim themselves so in the hope that loyalty might win for them relief from their penal disabilities. Where Catholic disloyalty was found it was only among the Irish, and they were disloyal to the throne not because it was Protestant but because it was English. The Jesuits of the second half of the eighteenth century had quite abdicated from any ambition to play a part in English politics, but of course they could not erase the tradition of their name and therefore as a consequence many English Catholics and all the Vicars Apostolic with the exception of John Milner were opposed to the restoration of the Society in England. They thought that its return would arouse old prejudices and make more difficult the removal of the penal laws. A congress was held at Aix-La-Chapelle to protest against the restoration and both a number of English Protestants, led by Sir John Hippisley, a west country Member of Parliament, and a number of English Catholics attended it.

It has been mentioned that in the general experience of the Society in the hundred and fifty years since its restoration it has enjoyed a much more tranquil life in Protestant than in Catholic countries – alike in mother countries and in their colonies. Consalvi imposed on the Church the formula of an alliance of throne and altar. The Jesuits with disastrous fidelity accepted the formula and as a result naturally became involved in party politics, and involved on a side which was inevitably destined to go down to defeat. They were the natural victims of every liberal victory in every continental country, and, though they boasted of their tribulations as a mark of their fidelity to their faith and though it was indeed true that many of the enemies of the Church were men filled with an insensate hatred that defied all reason, still it cannot be denied that the leaders of the Society on the continent in the nineteenth century were often men who championed reactionary political programmes that were not justified by any teaching of the Church. They were men of a somewhat different calibre from a Canisius or a Suarez in the Society's earlier years. They supported the Ultramontane cause which pressed for an extravagant

definition of the scope of the Pope's infallibility. It was fortunate
that they were defeated. Who shall say what the English and the
American Jesuits would have done had they been in a position to
act like their continental brethren? The Jesuits have a very strong
tradition of verbal loyalty and they might have acted as their
superiors instructed them to act had it been possible. Happily it
was not possible. Their record in the nineteenth century was on
the whole peculiar but beneficent. It is easy to find in their writings
strong verbal expressions of sympathy with the continental
Catholic policies. Fortunately the Catholic bodies in England and
America were so weak that they had no chance of interfering in
their nations' politics and indeed on the whole, in so far as they
expressed opinions, tended to give their support in England to
the Liberal party and in America to the Democrats because in the
first half of the century the Liberal party in Britain was more
favourable to Catholic Emancipation and in the second half more
favourable to Irish Home Rule, as also were the Democrats in
America, in so far as it was their concern at all. While the Jesuits in
Rome were in favour of a strong Ultramontane definition of papal
infallibility, the English Jesuits were for a moderate definition of
the type which Newman or Dupanloup favoured and which
indeed was eventually forthcoming, and of course they earned the
disfavour of Manning for what he considered to be their insufficient loyalty to the Pope.

In their teaching, the conservative loyalty of the Jesuits to old
traditions and to the *Ratio Studiorum* made them slow to change.
In the early part of the century Catholics were still excluded from
the most important positions in English society and still of course
excluded from the universities. It was natural under these circumstances that they should lack ambition and in consequence tend to
take their school lessons lightly, since they did not think that they
would be allowed to derive any worldly advantage from them.
It was natural also that, since the Catholic schools existed in complete isolation from the general educational life of the nation, they
did not learn of any new techniques of teaching through picking
up the ideas of others. The curriculum of Stonyhurst, as everywhere else then, was entirely classical. The old Renaissance names
of the classes – Rhetoric, Poetry, Syntax and the rest – were preserved, as indeed they still are. There was nothing but good in

that. Discipline was strict and punishment, by modern notions, severe and frequent, but when we remember the barbarity that was tolerated at English Protestant schools in the early years of the nineteenth century we should hesitate to say that the regimen at Stonyhurst was more severe than that elsewhere. The great difference on that score between Stonyhurst and the Protestant schools was beyond doubt that the boys at Stonyhurst were under more rigorous supervision.

In 1840, when Catholics were still excluded from the ancient universities, Stonyhurst became 'affiliated' to the new non-denominational London University and its pupils thenceforward and for half a century took the London matriculation examination and indeed had a high record of success. They excelled perhaps to some extent because it was only the very undistinguished among non-Catholic schools who sent their pupils in for it rather than sending them to Oxford or Cambridge. Yet taking the London matriculation did not of course bring the student into personal contact with the non-Catholics, as would have happened had he gone to Oxford or Cambridge, and the Stonyhurst boy at that time lived of necessity a life of extraordinary isolation from his fellow citizens, so many of whom would have thought it a disgrace to be seen speaking to a Catholic. The isolation broke down very slowly. It was by no means a matter of merely passing Acts of Emancipation. It was only in 1874 that Stonyhurst was able to play its first cricket match against a non-Catholic school – Rossall – and of that match the *Rock*, a well known Protestant paper of the period, wrote:

How the Rossall pupils could have desired, or the Rossall masters could have sanctioned any match of the kind we are entirely at a loss to conceive. However it is some comfort to know that the Protestant youths were thoroughly well beaten, as they richly deserved to be. But have the masters never read the Bible? or have they forgotten the consequence – as recorded in its pages – of allowing Israelites to mingle in the Moabite games and dances? All these comminglings with Papists act as so many enticements to idolatry, and the masters who do not see this are unfit to manage a Protestant school. We would advise parents who have sons at Rossall to keep a sharp look-out.*

* Gruggen and Keating, *History of Stonyhurst College,* New York, Kegan Paul, 1901, pp. 158–9.

H*

A result of taking the London matriculation was that, in order to meet its demands, the curriculum at Stonyhurst after 1840 had to be modified so as to include a good deal more of science and mathematics than heretofore. These changes were introduced rather under protest from the Jesuits than as desirable in themselves and when in 1895, with Catholics by then allowed to go to the old universities, the school substituted the Oxford and Cambridge Higher Certificate for the London examination, it was considered as an advantage that the curriculum could now once more become predominantly classical.

Newman, as we know, did not think that Englishmen would ever accept Jesuit continental habits of supervision which he considered to verge upon espionage, and therefore believed that, if all Catholic education was left in Jesuit hands, there would be an insurmountable obstacle to the conversion of Englishmen. He founded his Oratory school in order to give to the converts' children an education similar in all but the most strictly religious way to that which they would have received at a Protestant public school. But Newman had never himself been at a public school and had that reverence for public schools which is so common among those who never attended one. He greatly underestimated their brutality. The consequence of importing ex-public school men to teach the young Catholics at the Oratory was, as soon appeared, that the boys at the Oratory were beaten a great deal harder than they would ever have been beaten by the Jesuits. While Newman set up a rival school to the Jesuits on the ground that the Jesuits were too Ultramontane, Vaughan, afterwards the Cardinal but at that time Bishop of Salford, himself an old Stonyhurst boy, refused to allow them to establish a school in his diocese on the ground that they were too little respectful of episcopal authority.

There can be no question of the fact of the contrast between Jesuit schools and Protestant public schools in the matter of supervision. The rights and wrongs of the matter are less certain than is sometimes pretended. It was the fashion of a society that was imbued with an unquenchable prejudice against Jesuits to argue that what they called espionage was wholly evil and arose entirely out of a sadistic wish to prevent the development of any independence or individuality in the pupils. One need not deny that some of the Fathers had from their discipline imbibed an excessive respect for mere conformity and that it would have been well had they allowed more freedom to the boys. Things have moved in recent years, but it is the Jesuit, as indeed it is the Catholic, custom to move slowly, and they are therefore often found adopting the customs of Protestant schools just at the time when the Protestants themselves are beginning to modify them – as, for instance, in inculcating a great respect for the forms of political life and for success in it just when the magic such systems hold for the rest of the community has so largely evaporated.

An incidental consequence of the progress of industrialism in nineteenth-century England was to change the nature of the Catholic body. In the early years of the century the small Catholic population of England fell into two parts – a few old and well-to-do landowners and the very poor Irish immigrants. The Catholics had few members among the middle classes. Over the last hundred and fifty years a steady proportion of Catholic families have raised themselves up from the lower to the middle classes. In spite of a dribble of conversions, Catholics of English origin, however important the most distinguished of them such as Newman and Manning may have been, were and are few in number. The Catholics in England are predominantly Irish, but a reasonable proportion of them are now middle-class, and it has of course been necessary to provide appropriate schools for their children. The Jesuits with their big town day schools that have grown up in Preston, Liverpool, Leeds and elsewhere as well as in London have made their contribution to the satisfaction of that need, and it is notable that when they had to reduce their commitments, owing to a reduction in the number of members of the Society and the need to maintain the missions in Rhodesia and Guiana, it was the boarding school of Beaumont which they sacrificed rather than one of the big provincial day schools.

The general reader's notion of Irish Jesuit schools is probably mainly derived from James Joyce's pictures of Clongowes and Belvedere in his *Portrait of the Artist as a Young Man*. It is not, and it is not intended to be, a flattering picture. The Jesuit tradition allows for harsh punishment but insists that that punishment should be in accordance with an understood system. The random brutality ascribed to Father Dolan is certainly not in accordance with any Jesuit tradition and, had it ever been exercised by one

Jesuit, it is hard to believe that it would have been supported by a superior as Joyce depicts. The Irish take more readily to corporal punishment even than the English and one need not doubt that the nineteenth-century Irish Jesuit schools were often severe. But Joyce's basic assertion was of an utter refusal to serve, which obviously implied a total defiance of that fundamental Jesuit principle. It is therefore not reasonable to expect from him a wholly balanced picture.

In the continental tradition of the last two hundred years, education has always been looked on as a weapon of state. In the Middle Ages education was the business of the Church, but a consequence of the victory of the *politiques* was that it became predominantly a business of the state and the state only allowed to the religious, Jesuit or other, such influence over it as they judged to be to the interest of the state. This conception of education Napoleon inherited in an extreme form from the *ancien régime*, and throughout the nineteenth century it was the ambition of all continental governments to control the educational system for their own advantage. Conservative governments thought that they could use the Church as their spiritual policeman. Liberal governments thought that the Church was a rival and enemy who must be fought. But both had essentially the same purpose of increasing their own power; they differed only over means. The English policy was to use religion as an instrument of policy more completely than any Catholic or continental country, but the religion which the English thought to use was not of course the Catholic religion but the Church of England. That Church had until the middle of the last century a complete state-guaranteed monopoly of all important education in the country. This fact had the happy accident of throwing Catholics in general and the Jesuits in particular on to the liberal side in British educational controversies. They were compelled to demand some freedom for everybody as that was the only conditon of obtaining freedom for themselves. Whether they would have demanded such freedom had the situation been different is a matter of opinion.

Obviously in Britain or in America the Catholics were and are in so small a minority that the question of their imposing their opinion on others did not arise. There were those who prophesied that if ever the Catholics got equality in Ireland they would use it to discriminate against others. In so far as it was expected that they would put obstacles in the way of Protestant education for Protestant children, the expectation has been singularly falsified. Protestant schools receive much more generous support out of public funds in Catholic Ireland than they are doing in any Protestant country, as indeed the Catholic schools in Northern Ireland receive much more generous support out of public funds than do the Catholic schools in England. In so far as it was desirable, as Newman thought, that in an age of the laity an increasing proportion of the teaching in schools should be entrusted to laymen, this development, which has gone forward rapidly in Catholic schools in England and America and nowhere more than in Jesuit schools, has been less wholeheartedly adopted by the Irish Jesuits. Since the only Church in Ireland that received state support was not the Catholic Church but the strongly anti-Catholic Church of the Protestant minority, the Irish Jesuits were under no more temptation than any other Irish Catholics to look with favour on claims that the ideal pattern of Church-state relations was a pattern of concordat. This meant that there was an inevitable difference of attitude and approach, even though it was not always fully recognized and admitted, between the Irish Jesuit and the continental Jesuit and, though the allegiance to Rome was always vociferously admitted in honorific generalization, in practice much less attention was paid to the teachings of Rome than was commonly admitted. This of course proved of enormous importance as the bulk of the Catholic population in the new countries of America and Australia were of Irish origin. Owing to their history they had none of the difficulty which continental, as for instance Spanish, Catholics might have had in reconciling themselves to the acceptance of the formula of those countries of a separation of Church and state, and when in our time at the Second Vatican Council the Church committed itself to a policy of religious liberty for all people, the Irish Catholics, for all the fervour of their own faith, had no difficulty at all in accepting such a policy. The Irish Jesuits were leaders in its acceptance.

The United States was of course of its nature a pluralist society, dedicated to religious freedom and to the separation of Church and state. There was no tradition of a state-Church, whether Catholic or non-Catholic. Therefore there was never any question of the federal government imposing a curriculum. It contented itself with small patriotic demands as for a salute to the flag but otherwise left school authorities free. Therefore the Jesuits in America have been free to develop their own policies without interference by the state and, since the Jesuit and other ecclesiastical authorities in distant Rome have been too unfamiliar with American conditions to exercise any effective control, they have in fact been as free of the Church as they have of the state. They have been able to go their way, hampered only by Bishops. Their schools do of course operate in America (as also in Australia) under one grave handicap. They receive no direct financial aid from the public funds and, as schools and colleges with the elaborate scientific equipment which modern education demands become steadily more expensive, it is an increasingly heavy burden. Had it not been for the spectacularly rapid increase of prosperity in America and Australia, it would doubtless have been a burden that was insupportable. As it is, the financial burden on the Catholic population, if it can be borne at all, is probably an advantage rather than a disadvantage to the Church. There is no more important service to religion than to devise methods of preventing Catholics from getting rich.

The United States had no Jesuit history similar to that of England in the sixteenth and seventeenth centuries, and had established itself as a land of religious freedom. In its first years of independence, opinion was still hostile to Britain and mindful that the country largely owed its freedom to Catholic France and Spain. At the time of the American War of Independence, Canada had only been won from the French some thirteen years before. It was therefore both the hope and the ambition of the Americans that they would get the Canadians to join them and thus be able to expel the British entirely from the American continent. They could not look for whole-hearted support from the inhabitants of Canada, since there were American Tories who, opposed to secession and driven out from the eastern colonies, had gone up into Canada precisely in order to remain under the British flag. But it was not unreasonable to hope that the French at any rate would take the opportunity to repudiate their unwanted allegiance to George III. The only problem was that of religion – of the fervent Catholicism of the Quebecois. Therefore it was reasonable to send up Father Carroll along with Benjamin Franklin to ask for Canadian support. But Carroll's hand was not an easy one to play. He might talk to the Canadians about American freedom but the Catholics well knew that, though indeed Catholics in England or in Ireland received far from satisfactory treatment, yet the Canadians as one of the conditions of their capitulation had been specifically promised freedom for their religion, whereas the Americans at the time of the Declaration of Independence had in their Address to the English People made the promise to maintain what they called 'a papistical establishment on the banks of the St Lawrence' one of the grievances against George III. Naturally enough therefore, Carroll did not meet with much success in Quebec.

After the war, Carroll and the other ex-Jesuits in America had no formal status and no financial resources other than those which the Carroll family could supply to them out of their private wealth. Yet they were determined to carry on with their missionary work. They sent a petition to Rome begging the Pope to regularize their position and to give one of them the faculties for granting dispensations and the like. Pius VI replied that they should have a Bishop and bade them elect one of their number. They elected Carroll, who was consecrated Bishop of Baltimore at Lulworth in England in 1790 and held the first Synod of Baltimore in that same year. The Catholic immigrations from Ireland and afterwards from the continent were still in the future. In general, the first founders of America were high-minded agnostics who a little prided themselves on their superiority to prejudices, whether in favour of or against religion. Europe was in their view inhabited by bigots and the fact that the Jesuits had won enemies for themselves in Europe was a reason why America should treat them with tolerance. Father Grassi, unable to find his way to China, was allowed to enter America and was appointed President of Georgetown. It so happened that the Society was restored at a time when the war of 1812 was still raging between Britain and America, and it was only a few days before the restoration that Father Grassi had watched from his windows at Georgetown the British fleet's bombardment of Washington. Carroll lived until 1815, and was then succeeded as Bishop by another ex-Jesuit, Charles Neale. Neale only survived two years and in 1817 with the restoration of the Society it was not considered necessary or desirable to have an American-born Bishop. A French Sulpician who was by no means favourable to the Jesuits, Bishop Maréchal, was appointed. The years were unhappy years in American Catholic history, but the developments were not wholly unfavourable to the Jesuits. The very fact that the main hostility to the Jesuits came from French priests and Bishops and that most of the Jesuits were American meant that the Jesuits, who in so many other countries had been looked on as cosmopolites and anti-national, in America appeared as the American Catholics. Fenwick in particular, one of the first students at Georgetown, was winning for himself a great reputation in New York where he had built the New York Literary Institute on the site of the present St Patrick's Cathedral and had gained the high regard of such men as de Witt Clinton, the Governor of New York, and Governor Thompkins, afterwards the Vice-President, who looked on him as a good American who was doing an invaluable work in teaching American ways to the immigrants from a foreign culture who could not be reached except through a priest and, in the view of such politicians, could never be reached satisfactorily except through an American priest. De Witt Clinton as a judge was responsible for the ruling that a priest could not be compelled to reveal in court any secret of the confessional. (A Father Kuhlmann had been resposible for obtaining the restora-tion to its owner of some stolen property but was supported by de Witt Clinton in his refusal to reveal the name of the thief.)

The American squabble had been between the French and the Irish. Back in the English days British priests – English or Irish – were both few in number and hampered by penal disabilities. On the other hand, up till the Seven Years' War the French, estab-lished in Quebec in the north and in Louisiana in the south, had plans to hem the British into the sea by a line of forts and then eventually, if all went well, to drive them into it and make them-selves the masters of all North America. Therefore fervour and policy combined to make them ambitious to send into the country as many missionaries as possible. Thus it happened that most of the few early Catholic priests there were French. Their small con-gregations were often French or at least French-speaking and even after independence there were French ecclesiastics who wanted the Church in the United States to remain under French control.

It was the English Jesuit Father Plowden who with two of his friends called on Benjamin Franklin in Paris to persuade him to use his influence to prevent this.

When later the Irish came, they had no use for French habits. They challenged the claims of the French language and bitter internal conflicts broke out. These conflicts came to a head particularly in Charleston in South Carolina, where what amounted almost to a battle between the French and the Irish broke out. Charleston was at that time in the diocese of Baltimore, of which Archbishop Maréchal was ordinary. Maréchal had not up till then been very friendly to the Jesuits but he thought that they were the men who might compose this conflict. He appealed to the superior of the Jesuits to send some men of his Order there to help Bishop England, whom he had appointed as Bishop, and Father Fenwick, Grassi's successor as President of Georgetown, was selected. Fenwick composed the conflict between the two languages by ascending the pulpit and there preaching a sermon in which the sentences were alternately in French and English. A new diocese of Charleston was created and England, its first Bishop, who had previously had strong prejudices against Jesuits, was quite won over and made Fenwick his Vicar General.

When Bishop Cheverus, who had been Bishop of Boston, was recalled to France to become Archbishop of Bordeaux, Fenwick, in spite of the fact that he was a Jesuit, was appointed to succeed him and the Bulls were sent direct to him without giving him any opportunity to refuse them. Now that the United States was an independent country it was obviously essential, if the Church was to make any progress, that the Bishops should be American rather than French. However tactful Fenwick may have been in Charleston in not too brusquely insisting that the French residents there be broken of their traditional habits, yet he had fairly clearly shown that he understood that American Catholicism must be firmly American if it was to achieve any prosperity. The American temper was not such that Americans would accept their religion from imported foreigners. It was therefore a wise move to put an American in place of a Frenchman in the see of Boston, and the emergency abundantly justified waiving the normal rule against Jesuits accepting preferment.

Fenwick, though an American born and willing to give his

congregation an American Catholicism, was in no way a brutal racialist. Catholicism in America had inherited from the French missionaries, Jesuits and others, the tradition that it was a Christian duty to fight the battle of the Indians against exploitation by the white man. If any Americans had imagined that with the departure of the French that great Catholic tradition would be abandoned, they were very quickly undeceived. The Indians to whom the earlier missionaries had especially ministered in that part of the world were the Abenakis. The Massachusetts whites had in 1724 murdered the Jesuit Father Rasle along with his Indian defenders for his championship of them at Norridgewok on the Kennebec. Bishop Fenwick erected there as a monument a shaft of granite with an inscription recording what had happened. This was too much for Massachusetts Puritans and they overthrew the monument, but Bishop Fenwick re-erected it.

After the first decades of the nineteenth century, immigrants – particularly from Ireland – began to pour into the country in sufficient numbers substantially to change both the racial and religious proportions of the population. The Anglo-Saxon Protestants, who had at the nation's birth so nearly constituted the whole population that they could afford to look with a whimsical and benevolent tolerance on the eccentrics who were not of their way of thinking or origin, now found themselves – or thought that they found themselves – threatened in their mastery of the country by ill-conditioned immigrants. The Constitution forbade overt attacks or prohibitions. Religious freedom had been guaranteed to all and the promise could not be openly broken. Therefore the menace must be combated by secret means. So there grew up the Know-Nothing movement. It was a movement which organized secret attacks on Catholic and other allegedly un-American institutions and it derived its name from the fact that, if any questions were asked as to who was responsible for the outbreaks, all were agreed to say that they knew nothing. There was a particularly gross attack on the Ursuline Convent at Charleston in Massachusetts. The chapel was burnt to the ground and the nuns shot at. The blackened ruins remained there for another fifty years. This Know-Nothing attack was never particularly an attack on Jesuits. On the continent of Europe in the nineteenth century, movements that were anti-Catholic were always with a special

violence anti-Jesuit, and the Jesuits were regarded as the worst
sort of Catholics and the most dangerous enemies of liberty. That
was never so in the United States: there was to be plenty of anti-
Catholicism, and Catholics were attacked on the ground that they
were not properly American, but among Catholics the Jesuits
were thought to be on the whole more American than were other
ecclesiastics. This was largely owing to the example shown by
Fenwick in these early years in rescuing the Church in America
from French domination.

In the United States the Jesuits, though at times the victims of
sporadic and illegal riots, yet enjoyed toleration and for the most
part the protection of the authorities. The greater number of the
Jesuits worked in the settled parts of the country where from small
beginnings they grew into a numerous company with seven
provinces, many schools and colleges, and over five thousand
members, but others of them carried on the Society's tradition of
missionary work among the Indians. They earned from the
Indians the name of 'the Blackrobes'. No one else of comparable
culture was willing to undertake social and educational work
among these tribes. Fair-minded Protestants paid full tribute to
their work. Senator Vest, for instance, in the debate on the
Indian Appropriation Bill in 1900 said:

> Some years ago I was assigned by the Senate to examine the Indian
> schools in Wyoming and Montana. I visited every one of them. I wish to
> say now what I have said before in the Senate, and it is not the popular
> side of the question by any means, that I did not see in all my journey a
> single school that was doing any educational work worthy of the name
> educational work unless it was under the control of the Jesuits. I did not
> see a single government school, especially day schools, where there was
> any work done at all. The Jesuits have elevated the Indian wherever
> they have been allowed to do so without the interference of bigotry and
> fanaticism and the cowardice of politicians. They have made him a
> Christian, have made him a workman able to support himself and
> those dependent on him. Go to the Flathead in Montana and look at the
> work of the Jesuits, and what do you find? Comfortable dwellings,
> herds of cattle and horses, self-respecting Indians.

Undoubtedly the greatest Jesuit missionary of the nineteenth
century on the American continent was Peter de Smet. Peter de
Smet was born in Belgium in 1803. He went out to Maryland in

1821 and shortly afterwards went out West. He worked first among the Pottewotians and then among the Flatheads. During his career he preached the Gospel to almost every sort of North American Indian across the country, and his four-volume biography records an enormous series of atrocities and cannibal feasts, the risk of being involved in which he had fearlessly run. 'Never,' recorded Archbishop Purcell, 'since the days of Xavier, Brebeuf, Marquette and Lalemant had there been a missionary more clearly pointed out and called than Father de Smet.' Though he was no American himself, he accepted the American doctrine of 'manifest destiny' and thought it inevitable that the Indians should be absorbed within the American system. That being so, he thought it best that they should accept their inevitable fate with as little bloodshed as possible, and made it his business to persuade them to accept it peacefully. He was largely successful. 'You can do more for the welfare of the Indians,' said Senator Benton to him, 'in keeping them at peace and friendship with the United States than an army with banners.' His greatest achievement was to arrange in 1868 the peace between the most colourful of the Indian leaders, Sitting Bull, and the Americans in the Upper Missouri.

Jesuits at the invitation of Bishop Seghers also made their way up into Alaska, where in these early days they lived and worked under conditions of almost indescribable suffering and where indeed they still remain among the Eskimos to this day. Others worked under almost equally terrible conditions in the wilds of British Honduras. In these days of underdeveloped countries and of threats of overpopulation it is easy for the cold-blooded to ask whether it is desirable that primitive people should recklessly increase their numbers, whether it is not in truth better that under-developed countries should come under the control of those who have the intelligence and the skill to exploit them. Such arguments are certainly often difficult to answer, but one cannot but be struck by the difference between those who ask such questions and the Jesuit missionaries who never thought of asking them, and who without question accepted that every man, however primitive, had the right to live and reproduce himself simply because he was a man. There was a simple-minded, unquestioning acceptance of the doctrine of the equality of man which in the modern schemes it is not always so easy to find.

As we have seen, much of the greatest work of the Jesuits in the years before their suppression had been their missionary work overseas in almost every country of the world. In 1773 three thousand Jesuits were on the missions. It looked – indeed it was so intended by their enemies – as if the suppression would bring their work utterly to destruction. Things did not in fact turn out quite as badly as that, partly because in a number of distant places the Jesuits merely continued with their work unaffected by the suppression, partly because in some places – in India, China, both Americas and elsewhere – it proved that the faith had been so firmly planted that it survived even without priests. Nevertheless, the blow was grievous. When the Society was restored Father Fortis, its first General, was not at first willing to commit it to missionary enterprises. The first necessity, he thought, was to reorganize at home. Father Roothan, his successor, reversed this policy. He sent out missionaries to Bengal, to Madura, Argentine, Paraguay, the Rocky Mountains, China. At home in Europe, Gregory XVI was one of the most ineffective of all the Popes, but he was at the same time a great missionary Pope. It was during his papacy that Macaulay wrote his 'Essay on the Papacy' and expressed the judgement that the papacy had regained in the new world more than all that it had lost in the old. It was under Gregory XVI that slavery was for the first time unequivocally condemned by the Church.

No place had suffered more from the suppression of the Society than the Philippines, which with the departure of the Jesuits had fallen into disorganization and been laid wide open to the raids of Arab slave-owners. The Philippines were very remote, and it was not until 1859 that the Jesuits returned there and established among the Filipinos Reductions on the model of Paraguay. When the Spanish-American War came at the end of the century American aggression was denounced as a threat to the Philippines' Catholic freedom, but as a matter of fact the Jesuits have enjoyed much greater security from the Americans than they could ever have hoped for had Spanish rule continued.

During the years of the suppression there were numerous massacres of the few Christians who remained in China. It was not until 1841 that the Jesuits returned there in organized form. The second half of the century in China brought them considerable success but it was a time of great difficulty. China was in a condition of continuing chaos. All Chinese have a natural contempt for 'foreign devils'. Who can say whether things would have been different had the policies of the early Jesuits been continued and a European Society remained there which, as in America, could have fought the battle of the natives against the exploiting traders? But as it was it was only natural that the Chinese should look on Christianity as a foreign and anti-Chinese force and that the Jesuits should suffer for policies against which in fact they had most vigorously fought and for their opposition to which they had suffered. The second half of the nineteenth century in China was filled with constant civil wars in all of which the Jesuits suffered. The European powers, in order to protect their commercial interests, seized Chinese ports and imposed upon the Chinese the capitulation by which they were forced to recognize European rights to exemption from submission to Chinese authority. As one result the missionaries came under European protection. There was doubtless no alternative, but the consequence was that Chinese suspicion of missionaries as mere envoys of Western imperialism was greatly increased. Everywhere except in European-held Shanghai missionaries were in danger, and there were frequent massacres. At the turn of the century came the great Boxer rising. In this anti-foreign rising some four hundred Christian villages were destroyed, and thousands of Christians were killed, including five Jesuit priests.

Up till the end of the eighteenth century, the Protestants had sent virtually no missionaries to India. The only missionaries there were the Catholics who followed in the footsteps of Xavier – predominantly Jesuits. The early years of the nineteenth century showed the British finally victorious over the French and the masters of India. During that century – and particularly after the 1840s – Protestant missionaries in India increased, but the British government was not especially favourable to missionaries, whether Catholic or Protestant. It did not forbid them; where they succeeded in curbing or suppressing such obviously barbaric cults as suttee it even applauded them. But the general attitude of the British government was that the condition of peaceful British exploitation of India was that the British should refrain, and should make it clear that they refrained, from interference with the

customs and above all with the religion of the natives. As between
rival missionaries, the government's sympathies were naturally on
the whole Anglican since that was the religion of the government
officials themselves and since the Anglican missionaries were predominantly Englishmen who might be presumed to share the
imperialistic point of view, while the Catholic missionaries,
though there were a few English Jesuits for a short time in
Calcutta in the 1830s, were overwhelmingly foreign. For instance,
the Jesuits in the nineteenth century were German in Bombay,
Belgian in Calcutta, French in Madura and Italian in Mangalore.
With the 1914 war the Germans had to withdraw from Bombay
and the British government insisted that a British Jesuit, Archbishop Goodier, be sent out as Archbishop. Yet with these
reservations the government, while giving no assistance to the
Catholic missionaries, put no obstacles in their way. If they did not
meet with spectacular success it was not because of any ill will
from the British government but because of the Indian custom of
polygamy and their caste-system.

The main hostility to Catholic missions came indeed not from
the government or from any Protestant rivals but from the
Goanese who, even when the country at large had passed into
British hands, thought that the Portuguese and through the
Portuguese, the Goanese had the right to control all Catholic
activity in India, to hold all the ecclesiastical posts and to resent the
establishment anywhere in the country of any non-Portuguese
Catholics. In 1841 Gregory xvi ordered the Society to reopen its
Indian missions. The Pope created at once a number of Vicars-
General throughout India who were to be independent of the
Portuguese metropolitan Archbishop of Goa. The Goanese refused
to accept the arrangement and went into schism. Nevertheless the
Jesuits started their colleges in Calcutta and Bombay, but they received no support, financial or any other sort, from the Goanese
who formed the majority of those who had been Catholics there,
and it was uphill work. The only district of India in which the
Jesuits met with any very notable success in the nineteenth century
was Chota Nagpur, where the Jesuit Father Lievens learnt the local
language and law and made himself the champion of the exploited
peasants, thus winning considerable numbers to the faith.

In the Turkish Empire ever since the time of the Crusades

France had by tradition been recognized as the leading Christian power, and it was natural enough that the Jesuit work in Muslim countries should be entrusted predominantly to the French Jesuits. It was not easy work. The chances of converting Muslims to Christianity were very small indeed. On the other hand there are a variety of Christians of various rites scattered throughout these lands, some in communion, some out of communion with Rome. Two years after the restoration of the Society, the Bishops of the Levant petitioned the Pope to send back the Jesuits to their diocese and in 1831 Gregory XVI ordered the Society to undertake missions to Syria. For a time it looked as if the prospects for missionary work there and for the Jesuits were fairly rosy. The French and the Turks were in alliance against Russia in the Crimean campaign and – even though not for the best of reasons – it appeared that the consequence of that would be that the Turkish government would give generous treatment to Catholic missionaries, at any rate so long as they were French, as the Jesuits were. But it turned out, as was less fully understood at that time than it would be today, that there was a great difference between the Islam of the Turks and the Islam of their Arab subjects. The Arabs felt no need to concern themselves with the ambitions of the great powers. The only Christians that they saw were the unbelievers in their midst. The Sultan's policy was very unpopular with them and in 1860 the inhabitants of Syria rose up in protest against the Sultan's concessions to Christians. They massacred all the Christians of Damascus and the neighbourhood and among many thousands who perished were five French Jesuits. The Jesuits remained in the Turkish Empire throughout the remaining fifty years of its bloodstained and chaotic history.

Whatever the ups and downs of domestic French Catholic fortunes, anti-clericalism in French eyes was, as Gambetta said, 'not for export'. Just as the government sent the Jesuits to Turkey with the hope of increasing national influence there, so they sent them into France's new African colony of Algeria. The first notable Jesuit in Algeria was Father Brumauld, who established an orphanage there. It won the high praises of Marshal Bougeaud who, like Senator Benton with Father de Smet among the North American Indians, was of the opinion that judicious missionary work might be a very economical method of saving the expense

of military expeditions. 'Try to make Christians of these young-
sters,' he said. 'If you succeed they won't be shooting at us one
day from the undergrowth.' But it soon appeared that missionary
work among the American Indians and missionary work among
the Muslims were very different propositions. Muslims have
everywhere proved themselves much more strongly resistant to
proselytism than any other kind of non-Christian. To begin with
the Jesuits were allowed to mix with and to accept into their
orphanage the Muslim children, and to make friends with them.
But after a time the authorities reached the conclusion – rightly or
wrongly, and perhaps rightly – that their activities aroused more
hostility among the Muslims than they made converts. Cardinal
Lavigeries strongly supported the Jesuits in their missionary
efforts. Marshal MacMahon, the Governor, opposed them.
Napoleon III so long as he was on the throne supported the
Jesuits, and Cardinal Lavigeries was able to continue his support
in the years immediately after Napoleon's fall. Admiral de
Gueydon, who came out as Governor in 1872, when the republican
regime was still conservative, continued the support of the
Jesuits, but by 1880 anti-clericals were in power in France and
their belief was that it was only possible to hold Algeria by appeasing the Muslims, and the Jesuits with their unconcealed ambitions
of making converts were recalled from the land.

Other Jesuit missions were established in Africa in the nineteenth century, in outlandish places like Fernando Po or
Madagascar, and in sophisticated places like Egypt. In so far as
they were staffed by Fathers from the countries of continental
Europe, or were in European colonies, they all suffered from the
handicap of instability since they were at the mercy of the domestic
politics of their motherland. The mission of the English Jesuits in
Rhodesia was of course in this respect more fortunate and has
continued unbroken to this day. Though the Catholics in
Rhodesia, both white and black, are a minority, they have had at
least a continuity of history, and the Jesuits have succeeded in
building from heroic beginnings a stable Catholic community.
As long as Rhodesia was able to keep mercifully free of politics the
Jesuits there were able to continue on their way unimpeded. Later
less happy developments in the country have brought complica-
tions to them as to everybody else. In the Congo to the north of

Rhodesia Belgian Jesuits established themselves. It was their misfortune that they had no choice except to establish themselves to some extent as the protégés of King Leopold and therefore inevitably suffered as a consequence of his misdeeds. The war of 1914 of course dealt grievous blows to all the Jesuits in Africa, operating as they did with scanty money and scanty manpower.

THIRTEEN

The Jesuits and the *aggiornamento*

As the world moved towards the First World War, Father Wernz, the Society's General, gave in October 1910, with what seemed to some a strange optimism, his account of the 'flourishing condition' of the Society. He wrote:

There are five new provinces; a revival of the professed houses; new novitiates, scholasticates, tertianships and courses in the best colleges for students of special subjects; and a superior course for Jesuit students of canon law in the Gregorian University. Next year there are to be accommodations for 300 theologian [boarders] at Innsbruck, which institution will be a Collegium Maximum for philosophy, theology and special studies. The novitiate is to be moved to the suburbs of Vienna. In the province of Galicia sufficient ground has been bought to make the College of Cracow similar to Innsbruck and a beautiful church is being built there. The province of Germany though dispersed has built in Holland an immense novitiate and houses of retreat, and the Luxemburg house of writers is to be united to the Collegium Maximum of Valkenburg. The Holland province has more diplomated professors than any other in the Society and is about to build a new scholasticate. Louvain is becoming more and more a house of special studies. In England the Campion house at Oxford is continuing its success and there is question of moving St Beuno's. The Irish province is looking for another site for the novitiate and juniorate and is using the University to form better teachers. Canada is looking for another place for its novitiate and so are Mexico, Brazil and Argentina, while Maryland is trying to put its scholasticate near New York.

Not much remains to be done in Spain. However Toledo has established a scholasticate in Murcia, and Aragon is planning one for Tarragona. France is dispersed, but it has furnished excellent professors for the Biblical Institute and the Gregorian University. In the mission of Calcutta 130,000 pagans have been brought to the faith and in one Chinese mission 12,000. The numbers could be doubled if there were more workers.

It was somewhat ironical that within a week of this report the revolution in Portugal, leading among other things to the expulsion of the Jesuits, was to break out, but much more important of course is that the whole world was moving towards its catastrophe of four years later. The World War naturally enough brought suffering and inconvenience to Jesuits as to everybody else, but, whatever catastrophes in the shape of the growth of Communism and the rise of Nazism might be the final consequences of the war, the immediate pattern which it left was one less unfortunate for the Church and the Jesuits than was the pattern of the world immediately before the war. If it be true, as is often said – and with some plausibility – that Vatican opinion on the whole wanted a German victory in that war, yet German defeat, once the danger of a Communist rising in Bavaria and elsewhere had been contained, did not bring any attacks on the Church. The Church and the Jesuits enjoyed reasonable freedom during the years of the Weimar Republic. It is true that in the secession states of what had been Austria-Hungary the Catholic cause had been identified with the Hapsburg cause and therefore the new regime was not favourable to the Church in Czechoslovakia, and in the newly formed Yugoslavia the Catholic Croatia was harshly ruled from non-Catholic Serbia. The effect of the identification of the Church with Hapsburg politics was that intellectuals in the secession states were so complacent in their contempt for Catholicism that they were quite extraordinarily ignorant of it. Take, for instance, Thomas Mann's belief, confessed in *The Magic Mountain*, that there were laymen going about in the world who were 'secret Jesuits' – a notion culled out of the bogus *Monita Secreta* of three hundred years before.

On the other hand an independent Poland had risen again. In France, whether because of the superiority of Catholic generals or the patriotism of priests who had not attempted to evade and had gallantly performed their military service, there was a reaction against anti-clericalism and the Jesuits and other Orders were able to return. In Italy Benedict xv repealed the *non-expedit* which forbade Catholics to be either elected or electors in the nation's Parliamentary life and a Catholic party, the *Partito Popolare*, under the priest Dom Sturzo, was able to make itself the strongest party in the Italian Chamber. When Mussolini came in and made the

Lateran Treaty the Jesuits were able freely to return, and under the leadership of such men as Father Tacchi – Venturi played a part of the first prominence as advisers both to Pius XI and to Pius XII. But, as the wise Pope Benedict XV had seen, this was a brittle good fortune. The Church ever since 1815 had committed itself to the belief that the ideal relationship between Church and state was a relationship of concordat and that the Catholic who was compelled to live under a government that did not give special favours to the Church was a Catholic living under a certain handicap. The belief was not only held by the early nineteenth-century, not very intelligent, Popes, but was specifically reaffirmed by the much more far-seeing Leo XIII at the end of the century. Even at the time of the Lateran Treaty Pius XI seems greatly to have underrated the dangers of a concordat with Mussolini, though bitter experience was later to prove to him all too clearly how great were those dangers. When Hitler seized the German Chancellorship, although up till then Catholics had been forbidden to support the Nazi party, yet the Vatican with dubious wisdom made a concordat with the new government. In a world in which even in nominally Catholic countries only a proportion of the population believed or practised the Catholic religion – as, for better or worse, was the situation in Europe in the modern age – it was fairly obvious that a demand for special privileges from the state would inevitably lead to criticism, and a Church which made such demands in fact identified itself with a political party and could not hope for more than intermittent favour, interspersed with periods of discrimination as the other side took its turn to be in power.

By a curious paradox the only Catholic regions where in the nineteenth century, and indeed since, the Jesuits enjoyed security are countries under Protestant rule – Malta, Ireland and Quebec. In England and America their prosperity has been uninterrupted. The reason for this is that they have been there prevented by circumstances from involving themselves in controversy and taking political sides. They may as a matter of theory have professed that it was a misfortune that they did not live in a Catholic country and could not claim the full privileges of a concordat. They had had to accept their Constitutions and indeed to some extent have been inhibited by some of the conditions of canon law, such as that which demands that a superior only hold

office for a limited time; but in practice they have found a much
greater freedom to manage their own affairs and to lead their own
lives than in so-called Catholic countries, and the wiser of them
have been very well aware that they enjoyed much greater freedom
of action in a free, pluralist society. In fact, as Newman saw,
Catholicism can only really preach its gospel effectively in an
atmosphere of the free intercourse of minds, and such an atmosphere is much more likely to be found in a pluralist than in a
wholly Catholic society.

Jesuits in Catholic countries under the too strong discipline of
their rule tend too much, as indeed do religions of other Orders,
to give official text-book answers derived from conditions of a
past age that are no longer relevant. In modern times, confronted
as they generally are in Catholic countries with a mere rejection of
the faith, they have all too easily replied with a mere reiteration of
traditional answers. In Protestant countries they have not been
able to escape from the company of men with differing positive
ideas, and the more the old notion of two segregated communities living without contact with one another has waned, the more
have the Jesuits, whether they wished it or not, been compelled
to give their minds to the discovery of a new language in which
to answer new objections.

The relations of the Society to the Pope have of their nature
always been close, and, while Jesuits in some distant land are not
so intimately affected by the personality of the Pope of the
moment, the policy of Roman Jesuits is very much dependent on
this accident. Thus the Jesuits of the early half of the nineteenth
century were in general devoted to the absolutist policies of the
Popes of that day. When Pius IX ascended the throne with notions
of constitutional reform in his head, he for a time tended to be a
little critical of the attacks of some Jesuits such as Rozaven on
Rosmini's good will towards the Italian nationalist cause, but after
the débâcle of his anticipated reforms he turned to the Jesuits and
the Jesuits to him. Similarly when Leo XIII came to the throne
and more intellectual policies at the Vatican came into fashion,
these policies came also into fashion among the Jesuits. Roman
minds broadened and Roman interests widened with the death of
Pius IX, and Jesuit minds along with others. The Society in the
last quarter of the nineteenth century was certainly a Society of

more intellectual life than it had been in the previous three-quarters.

The Jesuits joined with the Pope in adumbrating a Catholic social policy. Jesuits were prominent in Leo's revival of Thomism and he raised to the cardinalate two of the leading Jesuits of the day, Mazzella and Franzelin. Under Pius x, with his Jesuit confessor, the Jesuits at Rome were prominent in the campaign against Modernism, while the Jesuit Father Tyrrell was the leading Modernist in England and the movement had a few Jesuit followers elsewhere. Under Benedict xv the Jesuits, who each with a few exceptions supported his own national cause in the First World War, were perhaps less influential. According to French law as it then was, all clerics were liable to military service, and the French Jesuits, though scattered in exile all over the world, returned to the number of 855 and accepted combatant posts under the colours. It was customary, at any rate in allied circles, to praise their patriotism, but in fact it was not altogether easy to see on what principles a dedicated religious should think it more important to fight in a war in which there was hardly a pretence that his side was more Catholic than that of his opponents than it was to spread the Gospel. It was an example of the curiously tense hold which nationalism had acquired at that time over minds, even over Jesuit minds, that such a thing should ever have been thought. It was doubly absurd when at the same time 534 exiled German Jesuits returned to fight on the German side, 293 as combatants, 180 as chaplains, and 151 as stretcher-bearers. At the same time Father Bernard Vaughan, the popular English Jesuit preacher of the day, was winning a reputation for his patriotic English sermons. The attitude of all of them was in somewhat marked contrast to the highly responsible Christian thought of Pope Benedict xv, who appreciated to the full, as few at that time did, the supreme catastrophe of the war and bent all his energies to bringing it to an end – unfortunately without success.

To Benedict xv a European war was essentially a civil war, the only result of which could be the destruction of the hegemony of European civilization. He bade the peoples of Europe rise above their national rivalries and recollect how much more they had in common than they had in difference. By Pius xi's time the world was faced with a new issue. Communism in Russia appeared to threaten the whole structure of Christian civilization. It could not be said of Communism, as it could have been said of the pre-war European governments, that as between it and its opponents both were a mixture of good and bad and it was a matter of six to one and half a dozen to the other. Under Pius XI and Pius XII the attitude of the Church towards Communism was one of stark antagonism. Under John XXIII and Paul VI there have been some modifications, but these involve no contradiction. Fanaticism usually lasts only for a period. With the Calvinists and the Jacobins there was for a time no alternative but to fight the Church's remorseless enemies. Then with a new generation fanaticism abated, people were willing to live and let live and the Church was able with the descendants of the fanatics to establish a certain measure of peaceful coexistence. So it has been in our time with the Communists – or at the least it has been the hope of the last two Popes that it is so. Whether their hopes will be realized is still not quite certain. Ripeness is all, and there is no reason to think that all four Popes were not quite right – each in his own day. In all four reigns the Jesuits have obediently co-operated with papal policy, but even under the two earlier Popes that policy was by no means one of mere blind antagonism, and there were no priests who played a more vigorous part in exploring the Catholic prospects in Communist countries than the two Jesuits, Father Walsh and Bishop D'Herbigny.

Under Pius XI the Jesuits played a large part in Vatican policies. Such priests as Father Tacchi-Venturi were prominent in the negotiations of the concordat with Mussolini. On the ideological plane Pius XI in no way abated from the rigour of Pius X. It was in these years – though the world knew little of it at the time – that Father Teilhard de Chardin met with his first difficulties at the hands of authority. The young Teilhard was by this time developing his belief that original sin was no more than a present flaw in a world in evolution and destined eventually to be overcome as creation moved towards its Omega point. By 1924 Teilhard's views had fallen under the disfavour of Cardinal Merry del Val, previously Pius X's Secretary of State and then Secretary of the Holy Office, the main architect of the anti-Modernist campaign. What is most unpleasant about the events of that year is not so much that Teilhard's views fell under scrutiny – for there was indeed much in them that required explanation – as the suspicion as to the methods used to incriminate him, the suspicion that a manuscript was stolen from his desk at the Institut Catholique and sent to Rome. On Merry del Val's command Teilhard was summoned before his Provincial, Father Costa de Beauregard, and required to sign a paper that he would neither say nor do anything 'against the traditional position of the Church on the matter of original sin'. He refused such a demand as altogether too vague. He was prepared to say, 'I undertake not to spread abroad or to proselytize on behalf of the explanations contained in my note'. The Jesuit authorities wished to be accommodating but Rome was implacable, and Teilhard was compelled to sign a document repudiating his views on original sin. Yet it was, he confessed eight years later, his opinion that 'original sin (under its present form) opposes at every point the expansion of our religion on the natural level'.

Whether Teilhard's views were correct or whether they were compatible with Catholic teaching is one matter, and a formidable case could be made out that they were not; but, as in all the Modernist controversies, the question was not so much whether the ecclesiastical authorities were right in what they were defending as whether by their methods of defence they were not doing incomparably more harm than any that they could possibly be preventing. It was not altogether surprising that as a result of his treatment Teilhard should have lost, as he confessed, belief 'in the immediate and tangible value of official directions and decisions'. But his grievance was of course against Rome – not against his Jesuit superiors whose only fault was that they had perhaps been too submissive to Rome's commands. The Jesuits were often spoken of as all-powerful at the court of Pius XI. But they had a price to pay for their high favour. Teilhard was sent out to China and commanded to confine himself to scientific work. He was unable to get his *Milieu Divin* published. There were further episodes of thefts of manuscripts from his desk in order to be sent to Rome. He was told that the Jesuit Order was not 'an Order of pioneers' – an extraordinary and illuminating remark considering the early history of the Jesuits, and indicative, one might have thought, had this judgement been general, of a very great departure from the original nature of the Society. In the event the

I

treatment of Teilhard has had exactly the opposite effect to that which was intended, as policies of repression usually do. There is much that is questionable in his beliefs, but, if it was thought desirable that such beliefs should not have been published, through posthumous publication they have received incomparably wider circulation than would otherwise have been the case, and indeed in certain circles have been accepted not merely as contributions to the debate but, in a manner that Teilhard would certainly have considered comic, almost as if they were infallible pronouncements.

The intimate ties between the Pope and the Society which had made it almost inevitable that, so long as conservative policies were in favour at the Vatican, these should also be the policies of the Society, meant equally that when Pius XII called for the first reforms and when Pope John XXIII called for an *aggiornamento*, the Jesuits should respond to that invitation. It was their vocation to be papal, but they had no vocation to be more papal than the Pope. It was natural enough that some among the Jesuits, as among other priests, found a certain difficulty in adjusting themselves to the new ways – in particular to the liturgical changes – and naturally it was as a general rule the old who were set in their ways who disliked changes and the young who were *avant garde*, but there was no inevitability about this. For instance, the Pope of the *aggiornamento* was an old man and in England the most prominent Jesuit advocate of moral reform and of the Church's involvement in a condemnation of nuclear weapons is the septuagenarian Archbishop Roberts.

It so happened that the General of the Jesuits, Father Janssens, died during the third session of the Vatican Council, and his death necessitated, according to the Constitutions, the summoning of a General Congregation – the thirty-first Congregation of the Society – to elect his successor. It met on 7 May 1965. The Congregation consisted of the Provincials and two elected representatives from each of the sixty provinces of the Society. Its first session lasted from 7 May to 5 July and was then adjourned until September 1966, so that its final decrees might be delayed until the Vatican Council had itself issued its decrees. In so far as the Council's task was to recognize the change from the Tridentine attitude of defence against a hostile world to the Johannine attitude of dialogue with the non-Catholic and non-Christian world, and in so far as the Tridentine pattern of the Church was so largely the pattern imposed upon it by the Jesuits, it was natural enough that the call for *aggiornamento* should carry with it a call to the Jesuits to re-examine their policies. The hundred and fifty years of the Society's second life had been years of a remarkable expansion by any statistical calculation. The reconstituted Society had grown to almost double the size which it had achieved at any previous time in its history. There were thirty thousand Jesuits, where in pre-suppression days they were never more than about twenty thousand (it is of course true that the world's population had greatly increased). They had taken up their missionary work to which their traditions had invited them and more than seven thousand had made their way into every continent of the world. They had more than doubled from seventeen thousand to thirty-six thousand since the First World War. Their growth had been most notable in North America and there were now eight thousand four hundred Jesuits in the United States. It was true that, as with other Orders, there had been a certain decline in the years since the war. Novices were not coming in as fast as they used to do and – what was more disturbing – the number of those who left during the course of their studies was alarmingly large. Their numbers were down over the years since the war by a hundred and nine.

The Congregation fully recognized, as perhaps the Jesuits at the time of the Society's restoration had not, the necessity for self-reform. The first problem to which they gave their minds was that of their highly centralized and authoritarian Constitutions. In the Ignatian system the General was elected for life by the Congregation, itself consisting exclusively of senior members. Nowhere else in the Society's life was there any trace of an election. All other posts were filled by the General's appointment. Superiors were changed at least every six years. Each Provincial had to make a report to the General once a month, each superior once every six months. The Congregation made no attempt to limit the powers of the General, but it recognized that beneath such an avalanche of paper the machinery must almost inevitably become clogged. The great disadvantage of overcentralization at Rome, whether among Jesuits or any other Order, was not so much that wrong or unjust decisions were made as that it took such an inordinately long time to get any decisions made at all. The Congregation

I*

therefore decided that the General should have a cabinet of four General Assistants and that they should not be appointed by the General but elected by the Congregation. Provincial Congregations hitherto had consisted of the forty senior professed Fathers of each province. The fact that longevity was the only qualification for membership meant that their influence was likely to be conservative. It was decided that in future the members of the Congregations should be elected. The exact method of their election was not settled, it is true, but at least this reform meant that the younger Fathers would have a chance of exerting influence. Father Arrupe, the General elected in succession to Father Janssens, strongly supported this change. 'We must certainly meet the needs of youth which are the demands of our time,' he said.*

The distinction between professed Fathers of the four vows and 'spiritual coadjutors' who took only the three vows, which had up till then been based almost entirely on examination results, was reduced almost to a rule of formality. On the other hand no attempt has been made as yet to give the General Congregation, even though it is in future to contain elected members, an individual equality of 'one man one vote' rather than an equality between provinces. The Congregation will consist of three members from each province irrespective of the strength of the province. The United States has eight thousand four hundred members divided into eleven provinces. Italy has two thousand members divided into five provinces. Thus the Italian Jesuit will be almost twice as heavily represented in a Congregation as the American.

The new General, Father Arrupe, is a Basque, the first since Ignatius, but though his origins are not dissimilar from those of the founder, his career has been very different. As he served his novitiate and did his studies during the time when for political reasons the Jesuits were expelled from Spain, he was brought up in Belgium and Holland. His working life has been spent mainly in Asia – particularly in Japan. He was at Hiroshima when the atom bomb was dropped. He has lived a life that has made him fully aware of the great development of our times which forbids the Catholic from any longer thinking of the Church as a predominantly European institution. His judgement on Teilhard de

* *Herder Correspondence,* November 1965, p. 321.

Chardin shows that he has travelled far beyond those who believed that truth is likely to be the outcome of policies of repression:*

It is possible that he did not foresee all the implications or consequences which could be drawn from certain of his views. It must however be affirmed that the positive elements far outnumber the negative or debatable in the work of Father Teilhard. He crowns his work with a spiritual doctrine where the person of Christ is not only at the centre of each Christian life but at the centre of the world's evolution – like St Paul who affirmed that 'all things are held together in Christ'. It is impossible not to see the value of Teilhard's message for our days.

Father Arrupe introduced a novelty into the customs of the Society by his readiness to hold press conferences and to give television interviews, which astonished a world that had been accustomed to think of Jesuit Generals as mysterious and secret men who issued orders for which they gave no reasons and demanded only 'blind obedience', as of a corpes, from their subordinates. He issued bulletins of his intentions to his subjects, which informed them not only of the reasons why he was doing what he was doing or saying what he was saying but also of the reasons which might be urged against him and by which he might conceivably be judged wrong. There were those who thought they could detect signs that the Society was moving towards some form of parliamentary constitution.

This was no doubt an exaggerated view, but it was more important to look at the changes in the educational system than in the Constitutions. Here of course the General's hands were to some extent tied. Pius XI in his *Deus Scientiarum Dominus* of 1931 had laid down the outline of the modern *Ratio Studiorum* within which reforms had to be contained. The two main points on which reform was possible were the unusual length of training imposed on the Jesuit and the highly 'scholastic' nature of their studies. The Jesuit's career up till now has consisted of two years' novitiate, from which all studies are excluded, then, in many provinces at any rate, three or four years of a university course, three years' philosophy, three years' teaching in a college, four years' theology and then finally a year's tertianship. For many the years of training were still further lengthened by special studies for a doctorate.

* *Herder Correspondence,* November 1965, p. 322.

The result is that the Jesuit who goes to his novitiate from school at eighteen or so is in his thirties before he becomes a priest.

There can be no dispute about the wisdom of the Council of Trent in checking the pre-Tridentine custom by which ordination was treated as a casual affair, requiring no preparation, and it is to the Council of Trent and very largely to the Jesuits that the Church owes its whole modern seminary system. Whatever the particular defects that may be today alleged against seminaries, it would not be reasonable to challenge the general virtue of the system. But it is clear that in the name of tradition, applied without discrimination in changed circumstances, the Jesuits were in fact enforcing a highly untraditional system. The Jesuits of the first generation were, as we have seen, almost all young men. Laynez and Salmeron were dominating the Council of Trent, Canisius was reconverting Germany, at ages at which under modern circumstances they would probably not yet have been ordained and certainly would not have been in any position of independent authority. The Society by its Constitutions has imposed upon itself an enormous handicap by denying itself the use of the untrammelled energy of its young men. The difficulty has arisen of course because under modern conditions it is correctly thought desirable to give as many Jesuits as possible a course at a secular university as a part of their training, and that course is simply added on to the Jesuit training, making the sum total inordinately long. The courses themselves were tied too closely to scholastic methods at a time when such philosophy was coming increasingly under criticism even in Catholic society and its methods increasingly unfamiliar to the world at large. Lectures in the Jesuit colleges were still in Latin. Tests were largely a matter of repetition in what were called 'scholastic circles'. Extreme rigidity of method meant that the Jesuit went out into the world talking to an unnecessary extent a language unfamiliar to those among whom he was to move.

To meet these criticisms, the Congregation issued a decree on the reform of studies consisting of forty-seven paragraphs. The most important of the reforms in studies were that in lectures the vernacular is substituted for Latin, the number of lectures is reduced, teaching will in future be tutorial rather than by formal lecture and 'circles' are abolished. Examinations can now be repeated so that the candidate is not automatically excluded from the *cursus academicus* by a single failure, nor will the admission to the full degree of the professed, henceforward rather a title of honour than a title to any real privileges, be in the future dependent solely on examination results. Instead of the total exclusion of all studies from the first two years of the novitiate a course of theology is to be taken. The lines between theology and philosophy are to be less rigidly drawn and the period of school-teaching between philosophy and theology is probably to be cut out. At the same time there was also decreed the abolition of the old rule by which houses of professed Fathers were forbidden to take stipends for saying Masses. In fact they had always been dispensed from the rule and the notion that a professed house could be entirely dependent on casual alms was not realistic. The abolition of the rule was little more than the removal of an anomaly and of course the individual Jesuit is still bound to personal poverty and even the revised rule forbids any Jesuit from refusing a spiritual service on the ground that no honorarium is forthcoming. But the old rule that forbade the acceptance of honoraria has been abolished.

The most dramatic outcome of the Congregation was the Pope's address in which he named the fight against 'atheism' as the special task to which the Society was called in the modern world. To this day it is not very clear exactly what the Pope meant or what he wanted the Fathers to do about it. Naturally any Jesuit is by his profession compelled to repudiate atheism and his dedication to the greater glory of God automatically involves him in an obligation to fight against the denial of God's existence. Did the Pope mean that in these ecumenical days those who thought that the battle of the day was against Protestantism or even against other religions were living in the past? That it was more important to defend the general cause of religion? It seems that he was concerned to protest not so much against those who professed a formal atheism as against the nihilists who deny any purpose in life beyond themselves, who use their 'weapons to destroy at the roots all sense of religion and all that is holy and pious'.

Father Arrupe in his press conference seemed at some pains to show that to fight against atheism did not in any way mean that the Jesuit was called upon to divide the world crudely into the sheep and the goats of good formal believers and bad formal unbelievers. 'The Pope's call,' said Father Arrupe, 'must make us direct our efforts to unbelievers as well as believers. We must draw closer to unbelievers than in the past, to help them to overcome the prejudice which keeps them from the faith. We must for pastoral reasons try to penetrate the mind of the modern atheist and look for the motives of his confusions and denials.'* There were, he argued, three possible attitudes of the Catholic and the Jesuit towards the society by which he was surrounded. There was the attitude of the ghetto – to shut himself away from the wickedness of a godless world. There was the attitude of the anathema – to denounce the wickedness of this godless world. And there was the attitude of the dialogue. It was this third which he and the Pope recommended. It imposes upon the members of the Society an obligation to play a most full part in the social work of the Church, in its work for combating racial antagonism, for breaking down the barriers of inequality, for helping the underdeveloped countries and for the prevention of war. 'The battle against atheism,' Father Arrupe was later to say during an interview given to the Bilbao *El Correo Espagnol*, 'is identical in part with the battle against poverty which was one of the causes of mass exodus of the working classes from the Church.'†

In the world outside the Society the question had been raised whether the special direct vow of the Jesuit to the Pope will be an obstacle to the full working of the new system of episcopal collegiality. In any normal circumstances the fact that the Jesuit is dedicated to the service of the Pope will in no way mean that he does not loyally work with the Bishop in whose diocese he finds himself. But the experience of Benedict xv when the Pope spoke out so bravely against the horrors of a world war and received so little support from national Bishops, each one dedicated to the patriotic acclamation of his own particular cause, seems eloquent of the dangers in allowing untrammelled authority to local Bishops. After all in the sixteenth and seventeenth centuries it was national Bishops who sold the Catholic cause alike in England and France and Germany. A Society whose dependence is directly upon the papacy may possibly have again in some exceptional circumstances a part to play even in this respect. Cardinal Spell-

* *Herder Correspondence*, November 1965, p. 324.
† Ibid.

man happily had no authority to speak even for the American hierarchy but his reckless defence of the American bombing in Vietnam as a holy action is evidence of the still surviving dangers. On that issue the majority of American Jesuits have, it is true, preserved a discreet silence. Some – mainly among the older members – took a traditionally patriotic line of 'My country right or wrong', but some, such as Father Berrigan and Father Kilfoyle, vigorously opposed the war. It is of course true – and not only true but inevitable and healthy – that there are differences of emphasis and approach between one Jesuit and another. Individuality is far more marked among members of religious Orders than in the secular world at large. An incident at Cambridge in the early months of 1967 when Father Christie prevented Archbishop Roberts from addressing an audience of undergraduates gave evidence of it in a somewhat ridiculous fashion. *The Tablet*'s Rome correspondent wrote at the time of the first session of the Congregation:*

It is part of the Jesuit genius to be many-sided and flexible. The spirit which sent Ricci to China, Nobili to South India, Xavier to Malacca, has always been completely integrated with that which built the mannerist and baroque churches of western Europe and gave a solid and sometimes rigid structure to neoscholasticism (in its Roman version at least). The same men who helped to produce a Catholic version of that indigenous, even idiosyncratic phenomenon, the English public school, could run slum parishes or preach fashionable missions. A Henri Perrin and a Teilhard de Chardin have been fashioned by the same Exercises; so have a Rahner and a Messineo, a Bea and a Lombardi.

The Congregation met again as arranged in October 1966, when Father Arrupe again addressed it. He argued that the Society was then facing a certain 'crisis of confidence'. The Society had its extreme critics who argued that it was of its nature an instrument for a Church under siege and for one in which the supreme need was for a rigid obedience. A Church of dialogue was a Church in which there was no place for such a Society. The more moderate argued that the Society could indeed find a place for itself in such a Church, but to do so it must be willing to adapt its ways. The rigid regulation of the amount of prayers to be said and the amount of asceticism to be practised, laid down by the *Spiritual*

* *The Tablet*, 12 August 1967.

Exercises, is cramping and destructive of freedom. The Society, it was said, must reform itself. Military obedience must give way to a system of democratic decisions.

Father Arrupe, refusing to surrender to panic, was yet willing calmly to consider the degree of truth that there was in each of these criticisms. With quiet humour he was able to point out that some of the supposedly novel demands were not really so novel as their proponents imagined. Progressives and conservatives alike all too often talk as if the highly special arrangements of the nineteenth century, whether in Jesuit life or in other forms of religious activity, are immemorial traditions which had been handed down from the very foundations of the Christian religion. Father Arrupe frankly confessed:

We cannot deny that we have experienced in dealing with our scholastics and priests a lack of ardour or enthusiasm, a lack of confidence in their vocation. The most serious business in our Congregation is to distil all the good contained in the numerous proposals and requests of our young men and properly to channel that force and dynamism. This is absolutely necessary. We are dealing with a biological or social law which is irresistible. We should not try to resist it unless we wish to bring a complete upheaval.*

He was willing to admit that directors of retreats had on occasion perhaps been guilty of wooden lack of imagination. Father John Roothan, General in the early years of the nineteenth century, had set on the *Exercises* an unfortunate parrot-like mark, and Victorian hagiology had dehumanized such characters as St Aloysius. The systematized and mechanized type of meditation satirized by James Joyce in his *Portrait of the Artist as a Young Man* was not to be uncritically accepted. Yet Father Arrupe was not prepared to admit any possibility that the Jesuit life could dispense with the *Spiritual Exercises,* or the examen of conscience or the annual eight-day retreat. It is of course certainly true that the Church of the ghetto of the nineteenth century did too readily equate obedience and humility with a wooden acceptance of the lightest word of a superior, and was strangely blind to the corrupting effect of uncriticized power on the superiors themselves and to the dangers and evils of a total loss of independence. Victorian Jesuits erred in this not so much because they were Jesuits as because they

* *Herder Correspondence,* April 1967, p. 119.

were Victorians. Power corrupted religious superiors in that age but power also corrupted tyrannical parents. Blindness to the corrupting force of power was the great evil of the age. As Yves Congar has written:

The Catholic Church since the sixteenth century has put into practice a genuine 'mystique' of authority in which the influence of the Society of Jesus has doubtless played its part. This 'mystique' may be characterized as the notion of a complete identification of God's will with that of the institutional form of authority. In the latter it is God himself whose voice we hear and heed. The fairly wide margin which the Middle Ages still left for the subordinate's appraisal was for all practical purposes reduced almost to nothing.*

Ignatius in the sixteenth century had demanded of the Jesuit a chivalrous loyalty to the Society and his superior. He had made no demand for an unreasoning literal obedience. Such an excess of subordination, if it was to be found at all, was a corruption of the nineteenth century, with its fear of a recrudescence of the Revolutionary spirit.

Of course long before the time of Pope John or of the General Congregation there had been alive in some quarters in the Society a reaction against any conception of a merely slavish obedience as the supreme virtue. 'The spirituality of St Ignatius,' said Father Arrupe, 'was not a martial or a military one.'† That reaction was most vigorous among some of the English Jesuits, to be found for instance in the works of Father Martindale and Archbishop Goodier. It was perhaps nowhere less prevalent than in Rome and in the Latin countries where every misfortune of the Society was too easily ascribed to the wickedness of its enemies and not sufficient consideration given to how far the members had sometimes brought their misfortunes on themselves by their obstinate adherence to conservative courses. Father Martindale, rejecting alike any notion of disloyalty or revolt against the *Exercises*, at the same time equally rejected the notion that they were a sort of *sortes Virgilianae* which contained within themselves the automatic solution to every passing problem. On the contrary, what the *Exercises* did was to teach a process of self-training, armed with which and guided by the Holy Spirit, the retreatant could then go

* *Herder Correspondence*, April 1967, p. 119.
† *The Tablet*, 12 August 1967, p. 873.

out and more confidently solve for himself the problems of the world. Ignatius' ideal of obedience, thought Father Rahner, was not a matter of drill-ground commands but a subtle method of persuasion based on a complex understanding of human nature. 'Today,' said Father Arrupe, 'it is not a question of revealing the light as it was formerly but rather of teaching men to live independently and developing their human personality.'* The greatest of the Jesuits – Ignatius himself at Rome, Canisius in Germany, Ricci in China – have been those who have taken the trouble most fully to understand those with whom they have been called upon to work, and have not sought to battle them down with anathemas but rather to discover what it was that they believed and to find methods to lead them on from their partial truths to the fuller and total truth of Christ. Mistakes have of course been made over the centuries. There have been overcautious superiors who have repressed what they should not have repressed and broken the spirits of the enthusiastic. There have been the imprudent improvisers who have not remembered the distinction between building on foundations that already exist and totally rejecting the past. What else was to be expected, human nature being what it is?

There had grown up in the seventeenth and eighteenth centuries a certain tradition of spirituality which, instead of teaching the Jesuit to preserve himself indeed from 'the vain honour of the world' while remaining physically in contact with the world, compelled the novice and the scholastic to shut himself away from the world, with the result that when later duties called on him to mix with the world, he came to it unnecessarily ignorant. The new reforms are designed to remedy these anomalies by increasing the facilities for contact with the world even during the early years of training, and by giving even the younger the opportunity to obtain representation and to express their opinions in their provincial congregations. The story of the Second Vatican Council itself is an ample refutation of any notion that the Jesuits in recent years have failed to produce their full quota of the Church's leaders. It is only necessary to point to such names as those of Bea, Jungmann, Daniélou, John Courtney Murray or Karl Rahner as examples to the contrary, all of them so prominent at the recent Council. If it be true of the nineteenth century that the Jesuit

* *The Tablet,* 12 August 1967, p. 873.

tradition of culture, though high, was somewhat narrow, and that superiors – not through ill will but through a philistine unfamiliarity with walks of life that they were not called upon directly to tread in their formal course of studies – were lamentably blind to the service to religion that might have been rendered by such a man as Gerard Manley Hopkins, that is certainly less true today. Happily the time has by no means come to make any final estimate of the standing of such a man as Father Peter Levi, but one can certainly say that his superiors have treated him with more understanding than their predecessors treated Hopkins.

'Christ chooses you. The Church sends you. The Pope blesses you', said Pope Paul VI to the Jesuits' Congregation, and the whole story might have passed off with no more dramatic verdict than that, in loyalty to a Pope who had called for *aggiornamento*, the Jesuits had set themselves to the task of reshaping their Society to meet the needs of the twentieth century or, it may be, even of the twenty-first. 'We must start to prepare our novices for the twenty-first century', said Father Arrupe to the Rome correspondent of *El Correo Espagnol* on 31 July 1967. It might be argued that the need to combine progress with a respect for tradition prevented such developments from being dramatic, but they were nevertheless real – if more rapid at some points than at others. And that would perhaps have remained about all that there was to be said. Nor indeed would much more have been said had it not been for the apparently surprising allocution which the Pope addressed to the Congregation at its closing session in November 1966.

Throughout the sessions of the Congregation the Pope had treated the Fathers with an especial consideration. He had concelebrated Mass with some of their leading members in the Sistine Chapel – a quite signal honour – and had warmly embraced them after his allocution. It was therefore a surprise to the world when the next day it read in the report of a News Agency:

Pope Paul reproached the Jesuits this morning and said that he had heard 'strange and sinister rumours involving spiritual slackness and worldliness.' He told Father Arrupe and 220 priests that he was 'astonished and grieved at the reports received'. He did not specify what the charges were. A résumé issued by the Jesuit Information Service said 'he had spoken frankly of the fears some had been communicating to him about the future course of the Jesuits. These rumours suggested that the Jesuits intended to embark upon revolutionary changes or were abandoning their traditions that had for centuries made them such a powerful force in the service of the Church. These rumours would never have arisen if the Order had remained faithful to St Ignatius.'

It is true that when one checked with the announcement from the Jesuit Information Service, one found that the Service only issued the words in quotes from 'he had spoken' to 'service of the Church'. The sentence about unfaithfulness to St Ignatius was a gloss of the secular agency. The words that followed the quoted passage in the release of the Jesuit Information Service were: 'He reassured his hearers that he was completely satisfied that the Society of Jesus had in fact simply worked out a programme of inner renewal and reform in its way of life and work that answered the demands of the Second Vatican Council.' It also included the words: 'He wished to take this occasion and the solemn setting of the historic Sistine Chapel to make a solemn declaration of confidence in the Society of Jesus and to renew the mandate first given by Pope Paul III to ecumenical work more than four centuries ago,' and other words of confidence. The full text is therefore a good deal less unqualified than the message which the secular agency released to the world, and the secular press of the next few days certainly indulged in its familiar habit of making the best it could out of a story. In a few days, as is also its habit, other news crowded it out of the headlines and the whole story was largely forgotten by the general world. Still, even when the qualifications are understood, there did remain the incontrovertible fact that the Pope had given some strong expressions of anxiety about what was going on in certain Jesuit circles. The story was made more puzzling but not less disturbing by the not uncommon Vatican habit of using language so vague that when the pronouncement had been made no one could be certain who was being censured or for what he was being censured. Yet it is commonly said that the Pope's strictures were especially directed to certain extravagances among some of the Dutch Jesuits, though neither they nor anybody else were mentioned by name.

As is known, the Dutch, who previously had a reputation of being outstanding among Catholics for their rigid obedience, have a little surprisingly in the post-war years constituted themselves the *enfants terribles* of the Church. Jesuits have long played a prominent part in this campaign of ultra-radical criticism. In September 1962 Father van Kilsdonk, S.J., chaplain to the Catholic undergraduates at the University of Amsterdam, delivered a very vigorous attack on the Roman curia. The Holy Office demanded his resignation but Cardinal Alfrink refused to support the demand. In 1964 there came up the affair of *De Nieuwe Linie*. The *Linie* was a well-established Jesuit paper which had for many years appeared under exclusively Jesuit control. When it ran into financial difficulties, that control was transferred to a lay body who continued to produce it under the name of *De Nieuwe Linie*. It was dedicated to the promotion of the dialogue between the laity and the clergy, but its editorial board still included three Jesuit Fathers, and four other Jesuits were regular contributors. It was outspokenly radical in its criticism of ecclesiastical policies and in April 1964 the then General of the Jesuits, Father Janssens, forbade the Jesuits to be associated with it any longer. Two months before he had closed down altogether the Flemish Jesuit paper, *De Vlaamse Linie*. It was said that the prohibition of *De Nieuwe Linie* was issued in defiance of the advice of Cardinal Alfrink and a number of prominent Dutch Jesuits. The Dutch Provincial, Father Terpstra, went to Rome to attempt to prevent it, but, according to reports, the General refused to see him.

It is generally believed that the General's action was taken as a result of three articles that had appeared in the paper. The first was an article discussing the raising of the ban on clerical celibacy. The second was an article by Father Arts, S.J. on the Eucharist, which seemed to call in question Christ's presence there – at any rate in any generally accepted sense. The third attacked the policy of censorship with special reference to some restrictions put on the activities of Father Rahner. Protests were particularly strong among the younger Jesuits, and Father Terpstra on his return from Rome took the unusual step for a Jesuit superior of meeting his theological students and giving them an explanation of why he had accepted the orders of Rome. Father Schoenmaeckers in an article in the Zurich paper *Orientierung** argued in explanation of the young men's protest that 'what is lacking is a spirit of internal liberty needed to confront the tasks of the moment'. He spoke of

* *Herder Correspondence*, August 1964, p. 242.

the lessons which the older men had learnt from the sufferings of the war but added: 'The younger generation who have grown up since the end of the war never experienced similar conflicts and cannot quite accept as genuine what is expressed with so much fervour by their elders.' Father Schoenmaeckers fears that he finds in Dutch Catholics:

An attitude which would abolish all tensions between Church and world, hierarchy and laity, nature and grace. This is always the great temptation of highly developed civilizations, indeed of the rich, to submit God to a given situation instead of submitting the situation to God. The effect is to turn the service of God into a service of man, to regard evolution as the source of revelation and to degrade Christianity to a mere ideal method for the improvement of human relations.

These controversies have been fanned to a yet more angry blaze by the controversies that have broken out over the so-called Dutch catechism which was produced in the closing month of 1966. This document was not a catechism in the sense in which that word is commonly used – not a record of questions to be asked of and the answers to be given by the orthodox. It is rather an exposition of the teaching of the Church as it emerged from the Second Vatican Council. Most of it is quite unexceptional and it has been issued with the full approval of the Bishops, but there are a few passages which it is surprising to find in a document that claims to be an official apologetic of the Catholic Church – most surprising among them that which suggests that the virginity of Our Lady is an open question. A group of conservative Dutch Catholics were disturbed at the catechism's untraditional expressions and sent a protest against it to the Pope. The Jesuit Father Schoenenberg, professor of dogmatic theology at the University of Nijmegen, has replied with articles which, though far from clear, seem to consider at least as open such questions as the virgin birth and the Resurrection. There is a danger of a school of Dutch Catholicism, to which some Jesuits are attached, attenuating their faith until it is concerned only with the affairs of this life and seems to differ but little from popular humanism.

Whether the Pope's criticisms were directed at the Dutch Jesuits or elsewhere, whether it would have been better if he had made them more explicit, the object of them more clearly pointed – these things are as they may be. But the general purport of the allocution, taking one sentence with another, was clear enough. There were causes for concern, but it was by no means the Pope's mind that the day for the Society had passed or that its members deserved some general censure. Warnings were indeed to be issued against excesses, but in general the Society was to go bravely forward into the new age, confident that in that age new and essential tasks awaited it.

The future

In such times as these, when the future of the world and the future of organized religion are both so wholly unpredictable who can say in what shape the Catholic Church will survive this century and, still more, what future is likely to await a particular Order such as the Society of Jesus? The prophets of today have strangely reversed the roles which they have been accustomed to assume throughout the greater part of history. In the past it was the worldly, indifferent to religion, who were content to eat and drink and be merry, to bid the morrow take care of itself, having no doubt at all that it would securely come, nor was there ever a time when civilization felt more sure that it had finally and irrevocably established itself than during the second half of the last century and the years of this century up till 1914. Men were willing out of curiosity to listen to the calculations of the physicists who told them that the solar system would burn itself out – but that was some comfortable millions of years away. H. G. Wells told them that we might be invaded by men from Mars, but it was thought of as no more than an exercise in ingenuity. Nobody really believed it or thought that Wells really believed it. His readers who asked for serious prophecy preferred his demonstration that the aeroplane could never play a significant part in war – which seemed to them more in tune with common sense. Among Christian writers there were those who like Chesterton in his *Napoleon of Notting Hill* light-heartedly prophesied the coming of civil war, when:

> the barricades shall blare
> Slaughter below and smoke above
> And death and hate and hell declare
> That men have found a thing to love.

but no one imagined, any more than Chesterton did that, even at the height of civil war the omnibuses would cease to run on time or it would be impossible to order a five-course luncheon at a restaurant.

As the early years of this century slipped by, the probability of an Anglo-German war visibly increased. English Christians assumed that there would be such a war and that the English would win it. German Christians assumed that there would be such a war and that the Germans would win it. There would doubtless be a transfer of some colonial possessions from the vanquished to the victor, but few – save Pope Benedict xv – thought that the general hegemony of Europe over the world would be challenged. The worldly took the security of civilization entirely for granted. It was only a few among the religious-minded – and some among them commonly thought of as cracked – who warned of an imminent second coming of Christ and a world in immediate danger of destruction. Man, it was thought, had made the world secure. Only God could shake its security and He happily was not at all likely to do so.

Today it is just the other way round. Though now people do not talk constantly about it any more than they talk of the imminence of their personal death, yet if by chance the conversation strays that way, it is often the secularly-minded who confesses that he thinks it almost inevitable that sooner or later hydrogen weapons will be employed and the whole human race destroyed, or at the least the fabric of civilization be shattered, and it is only among men of religion that we hear the robust voice of a John xxiii pouring scorn on the 'prophets of doom' or of a Teilhard de Chardin professing to perceive the traces of an inevitable evolution. The attempt to build an Order independent of God has proved clearly a failure. In face of its failure the nihilists abandon hope, while it is the believers who look to God to save man from his own incompetence.

Though robust faith may justly rebuke the prophets of ultimate catastrophe, it is of course merely a fatuous optimism which foresees an easy triumph over all difficulties. The Church is perhaps

Though doomed to death, yet fated not to die.

Yet no one could deny that, by superficial tests at any rate, the

Catholic Church and all other forms of organized religion are today steadily losing ground. The proportion that attends churches is everywhere on the decline, the number that rejects the religious solutions is on the increase. On the moral conduct of men and women it is not easy to pass statistical judgements as it has always been the custom of all men, and was particularly the custom of the Victorians, to sin but to be careful not to publish their sins. Defiance of the Christian code is certainly more publicly proclaimed than it was in previous ages, and, even though one cannot be certain, few would doubt that defiance is also more common in practice.

Naturally enough the serious thinker does not draw from such facts the dramatic conclusions which might be drawn by the superficial. He is neither so alarmed as those who are but superficially religious nor of course prepared to join with those who welcome a decline of religion as a triumph for freedom. He accepts and faces the fact that, for instance, religious vocations among the Jesuits and other Orders are for the moment somewhat on the decline. He feels less certainty that the decline will persist. There is a pulse of rise and fall in such matters over the generations and it is as probable that people will after a time grow weary of the pace and racket of modern life and will turn once more to the tranquillity of religion. The phenomena are too complex for facile interpretations. The religious instincts are fundamental to man. They are of course sometimes denounced by religion's overt enemies, but religion has little to fear from the professed atheist. The very violence of his repudiation of God is a certain tribute to God's reality. Who would bother so much with quarrelling with mere nonsense?

A far more dangerous attack on religion is the attack of those who assent to religion, take it for granted, forget to be surprised at its mystery and accept it as a part of the established order. Religious bodies have always been betrayed from within far more effectively than they have been attacked from without. It is because of this danger that the Christian religion throughout all its history has required from time to time to be purged by attacks from without and has emerged the stronger from the attacks. It is suffering from those attacks at the moment, and, short of the world being physically destroyed by man's use of his new weapons, there is no reason to doubt that religion will, as in the past, emerge the stronger from being purged by the attacks upon it, and then again in its turn be damaged by the corruptions of success. What the details of its new organization will be, no one can say. Yet there is no reason not to expect that the Society of Jesus, whatever its future numbers, will have an important part to play in the shaping of the organization. The Society is ideally formed for such a task. Whatever the verdicts to be passed on particular opinions of Teilhard de Chardin, the warning to him that the Society was not 'an Order of pioneers' was an extraordinary one. To pioneer was exactly the task for which the Society was founded and it is a commentary on how far the Society had temporarily lapsed from its true nature that members of it should at that time have used such a warning.

Heresy, it has often been said, is an exaggeration of one aspect of truth at the expense of the balance of the whole, and therefore it is the natural business of the Church always to be suspicious of mere fashion. In every age certain truths are in fashion and certain truths are neglected. It is the business of the Church – and of such an organization within the Church as the Society of Jesus – to redress the balance by insisting on the unfashionable truths. It was for this reason and not out of an unhealthy masochism that St Ignatius prayed that his Company might always be unpopular. So today when Pope John has called on the Church for its *aggiornamento* it has certainly been the duty of the members of the Society, along with other Orders and with every individual Catholic, to reform their own house and to purge their lives of those mere inheritances from the past or habits of language which may be an obstacle to the performance of their tasks in the modern world. Yet fashion is a double danger. There is a danger of being behind the times. There is an equal danger in a too great eagerness to be up to date – to be merely, as the phrase goes, 'with it'. Whatever the merits or demerits of the particular contentions of the Modernists, no religious movement has ever chosen for itself a more ridiculous title than they – as if it could be the task of a religious leader merely to discover what his contemporaries were saying and to repeat it. The fate of the Modernists has been, as anyone could have foreseen for them, that they have become very rapidly out of date. So among the Jesuits in our time there have doubtless been some who, formed in their ways, have been too reluctant to change with the times. Indeed, the Society's critics until recently most commonly criticized it for being too conservative – determined to impose upon its members and its pupils a rigidity of discipline which the modern world neither needed nor was prepared to accept. There have apparently been others, so the Pope tells us, who have changed too rapidly and been too anxious to adapt themselves to the mere fashions of the world. But the solid programme of the Society is concerned, as Father Arrupe's words show, not with the past nor even exclusively with the present. A new age is coming as a new age was coming four hundred years ago. And just as in the sixteenth century Ignatius forged the weapons that were to conquer in the seventeenth, so it is now the task of the Jesuits to prepare themselves to play their part in the world that is coming. The Society, as Father Arrupe has said, is working for the twenty-first century. It is for that that it is now preparing its novices.

The Jesuit Order is very far from being monolithic, as its external critics imagine or as some of its members have at times pretended. There is no body wherein a greater divergence of character is to be found. That being so, it is peculiarly difficult to prophesy with any confidence the future of the Society. Within it, as everywhere else in the Church, are to be found in the present crisis the so-called integralists and the so-called progressives – those whose first anxiety is to preserve the traditional structure of the Church and those whose passion it is to throw as wide open as possible the doors of salvation and to welcome in all who can possibly be welcomed. It is natural that on the whole among the Jesuits as elsewhere in the Church it is the elderly, who have been brought up in the old ways, who are most reluctant to change and the young who are impatient of traditional restrictions, but the very fact that the octogenarian Jesuit Cardinal Bea – to take only one example – has been the leader in the battle for Christian unity is an ample proof that this is more than a mere conflict of the generations. It is a battle that could not expect to be fought out without its casualties. There were bound to be those who fell by the wayside – some discouraged because the Church seemed to them to be losing its moorings, others discouraged because it did not seem to them to be moving fast enough. Such there have been both among the Jesuits and elsewhere. They have not been especially prevalent among the Jesuits, but they, with others, have had their casualties. It is inevitable that in a time of readjustment and *aggiornamento* there should be a certain falling off in the numbers of vocations. It would have been unhealthy – an evidence of excessive formalism – had it not been so. What the future will provide, who shall say? It may be as some think, that in the bustle of the modern world there is no place for the contemplative. It seems more probable that after a time some people will find the very bustle of life intolerable and will demand in increasing numbers a refuge from it. These things as a general rule go with an ebb and flow like a tide. The phase in the nineteenth century when the Society allowed itself to be identified with conservative and excessively authoritarian causes was an untypical one, and no matter how detailed problems may be settled, there can be little doubt that the Society will broadly associate itself with the new ways of *aggiornamento*, destined to conquer alike in the Church and in the Society. There is every probability that the Society will with its accustomed flexibility adjust itself to the new world and play in it a part as large as that which it played in the old.

✦

Bibliography

The bibliography of the history of the Society of Jesus is immense. In his *The Jesuits in History*, America Press, 1941, Loyola University Press, 1962, Father Martin F. Harney has listed some thousands of books on the subject in a bibliography entitled 'Partial bibliography of the Society of Jesus'. No purpose would be served by producing Father Harney's full list since anyone wishing to consult it can turn to his book. It will be sufficient to state the main basic sources of the history.

The two sources of general bibliography are Heimbucher's *Die Orden und Kongregationen der Katholischen Kirche*, Paderborn, 1934, which contains a large bibliography in its second volume; and, in French, Sommervogel's *Bibliothèque de la Compagnie de Jésus*, Toulouse, 1930, brought finally up to date by Father Rivière.

The basic general history is covered by the *Monumenta Historica Societatis Jesu* begun in 1899 by the Spanish Jesuits in Madrid and now published by the Institutum Historicum in Rome, the *Acta Romana Societatis Jesu*, begun in 1913 and published in Rome, and the *Archivum Historicum Societatis Jesu*, also published in Rome. There is also Albers' *Liber Secularis*, published in Rome in 1914. Prior to Father Harney's book, the most recent general American-written history of the Society was Father Campbell's *The Jesuits*, New York, 1921. Fülop-Miller's *The Power and Secret of the Jesuits*, New York, 1930 (English translation) is also of interest.

In every country the Society has produced the history of its own fortunes. It would take too much space to attempt anything like a full list, but Father Tacchi-Venturi's *Storia della Compagnia di Gesù in Italia*, Rome, Milan, 1910–22, Father Astrain's *Historia della Compania de Jesus en la assistencia de España*, Madrid, 1912–25 and Father Rodrigues' *Historia de Compania de Jesus na Assistencia de Portugal*, Porto, 1931, have won fame outside their own countries. Janssen's *History of the German People*, London, 1896–1910 (English translation), deals with the fortunes of the Society in that country at length, and Father Fouqueray's *Histoire de la Compagnie de Jésus en France*, Paris, 1910–25 tells the story of the Society in his country up till the time of its suppression there. The official history of the Society in the British Isles is to be found in Foley's *Records of the English Province of the Society of Jesus*, London, 1877–83 (7 vols. [in 8]). The story has recently been retold in more popular form by Father Bernard Basset, *The English Jesuits*, London, 1967. The American story is to be found in Father T. Hughes' *History of the Society of Jesus in North America* (*1580–1773*), London 1907–17 (4 vols.).

The story of the suppression has been most notably told by Crètineau-Joly in *Clément XIV et les Jésuites*, Paris, 1856, and Father de Ravignan in *Clément XIII et Clément XIV*, Paris, 1854; and of the Society's survival in Russia in Father Zalenski's *Les Jésuites de la Russie-Blanche*, Paris, 1886 (French translation).

The volume of work on the foreign missions is overwhelming. It would perhaps be best to confine one's mention to works of general writing as, for instance, Cunningham's *A Vanished Arcadia*, New York, 1924, about Paraguay, or even the more modern play on that topic, Fritz Hochwaelder's *The Strong are Lonely*. Incomparably the best source for early Jesuit activity in North America is, of course, *Jesuit Relations and Allied Documents*, edited by Reuben Gold-Thwaites and published in Cleveland, 1896–1901 (73 vols.).

Jesuit educational policies have been studied by Fitzpatrick in *St Ignatius and the Ratio Studiorum*, New York, 1933, by Father Donnelly in *Principles of Jesuit Education in Practice*, New York, 1934, in Father Farrell's *The Jesuit Code of Liberal Education*, Milwaukee, 1938, and in Father McGucken's *The Jesuits and Education*, Milwaukee, 1932.

The three basic works on the Society's constitution are *Institutum Societatis Jesu*, Florence, 1892, *Constitutiones Societatis Jesu*, Rome, 1908, and *Rules of the Society of Jesus*, Roehampton, 1926.

Of criticisms of the Society perhaps the most powerful is that of Bohmer, *The Jesuits, an Historical Study*, Philadelphia, 1928 (English translation). There is Boyd Barrett's *The Jesuit Enigma*, New York, 1927, Hoensbroech's *Vierzehn Jahre Jesuit*, Leipzig, 1910, and his article 'Der Jesuitenorden' published in *Enzyklopädie*,

Bern and Leipzig, 1926–7. The most recent general English criticism from a Catholic but anti-Jesuit point of view has been Taunton's *History of the Jesuits in England, 1580–1773*, London, 1901. Among apologists there has been Brière's *L'Apologétique de Pascal et la Mort de Pascal*, Paris, 1911, Father Brou's *Les Jésuites et la légende*, Paris, 1906, Father La Farge's *The Jesuits in Modern Times*, New York, 1928, Father Brodrick's *Origin of the Jesuits*, London, 1940, and, also by Father Brodrick, *Progress of the Jesuits*, London, 1946.

The lives of many of the great Jesuit saints are to be found in *Acta Sanctorum*, published in Brussels. Numerous biographies have been written on them. In English the most noteworthy of recent years have been *St Ignatius*, London, 1956, *St Francis Xavier*, London, 1952, and *St Peter Canisius*, London, 1935, all by Father Brodrick. Father Philip Caraman has written on the seventeenth-century English Jesuits – particularly *Henry Garnet and the Gunpowder Plot*, London, 1964. On St Ignatius himself Father Pollen's *St Ignatius Loyola*, New York, 1922, Christopher Hollis' *St Ignatius*, London, 1931, Stewart Rose's *Saint Ignatius Loyola and the Early Jesuits*, London, 1891, Sedgwick's *Ignatius Loyola. An Attempt at an Impartial Biography*, New York, 1923, and Van Dyke's *Ignatius Loyola, the Founder of the Jesuits*, New York, 1926, may be mentioned.

The most recent addition to major works on the Society is Father Laszlo Polgar's *Bibliography of the Society of Jesus* (Sources and Studies for the History of the Jesuits, vol. 1), Rome, Jesuit Historical Institute, 1967.

INDEX